# The End of Conduct

# The End of Conduct

*Grobianus* and the Renaissance
Text of the Subject

BARBARA CORRELL

*Cornell University Press* · Ithaca and London

THIS BOOK HAS BEEN PUBLISHED WITH THE AID OF A GRANT FROM
THE HULL MEMORIAL PUBLICATION FUND OF CORNELL UNIVERSITY.

First published 1996 by Cornell University Press.

*Library of Congress Cataloging-in-Publication Data*

Correll, Barbara A.
   The end of conduct : Grobianus and the Renaissance text of the
subject / Barbara A. Correll.
      p.  cm.
   Includes bibliographical references and index.
   ISBN 0-8014-3101-8 (cl. : alk. paper)
   1. Dedekind, Friedrich, d. 1598. Grobianus et Grobiana.
2. Didactic poetry, Latin (Medieval and modern)—Germany—History
and criticism.  3. Erasmus, Desiderius, d. 1536—Knowledge—
Education.  4. Dekker, Thomas, ca. 1572–1632. Guls horne-booke.
5. Dedekind, Friedrich, d. 1598—Influence.  6. Conduct of life in
literature.  7. Body, Human, in literature.  8. Scheidt, Caspar, d.
1565.  9. Courtesy in literature.  10. Renaissance—Europe.
11. Humanists—Europe.  I. Title.
PA8485.D6G7634   1996                                    96-13885
871'.04—dc20

Printed in the United States of America

♾  The paper in this book meets the minimum requirements
of the American National Standard for Permanence of Paper
for Printed Library Materials, ANSI Z39.48–1984.

*An die Zukunft*
*in der Vergangenheit.*

# Contents

# Preface

This work was the outcome of an investigative detour. It began when my interests in the records of early modern witchcraft and misogyny led me to question what it was, or what it might be, that sixteenth-century women were doing in their everyday lives and actions to provoke such negative and destructive attention. Finding no satisfactory answers to my questions, I began to ask others. It was only then, in reading texts from the genre of conduct literature, that I redirected my efforts to less limiting questions of gender and subject formation and found myself on the way to making some contribution to the study of the subject. Although I wandered from my investigation of misogyny, I thought my work might offer ideas that could be linked to the destructive effects of the historical hostility toward women and other marginalized groups.

Reading the sixteenth-century *Grobianus* became a labor in cultural genealogy. It drastically altered my ideas on Renaissance texts, on conduct literature, and on the position and power of marginal texts. Although not themselves subversive or dissident, the *Grobianus* texts pried open an area that a more conventional study of conduct, civility, and courtesy seemed to resist and repress. The consequence of bringing *Grobianus* into more serious study was an unsettling and revisionary rereading of conduct literature, one that, following a genealogical itinerary, both problematized and pluralized the study of conduct and the subject.

So much intellectual work comes from monkish solitude. This book is no exception; yet there are friends and colleagues whose help has been much appreciated in the completion of this project. The staff members of libraries at the University of Wisconsin, the University of Chicago, the Newberry Library, Columbia University, the University of Illinois, the Beinecke Rare Book and Manuscript Library of Yale University, and Olin Library at Cornell University were helpful and generous with resources, offering access to facilities, microfilm, and rare texts. An earlier version of Chapter 2, titled "Malleable Material, Models of Power: Women in Erasmus's 'Marriage Group' and *Civility in Boys*," was published in *ELH* 57 (1990); it is reprinted by permission of Johns Hopkins University Press. An earlier version of Chapter 4, titled "The Politics of Civility in Renaissance Texts: Grobiana in *Grobianus*," was published in *Exemplaria* 2 (1990), copyright Center for Medieval and Early Renaissance Studies, SUNY Binghamton. I am grateful to the publishers for permission to make use of this material. For permission to publish photographed text illustrations, I am grateful to the Beinecke Library. At a very early stage of my work, Max Baeumer of the University of Wisconsin was remarkably supportive of an approach that was by no means always congenial to his own. At a critical moment Jonathan Goldberg rescued from obscurity the work on Erasmus; his own example as scholar, stylist, and risky thinker has proved invaluable in affirming my own aspirations. Members of my 1991 seminar, "Conduct/ Identity/Discovery," were adventurous, curious, irreverent, and unfailingly polite in negotiating cultural concerns; I thank especially Bernadette Andrea, Timothy Billings, Mark Blackwell, Nate Johnson, and Rich Weldgen for their participation. Jonathan Crewe, Walter Cohen, and Peter Stallybrass read the work in manuscript and, with characteristic critical rigor and generosity, provided important encouragement and suggestions; I cannot adequately acknowledge what, as a sort of intellectual community, they gave. Pete Wetherbee offered help with questions of Latin, and Art Groos was also generous with advice on early modern German.

B. C.

*Ithaca, New York*

# Author's Note:
## Texts, Translations, *translatio*

Unless otherwise noted, translations in this book are my own. The following editions of *Grobianus* and other texts have been used and will be cited parenthetically in the text:

Fridericus Dedekindus. *Grobianus et Grobiana, de morum simplicitate, libri tres.* Frankfurt am Main: Christian Egendorphius, 1584. This edition reprints the third revised edition (1554) of the work. In citing this text, I have given numbers to the lines.

Kaspar Scheidt. *Grobianus, von groben sitten, und unhöflichen geberden.* Worms: Gregorius Hoffman, 1551. Edited by Gustav Milchsack as *Friedrich Dedekinds "Grobianus" verdeutscht von Kaspar Scheidt. Neudrücke der deutschen Litteraturwerke des XVI. und XVII. Jahrhunderts,* no. 34–35. Halle: M. Niemeyer, 1882. Quotations have been checked for accuracy against the photographic reproduction of the first edition of 1551, published by the Zentralantiquariat der Deutschen Demokratischen Republik, Leipzig, 1979.[1]

R. F. gent. [pseud.]. *The Schoole of Slovenrie, or Cato turnd Wrong Side Outward.* London: [Valentine Simmes], 1605. Published in Ernst Rühl, *Grobianus in England: Nebst Neudruck der ersten Übersetzung "The Schoole of Slovenrie" (1605) und erster Herausgabe des Schwankes "Grobiana's Nuptials" (c. 1640) aus Ms. 30. Bodl. Oxf. Palaestra,* 38. Berlin: Mayer und Müller, 1904.

Desiderius Erasmus. *De civilitate morum puerilium libellus*. Ed. Jean LeClerc. Amsterdam, 1706. *On Good Manners in Boys*. In *Collected Works of Erasmus*, vols. 25 and 26, *Literary and Educational Writings*, vol. 3, and *De pueris instituendis*, vol. 4, ed. J. K. Sowards (Toronto: University of Toronto Press, 1985).

Desiderius Erasmus. *Colloquia familiaria*. In *Opera Omnia*, series I, vol. 3 (Amsterdam: North Holland, 1972). *The Colloquies*, ed. and trans. Craig Thompson (Chicago: University of Chicago Press, 1965).

Thomas Dekker. *The Guls Horne-booke: Stultorum plena sunt omnia*. London, 1609. In Thomas Dekker, *The Wonderful Year, The Gull's Horn-Book, et al.*, ed. E. D. Pendry (Cambridge: Harvard University Press, 1968).

Baldassare Castiglione. *Il libro del cortegiano*. In *Opere di Baldassare Castiglione, Giovanni della Casa, Benvenuto Cellini*, ed. Carlo Cordié (Milan: Riccardo Ricciardi, 1960). *The Book of the Courtier*. Trans. George Bull. Harmondsworth, U.K.: Penguin, 1967.

=====

In making my discussion of minor texts and major cultural problems accessible to those who do not read neo-Latin or early modern German literature, it has been a great help to have R.F.'s English verse translation of Dedekind's (1554) *Grobianus,* which enables me to present parallel texts. There will undoubtedly be those who find the English translation insufficiently accurate, but R.F.'s translation, which seems to have been an extracurricular student exercise, attempts to reproduce Dedekind's text as faithfully as possible, transmitting the Latin elegiacs in the form of heptameter couplets ("fourteeners").[2] Given the difficulties, it is a remarkable achievement—if in its time unrecognized—of more than 4,500 lines of translation.[3] Simply in translating the meter from elegiacs to heptameter R.F.'s version coarsens the model somewhat; he also takes some liberties with the text to render passages livelier, more graphic, more colloquial and coarser. Rühl, who stresses R.F.'s "efforts to reproduce the Latin model in a lively and vivid manner," also offers a summary of changes (xxii–xxv).

(1) "The translator uses concrete and vivid expressions for formulaic Latin expressions, abstract nouns, personal pronouns or impersonal passive constructions"; for example, "An dubium est unum cunctos ha-

buisse parentem?" (1.4.513) becomes "had we not all one father Adam
and one mother Eve?" (1.4.424); and the simile "Aut velut exciso quondam sub Monte Metallum / Quaeritur in venis terra benigna tuis"
(1.4.559–60) becomes the more dramatic and exploitative "Or as our
Mettal-mongers do, with their industrious paines, / By digging mountaines, rob the earth of her rich mettall vaines" (460-61). (2) Additional
synonyms, images, and comparisons appear. (3) "Reasons or observations given in the third person are put in the mouth of one of the
participants, situations are filled out in a lively fashion, here and there
a witty reason is added, indirect speech becomes direct, exclamations
or protestations are inserted"; for example, "Inde adeas recta (pudor
omnis inutilis hic est) / Curaque sit blando molliter ore loqui" (1.6.775–
76), becomes "Then go strait to her, and in this case lay aside all shame
/ And with a pleasant smiling looke, demand the virgins name" (1.6.746–
47). (4) "The translator concisely and pregnantly renders awkward Latin
phrases: vestis vincula (1.5.724): gerdle (604), Impositam mensae . . .
mappam (1.4.587): table cloth (486), . . . Cereali litho (1.9.1235–36):
beere (1.9.1134)." (5) "He avoids Dedekind's verbose repetitions and
shortens these where they simply return to the same point without
adding anything new to the text." Thus in 1.6 advice to wear a short
gown that bares the buttocks and imitates noble fashion (1.6.317–22) is
shortened to a couplet (1.6.264–65), and Dedekind's six lines of advice
on the futility of cleaning shoes (1.6.807–12) are similarly condensed in
the English (1.6.688–89).

   In addition, R.F. is not unwilling occasionally to update the vocabulary and even to add contemporary allusions. Thus, "Hac potes urbani
nomen ratione mereri" (2.2.221) becomes "thou wilt deserve a civill
yonkers name" (2.2.1684); a dinner that ends raucously, "in tantis mo-
tibus" (2.2.302), becomes "in such a hurlie burlie" (2.2.1743); Erasmus
is referred to as "Olde sage 'Erasmus' " (1.2.266) or "old Roterodamus"
(title page) and the Latin speaker's praise of stained teeth—

> Iste color fulvo quoque non culpatur in auro,
> Auro quod nunquam non amat omnis homo,
> Dentibus ergo tuis cur sit color ille pudendus?
> Si sapis, hanc a te fac proculire fidem.
>                         (1.1.121–24)

—gains a timely, moral-economic coloring:

> That is a perfect saffron colour, t'will much credite you.
> What other colour then this red hath the bright glittering gold,
> *For which possessions, tenements, lands, lives, and all are sold?*
> Then thinke not that golds perfect colour doth your teeth disgrace,
> That colour *which in few mens purses*, in your teeth hath place.
> (1.1.103–6; emphasis added)

But R.F. is not the only one to alter the text; Dedekind himself must be regarded as a translator of sorts. *Grobianus* is very much the product of and a case of translation and *translatio*, that rhetorical figure of transport also known as metaphor.[4] Our texts look back on classical models of virtue, behavior, and a father tongue, transported to be "reborn" as living heritage in the sixteenth-century humanist activity of educating and refining boys and men; *Grobianus* is a translation from the classical past. At the same time, the *Grobianus* texts are embedded in a period of transition and mobility, in which the classical past was appropriated, transported, and used to further specific, power-related ends. Perhaps nowhere can this mobility be seen more convincingly than in conduct literature, which inscribes the bourgeois aspiration to cast off what its imaginary constructs as a coarse and unaristocratic ancestry and assimilate itself to the noble models it sees itself embracing with an aggressive but uneasy sense of entitlement. The crossed and socially inflected etymology of *Grobianus* itself discloses this cultural hybridity: the name Latinizes the German noun (*Grobian*) for a coarse and common man, *grob* (coarse) Hans. The text therefore transports something regarded as common and coarse from the past and displaces it into present erudite vulgarity. Thus several cultural heritages are carried by the vehicle of the texts—classical, aristocratic-feudal, agricultural-peasant—along with a traditional legacy of masculinity and its familiar fears of the feminine Other that both threatens and defines it. If *translatio* is "primarily a term for aligning cultural-linguistic production (and displacement) with political power, both conceived as mobile," then *Grobianus* is a rather special instance.[5]

Mobility in the *Grobianus* texts runs in several directions. Not only the translation practices of Kaspar Scheidt, who adapts and transports, and R.F., who tries to transmit faithfully, not only Dekker's remarkable transformation of the grobian into the English gull, but Dedekind's own revisions to his first edition suggest the compulsion to revise and translate which this text seems to produce.

In adapting Dedekind's text, Scheidt set out to "improve" it; the Latin, he complained, was "nit grob genug" (not coarse enough). His success is discussed in Chapter 5, but for now it is important to note that Scheidt was not alone in his concern. He simply articulated the tacit concerns and evident strategies of Dedekind himself. His revisions of 1552 and 1554, which Adolf Hauffen describes as sweeping changes that "leave no stone unturned,"[6] lengthen the work by coarsening what is already there and adding coarser material in a third book and chapter titles to underscore content and offer a reader's guide to the indecency of the verses. Aloys Bömer's introduction to his edition of *Grobianus* (1549 edition) notes the addition of new anecdotal material and the expansion of the original with coarser formulations and descriptions.[7] These problems and opportunities of translation should be kept in mind as the discussion progresses.

# The End of Conduct

# Introduction:
# Indecent Ironies and the
# End of Conduct

Abject and abjection are my safeguards. The primers of my culture.
—Julia Kristeva, *Powers of Horror*

Book 2 of *Il libro del cortegiano*, Castiglione's work devoted to the construction of the ideal courtier, briefly points toward the other, murkier side of the ideal when Federico Fregoso cautions his audience to "take great care to make a good impression at the start, and consider how damaging and fatal a thing it is to do otherwise." He cites examples: courtiers' food fights, horseplay, "filthy and indecent language," "shameful and shocking discourtesies"; he hints that he knows of those at court who "concoct things so abhorrent to human sense that it is impossible to mention them without the greatest disgust" (2.37.145–46). Although it is Federico who brings the matter of the indecent to the attention of the group at the castle of Urbino, he treats his contribution to the evening's conversation as a negative digression, material to "consider" but which he would be reluctant to consider further. His manner indicates that, as earlier, he "would not have us enter into unpleasant matters," for "it would be too long and wearisome to attempt to speak of all the faults that can occur." Refocused on those discreet techniques for making the all-important good first impression, seeking to avoid— we will consider whether successfully or not—topics so much less than proper, the discussion on the courtier continues in a work that is considered both representative of Renaissance courtesy literature and a major literary achievement.

Such is not the case with another, far more obscure text from the Renaissance genre of conduct literature, the neo-Latin *Grobianus*, that strange verse compendium of bad manners first written thirty years after *The Courtier* by the minor German humanist Friedrich Dedekind. I offer an excerpt from the Latin with R.F.'s English version in order to introduce readers to the relationship between *Grobianus* and *The Courtier*. In stark contrast to Castiglione's book and to other Renaissance books of courtesy, civility, or conduct, Dedekind's *Grobianus* keeps its readers precisely, insistently, relentlessly in the wearisome realm of unpleasant matters:

> Non sat eris simplex, si vestimenta ligare
>    Coeperis, et ventri vincula dura nocent.
> Ne nimus evadas moratus, pectere crines
>    Neglige, neglecta est forma decora viro,
> Foeminae crines ornare reliquito turbae:
>    Comantur iuvenes, quos levis urit amor.
> Crede mihi Dominum te nulla puella vocabit,
>    Si te composito viderit esse pilo.
> Sint procul a nobis iuvenes ut foemina compti,
>    Scribit Amazonio Cressa puella viro.
> Eximio tibi erit decori, si pluma capillis
>    Mixta erit, et laudem providus inde feres.
> Scilicet hoc homines poteris convincere signo,
>    Non in stramineo te cubuisse toro.
> Sint capitis crines longi, nec forcipe tonsi,
>    Caesaries humeros tangat ut alta tuos.
> Tutus ut a tristi rigidae sis frigore brumae,
>    Vertice prolixus crinis alendus erit.
> Cuncti homines quondam longos habuere capillos,
>    Quos modo virgineus curat habere chorus.
> Regna pater quando Saturnus prisca tenebat,
>    Tunc fuit in longis gloria magna comis.
> Simplicitas veterum laudatur ubique virorum:
>    Qua potes, hos semper sit tibi cura sequi.
> Dedecus esse puta faciemue manusue lavare,
>    Commodius crasso sordet utrunque luto.

Qui volet his vesci, per me licet, ipse lavabit,
   Dicito: res curae non erit illa mihi.
Forsan erit dentes qui te mundare monebit.
   Sed monitis parens inveniare cave.
Recta valetudo corrumpi dicitur oris,
   Saepe nova si quis proluat illud aqua.
Quid noceat, dentes quod sunt fuligine flavi:
   Iste color rubei cernitur esse croci.
Iste color fulvo quoque non culpatur in auro,
   Auro quod nunquam non amat omnis homo,
Dentibus ergo tuis cur sit color ille pudendus?
   Si sapis, hanc a te fac procul ire fidem.
                         (1.1.87–124)

Simplicity commands that you forget to trusse your pointes.
Hard tying is an enemie to bellie and to ioynts.
Lest some men say you are too hansome, ne're combe your haire,
As Nature sets it, and bed leaves it, use it so to weare:
Leave plaited haires and curled lockes unto the female sex,
And let them use to combe their haire whom cruell love doth vex.
Beleeve me, not a wench unto thee will affection beare,
If she perceive that thou observ'st such nicenesse in thy haire.
Who can abide yong men that dresse themselves as female crew,
A Creetish dame writ to an Amazonion lover true.
Tis praise and credite to have feathers store upon your head,
For thereby men may well perceive you scorne straw in your bed.
In any case cut not your haire, but let it hang at length,
Fort'will both keepe away the colde, and argue "Sampsons" strength.
When father "Saturne" rulde the world, all men did use long haire,
And gloried in it, though now wenches use it most to weare.
Fore-fathers plaine simplicitie is prais'd in every place,
Then let not us disdaine to use it, it is no disgrace.
Thy face and hands too oft to wash is cause of mickle hurt,
Therefore (a Gods name) let them both have ever store of durt.
Let other men that with hands they have care to wash them cleane,
But as for washing of my hands, to take no care I meane.
What though your teeth through o're much rust are dide to a red hue
That is a perfect saffron colour, t'will much credite you.
What other colour then this red hath the bright glittering gold,

For which possessions, tenements, lands, lives, and all are sold?
Then thinke not that golds perfect colour doth your teeth disgrace,
That colour which in few mens purses, in your teeth hath place.

(1.1.77–106)

Readers who recognize the Ovidian elegiacs may also see an ironizing imitation of "Magister Naso" counseling aspiring male lovers in the *Ars amatoria*.[1] Dedekind's borrowing appropriates parts of the classical model and transports them to the arena of the Renaissance conduct manual and its mixed lineage where debts to sources are drastically discharged in grobianism. What the excerpt should illustrate, both graphically (in its vivid representation) and viscerally (in the strongly negative response it elicits), is that unlike his Italian predecessor Castiglione, Dedekind was not averse to speaking the unspeakable, and speaking it copiously. On the contrary, in a text known for enthusiastically and ironically recommending the worst conduct imaginable, aversive conditioning was his mission, producing an aversive reaction his strategy for teaching civil manners.

For traditional interpreters such as Jakob Burckhardt or Ernst Cassirer, the renewed examination of the "self" in the Renaissance represented another step in casting off the chains of an ascetic and self-denying medieval past, in moving inexorably toward a more modern, individualized freedom and human autonomy.[2] For them, a *locus classicus* of the new ideology of the sovereign and transcendental subject and of its claims of a male individual's ability to shape and determine his life and actions independently can be seen in the following passage from Pico della Mirandola's fifteenth-century *Oration on the Dignity of Man*:

Thou, constrained by no limits, in accordance with thine own free will, in whose hand We have placed thee, shalt ordain for thyself the limits of thy nature. . . . We have made thee neither of heaven nor of earth, neither mortal nor immortal, so that with freedom of choice and with honor, as though the maker and molder of thyself, thou mayest fashion thyself in whatever shape thou shalt prefer. Thou shalt have the power to degenerate into the lower forms of life, which are brutish. Thou shalt have the power, out of the soul's judgment, to be reborn into the higher forms, which are divine.[3]

Pico's *Oration* has long been held to be the quintessential expression of that secular, optimistic spirit conventionally associated with Renaissance humanism, held to be a work marking the transition from a medieval theocentric and fatalistic world view to an anthropocentric—or at least androcentric—one, anchored by its professed belief in the perfectibility (but we might also call it the malleability) of human nature, the confidence that men have the freedom and ability to make their identities and their destinies.[4]

Increasingly, literary and cultural criticism has been deliberately distanced from idealist and essentialist positions; Renaissance scholars, applying and developing poststructuralist, new historicist, cultural materialist, or feminist methods, see the phenomenon of early modern identity formation less teleologically and more problematically.[5] In part we are dealing with what Stephen Greenblatt in his pathbreaking study of the English Renaissance called "self-fashioning," a shaping of human behavior and the conscious structuring of an outward, official identity, a deliberate, self-reflexive composition of the self as a text or a work of art.[6] Greenblatt's critical study of a historical transformation of human identity at one of its most crucial stages produced a breakthrough that has moved scholarship from the idealist-humanist tradition and is still producing effects and reactions.[7]

While much of the newer Renaissance scholarship has followed Greenblatt's interpretive itinerary, from attention to anecdotal or "nonliterary" material to fresh readings of major texts, attention to social history and to the so-called marginal or noncanonical texts of early modernity has also altered the terrain of Renaissance studies. Writers like Greenblatt are certainly aware of more obscure voices in the Renaissance of England, France, and Italy, but Reformation Germany also offers cultural material that complicates the picture of an aestheticized, high-cultural Renaissance and its reception in current interpretive and literary-historical practices; it also points to certain operative limitations in methods that restrict themselves to a canonical trajectory, to aesthetic preconceptions, or to neglect of gender and class questions.

In addition to making its own contribution to the newer and more

open spaces of historical and interpretive inquiry, German grobianism
also offers a far less than optimistic response to what Pico acclaimed as
options for human aspiration. Consider, for example, Kaspar Scheidt's
conclusion to his vernacular adaptation of Dedekind's *Grobianus*:

> Will man den menschen recht auß streichen,
>    Soll man jn mit einr saw vergleichen?
> Ja noch vil erger helt er sich,
>    Dann sunst kein unvernünfftig vich:
> Dasselbig bleibt in seim beruoff
>    Wie es Gott der Allmechtig schuoff
> Daß es arbeit, und dultigklich
>    Auffs erdtrich sehe undersich
> Dem menschen aber daß er kan,
>    Das gstirn und himel sehen an,
> Darbey gedencken seines Herrn
>    Der jn hat bracht zu solchen ehrn.
>                                    (4955–66)

(Should we compare man with a swine? Why, he behaves far worse
than some dumb, irrational animal. The beast knows its place and
only does what the Almighty created it to do: it labors and patiently
sees the earth beneath it. But man, who can see the stars and heav-
ens, should remember the Master who has brought him such honors.)

Like Dedekind in his neo-Latin text, Scheidt certainly means to exhort
the readers of his own ironic-didactic work to fashion a better shape for
themselves; unlike Pico, he emphasizes their failings rather than any
divine or superhuman potential or, for that matter, aspiration; and instead of Pico's spirited and sunnily optimistic oration, he chooses other
means of persuasion: satire and didactic irony. Nonetheless, Scheidt's
*Grobianus*, like the neo-Latin work it adapts in the doggerel rhyme
(*Knittelvers*) of the *Meistersang*, is also an important manifestation of
the self-fashioning process. The reverse precepts of the *Grobianus* texts
make their strong and visceral appeal to an individual sense of shame
and abjection as the motivators of personal change toward refinement
and civility. For these authors, irony is a mode of containment, but it

has a double edge. That is, it both constrains and preserves an excess without which civil discipline, always striving to suppress it, cannot exist. In reading the *Grobianus* texts and adding them to the history of conduct literature, we deal with the civilizing process as a problem of culture's constitutive unmentionables.

Altering the literary-historical lineage of the courtesy and conduct genre to suggest the importance of developments in the more obscure cultural arena of Renaissance and Reformation Germany opens up the discussion of early modern subject formation and of the constitution of cultural manhood and the tensions embedded in it in a way that, I would claim, marks a kind of final word. Dedekind's remarkable but now obscure work and its translations and adaptations disclose the techniques of other conduct books. Like them, too, they present a compelling picture of a historical crisis of masculine cultural identity. Conduct formation, then, is not affirmative and progressive movement toward civility and social consideration; rather, civility is unveiled as the product and precipitate of harsh, aversive conditioning in which male subjects cultivate anxieties about the very bodies they inhabit.

What could be the relationship between Castiglione's seminal text on courtly behavior, so influential for English Renaissance literature, so unquestionably and enduringly canonical in status, and Dedekind's ironic and rather unsavory, resolutely countercanonical treatment of manners and conduct? *The Book of the Courtier* offers its readers an ideal toward which to aspire; *Grobianus*, its nightmarish inversion, inspires disgust. It is little wonder, to be sure, that Castiglione's is the more influential text of early modern masculine identity formation; yet Federico Fregoso's raising and quick dismissal of indecent possibilities, his making unmentionable the actions he names, indicates that something of the "grobian" is really never absent from the ideal with which Castiglione and his successors and adapters, both German and English, were so preoccupied. For what we could call the grobian within—the recognition that good behavior is predicated on militantly remembering a worst-case scenario—is also the lesson they teach. It is certainly present in Castiglione's concern for making a good impression and for locating the elusive "happy mean" of *sprezzatura* by knowing how to "withdraw, little by little, away from the extreme to which we know we usually tend" (2.47.314). Castiglione's small gestures of withdrawal, gestures that even in turning from an unnamed extreme continue to point toward it, already name the grobian who haunts the ideal courtier.

On the one hand, then, we have the literary institutionalization of a courtly ideal; on the other, its negative complement. Despite the really vast and likely unbridgeable distance between them in canonical standing, *Grobianus* is not counter to, so much as in excess of Castiglione's courtier's exemplarity. But, or so I argue in the pages that follow, it is that very excess—the excess of the body which exceeds the civil discourses that construct the early modern masculine subject's body even as it is molded and disciplined by them—which constitutes the structure of the literature of conduct and courtesy in the first place.

What is the relationship, then, between courtly ideals and the worst-case scenario of an ironic conduct book? Between courtesy and conduct? Castiglione's work is instrumental in the dissemination of discourses on courtesy in England; Dedekind's tears the veil from those discourses of courtesy, exposes the constitutive unmentionables of courtesy and, as well, of humanist civility.[8] His modes of presentation and persuasion may seem incompatible with those of other reformers, civilizers, and shapers of civil and courteous behavior (Erasmus, Juan Vives, Thomas Elyot, Roger Ascham);[9] yet his ironic text addresses and anatomizes what emerges as the early modern process of subject formation in bodily *régimes du savoir-faire*. In a text thus fully complicit with the pedagogical and political goals of its predecessors, fully continuous with the traditions and contexts from which the genre of the conduct book develops, Dedekind presents a lesson in how to read conduct literature itself. Since the lessons he presents give the game away on the cultural inscription of the body in regimes of conduct, civility, and courtesy and undermine their ideological and legitimating operations, it is thus possible—and assuredly ironic—to say not only that *Grobianus* alters our understanding of the textual lineage of the conduct genre but also that it marks the end of conduct.

My concern in this book is with the category of conduct and the role of indecency in early modern subject formation. Following a by now well-traveled historical itinerary, aided by a particular methodological itinerary, and addressing a less familiar itinerary of readings in Renaissance texts, I want to refocus attention on a body of literature and its distinctive (if, finally, still repressed) contribution to traditions of bodily discipline and representation in European cultural history: Renaissance conduct literature, under the rubric of which I include courtesy literature. Through this rechanneled investigative gaze, I want to pry open questions still being posed in the reexamination of subject formation and cultural inscription of the body in early modern Europe, examine constructions of masculinity and their significance for gender and class at a crucial historical moment.[10]

It is the refocusing on the margins which is important to my project. Attention to conduct literature and the body is not new, of course; indebted references to the pathbreaking work of Mikhail Bakhtin on Rabelais and late medieval carnival, as well as to Norbert Elias's work on the civilizing process and Michael Foucault's work on discipline and bodily regimes in the seventeenth century, frequently mark the richness and diversity of newer Renaissance scholarship. Nor, to be sure, is the notion that conduct literature writes a text of the subject with far-reaching consequences for Renaissance literature and cultural history an unprecedented claim.[11] But here I am particularly concerned with Friedrich Dedekind's ironic-didactic poem *Grobianus et Grobiana*, composed of reverse precepts that systematically recommend the most disgusting behavior—indecency—as the way to teach decent behavior. The goal of Dedekind's text, as of those subsequent translations and adaptations that will also find place in this book, is to secure normative masculine identity and construct the gendered subject of civility by means of the labor of aversion, reading through reversals in a text that (ironically) authorizes indecency.

The history of the text itself is not complicated. Dedekind's first edition of *Grobianus, de morum simplicitate* appeared in 1549. In 1551 Kaspar Scheidt produced a vernacular adaptation, *Grobianus, von groben sitten und unhöflichen geberden* (Grobianus, on coarse manners and impolite behavior), in the early modern High German of Luther, which nearly doubled the length of the Latin original, adding marginal commentary in several languages. It was followed in turn by Dedekind's second edition in 1552, in which he altered and lengthened the text and added a third book. In 1554 this version became the third edition, now bearing descriptive chapter titles and retitled *Grobianus et Grobiana* to call attention to Dedekind's addition of "Grobiana," a chapter

of advice to women which concludes the third book. It was one of the
better-known works of the sixteenth century in Germany and indeed in
much of Europe, going through some twenty-three Latin editions and
several translations in the first fifty years of its existence, including
Scheidt's renowned adaptation. Early in the seventeenth century its Roman elegiacs (alternating lines of hexameter and pentameter) were skillfully translated into jaunty English fourteeners by one known to us only
as "R.F. gent." (1605), and shortly thereafter Thomas Dekker incorporated and adapted a good part of the work to English conditions and
prose in *The Guls Horne-booke* (1609).[12]

As for Dedekind and Scheidt, the two chief authors of the *Grobianus*
texts, who never met, what little we know about their lives shows them
to be typical early modern German bourgeois intellectuals, third-
generation humanists who rose from undistinguished, even (in the case
of Dedekind) humble origins through education and the opportunities
made available by the Reformation's polemical and pedagogically directed energies, combined with the economic and psychic impulses of
an emerging German Protestant bourgeoisie.[13] Characteristically, both
wrote and published civil-didactic works, on the one hand, while, on
the other, they pursued patronage from the regional nobility by com-
posing and dedicating occasional verses to them.

Friedrich Dedekind (c. 1524–1598) was born the son of a butcher in
Neustadt am Rübenberg and studied in the Protestant university towns
of Marburg and Wittenberg, his education most likely sponsored by a
noble household. As pastor in Neustadt, he made a career as a minor
Protestant theologian and the author of some obscure Reformation
plays.[14] Aside from the customary assumption that the text was published when Dedekind was no older than twenty-five and thus that it
was written at a young age, and his concluding apologia to book 3, in
which he confesses to witnessing certain excesses of behavior and being
occasionally guilty of them himself as student, we know almost nothing
about the circumstances surrounding the writing of *Grobianus*. Considering his slight credentials, scholars have expressed some wonder at
Dedekind's achievement, Ernst Rühl calling it "a remarkable but not
isolated phenomenon that a writer so apparently untalented as Dedekind wrote one of the chief poetic works of the sixteenth century in his
youth."[15]

Most details about Scheidt's brief life remain unknown, and were it not for the far greater success of his student Johann Fischart, best known among Germanists for his adaptation of Rabelais's *Gargantua and Pantagruel* (*Die Geschichtklitterung*, 1575), knowledge of his life would be even more fragmentary.[16] Gustav Milchsack describes him simply as "a schoolmaster from Worms, of whom not much more is known than that he penned a few other insignificant little pieces and died, with wife and child, in 1565 of the plague."[17] As a humanist scholar, however, he was as engaged and familiar with the classical Greek and Latin tradition as with the vernacular literature of Germany, France, and Italy, but he consciously applied and dedicated his erudition to the project of Reformation vernacular culture. Active as moral reformer and proselytizer of Protestant culture, he translated and adapted biblical stories to the meter of the *Meistersang* and wrote pamphlets on moral topics, in particular against drunkenness.[18]

Like Dedekind's neo-Latin original, Kaspar Scheidt's *Grobianus* enjoyed great popularity in its time. Together the two texts represent something of a milestone in the development of both manners and literature and in the relationship between a style of life and a style of writing. *Grobianus* was widely read for two centuries. Yet today the work is considered something of a historical curiosity, virtually unread in contrast to comparable works of the same period, not only courtesy literature but satirical and humorous works such as Sebastian Brant's *Das Narrenschiff* (1494) (*Ship of Fools* [1497]), in which a "Sankt Grobian" is first popularized, Erasmus's *Stultitia laus* (*Praise of Folly* [1509]), or Rabelais's *Gargantua and Pantagruel* (1534). Today few of us know of *Grobianus*, in any version. Even fewer have actually read it—admittedly for some good reasons. If the theme of social propriety is no less "universal" than Brant's and Rabelais's thematic material, *Grobianus* is not an edifying work to read. As an early example of bourgeois literature, it does not represent its class in its most progressive light.[19] Like Rabelais's acknowledged masterpiece, it focuses intensely on the materiality of the body, but its use of humor is not generous or "Rabelaisian"; it offers neither heroism nor optimism. Nor (except in "Grobiana") does its intense investment in the indecent and scatological include the obscene or erotic.[20] Perhaps obsessively repetitive, more than merely bordering on or crossing the border into the tasteless, it is not the sort of work one might wish to view, much less embrace, as representative of Renaissance humanism. Indeed, it seems to contradict commonly held notions of humanist literature and Renaissance faith in human possibility and perfectibility. Even as an early antihero, the grobian lacks something in comparison to the earlier folk-book heroes or to the later *picaros*. In fact, the work is rather snide and unpleasant. It mocks not only what it considers human vices and faults but human drives and appetites in general. Insofar as it mocks its own lesson—in its exaggerated and ironic praise of bad manners and indecent behavior, dependent on humor and powerful, grotesque images—it seems to mock teaching itself and might thereby subvert its own didactic intentions. Yet *Grobianus* has been called "the most widespread satire of the sixteenth century."[21] It has been described as "the book that, despite all its grotesque exaggerations, is representative of social life in sixteenth-century Germany."[22] It has even been paired with the *Faustbuch* as the wrong end of a binary opposition that supposedly distills all that is the best and worst from the age.[23]

Surveys of sixteenth-century German literature give this meager but obstreperous body of work a position both awkward and obscure. Accompanied by the brief catalog of a literary-cultural phenomenon conventionally and rather dismissively referred to as grobianism (*Grobianismus*) and grobian literature (*grobianische Dichtung*), it is not always apparent whether these classifications refer to the *Grobianus* texts or others that use coarseness and indecency as techniques to attack coarseness and indecency; whether they simply signify a revisionary evaluation of popular sixteenth-century texts such as the folk books (*Tyl Ulenspiegel, Salmon und Marcolf, Neidhart Fuchs*, etc.) as coarse and indecent *tout court*; or whether they mean something else. Since their treatment in historical and comparative studies by the late nineteenth- and early twentieth-century philologists and positivists, the work and the topic have received very little attention.[24] There are those who would add, and rightly so.

It is certainly not a question of rediscovering a long-lost masterpiece of the Western tradition or, as in the case of retrieving Renaissance texts by women authors, of rectifying an oversight and making the Renaissance literary canon more inclusive. The *Grobianus* texts defy canonical incorporation, are resolutely antiaesthetic. Yet could we set

aside traditional evaluative practices, the historically developed hierarchy and separation of genres and the practices of canonization, or more
rigorously include in them questions of the subject and the disciplinary
regimes that construct the subject, the work records effects on a micropolitical and cultural scale which are far from inconsequential.[25]

*Grobianus*, as Dedekind wrote it in neo-Latin, as Kaspar Scheidt
adapted and vernacularized it into German, as the otherwise anonymous
"R.F. gent." translated it into English, and then as further adapted and
dispersed by Dekker in *The Guls Horne-booke*, presents, from the literary margins, not only a revision of literary history but a remarkable
reading of the humanist conduct tradition. In addition to its uncanny
familiarity and derivativeness—ventriloquized not only by conduct
books but by classical authority and popular literature—it offers a compelling reflection on the problematics of civility, subject formation, and
cultural masculinity in the early modern period.

In order to examine that reflection, I suggest a way to read *Grobianus*
that crosses texts, methods and histories. First, in the framework of this
book, a literary-historical itinerary begins with this introductory comparison of Castiglione and Dedekind, proceeds to Erasmus, then to a
two-part reading of Dedekind; follows from Dedekind to Scheidt's
German adaptation to R.F.'s English translation and from these *Grobianus* texts to versions and cultural "translations" of the grobian in Sir
John Davies' *Gullinge Sonnets* and Dekker's *Guls Horne-booke*. This
itinerary departs from the usual lineage of the conduct genre and positions the texts of two German Reformation humanists in a continental
tradition—aristocratic and humanist—of literary conduct texts, then
charts the transcontinental reception in Renaissance England.

Second, because *Grobianus* rereads and rewrites a tradition of high-
humanist conduct literature, I emphasize a reading that requires a
methodological and conceptual itinerary with overlapping, continuous,
and interdisciplinary concerns: psychosocial, historical, and poststructuralist. Through these itineraries and crossings I hope to present a
vantage point, situated at the margins where we locate *Grobianus* as a
countercanonical artifact, from which we may view conduct literature
in a new light. We may even add something to a still-developing speculative history of the early modern Western subject.

Conduct literature seeks to transform, subjugate, and produce the body it inscribes with the signs of civility. Embedded in this subjectification and cultural inscription are issues of class and sexual difference. The texts under discussion—even (as in the case of Erasmus's *Colloquies* or Dedekind's "Grobiana") when they seem to speak to or about women—are written for and about men. But the literature of conduct resonates profoundly with masculinist anxieties about the uncertainty of difference, is structured by an agenda that would pin down questions of difference in an effort to secure cultural-masculine identity, and bears consequences. Certainly it is status that is at stake, for the texts are the products of the aspirations and anxieties of the emerging bourgeois classes; often, too, as we will see with Scheidt and Dekker, status is linked to national stakes. Even when status and nation enter the picture, however, the constitution of cultural manhood in Renaissance conduct literature is achieved through temporary victory over ungovernable qualities of the body which come to signify the feminine and the alien.

*Grobianus* stands as a kind of end point in the development of conduct books, and thus I speak of the *Grobianus* texts and the phenomenon of "grobianism" as the end of conduct. In speaking of conduct, I see discourses of courtesy, contrary to many notable treatments of Renaissance courtesy literature, not as distinct from but rather as belonging to the cultural, socioeconomic context and psychic terrain of conduct. My reasons for this view, clearly much indebted to a Foucauldian understanding of power, should become more fully apparent in the discussions of Castiglione and Erasmus. They have to do with what I see as the "bourgeoisified" character of courtiers, who, regardless of official class status (usually aristocratic), circulate and trade on the cultural capital of courteous manners in the court. The term "courtesy" tends to reify the aristocratic presence in the court, rather than to contextualize court dynamics in the early modern period.[26] It also risks euphemizing and aestheticizing what are behavioral and communicative practices, socially embedded and political. I therefore argue for conduct as the more inclusive and critically more productive term.

In treating the minor genre of Renaissance conduct literature, I see the early modern discourses of conduct producing *régimes du savoir-faire* in which the masculine subject learns self-control, and the subjectifying mechanisms of self-governance and self-repression are "translated" into colonizing behavior in relation to encountered others whose (always projected) threats have already been called into the service of subjectification. As a reflexive literary treatment of self-governance treatises and handbooks, *Grobianus* (like them) contributes to an often more fluid than specifically sited discourse on the Other: women, animals, peasants. It both reflects and reenacts the incorporation of women in early modern masculinist culture, constitutes a double text of bourgeois embodiment, with the sanitized, docile body of the male civil subject; and the raging, delinquent body—with its female, bestial, vulgar signs—which speaks (only) the necessity for manners.[27]

In *The Civilizing Process* Norbert Elias argues for the study of conduct texts as "a literary genre in their own right."[28] Work done since the republication of his great work has produced a body of scholarship on Renaissance cultural politics which has established the key role of discourses of conduct and civility in early modern cultural and literary production.[29] My own work falls within that history of work on courtesy and employs the methodological and conceptual tools developed in it.

Daniel Javitch is rightly credited as the first to call attention to the relationship between modes of courtly conduct and literary production. In *Poetry and Courtliness in Renaissance England*, he breaks new ground in studying the connections between courtly culture and literary production in the Elizabethan period.[30] He sees courtiers as patrons and producers of literary art ("poetic entertainment" [4]) and contends that their actions stemmed from a courtier code of conduct modeled on Castiglione's ideal and altering or ameliorating the harsher and more pedantic effects of the humanist program. Once that humanist pedagogy, adequately nurtured by the conditions of monarchical rule, was "reoriented into more playful, more aesthetic modes of discourse" (13), the flowering of Elizabethan lyric poetry was the happy result.[31]

Javitch's affirmative evaluation of courtly ludification and aestheticization (fully indebted to, perhaps even mimetic of what Javitch himself sees as Castiglione's aestheticizing work in *The Book of the Courtier*) comes under more critical scrutiny when Frank Whigham adds Foucauldian concerns with power relations in his *Ambition and Privilege: The Social Tropes of Elizabethan Courtesy Literature*. Invoking the authority of Foucault, whose work on power, discipline, docile bodies, and subject formation is so influential for current Renaissance studies, Whigham sees courtesy literature as a "prime specimen of . . . a subjugated or marginal knowledge" which has embedded in it the "historical knowledge of struggles," "the memory of hostile encounters" (3).[32] In taking steps to construct a Foucauldian countermemory and to restore courtesy literature to a more prominent position in cultural history (without returning to the achievement model of Javitch), however, Whigham neglects some important questions of class and gender, even some addressed by his theoretical mentors, Kenneth Burke, Foucault, and Pierre Bourdieu. While not wishing unnecessarily to belabor points of disagreement that have so clearly helped my thinking, I want to discuss them briefly in order to indicate my own operations and critical agenda.[33]

Observing the social context of historical transition and class conflict, Whigham sees a fundamentally troubled, competitive relationship between the courtly ambitions of aspiring bourgeois contenders and the aristocratic elites whose privileges and prerogatives are threatened by the engine of early modern social mobility. Whigham's approach reads the binary opposition of ambition and privilege as a two-sided conflict, almost a cultural soap opera of "The Ambitious and the Privileged."[34] Courtly life was "lived under the surveillance of a queen and class whose entire style of rule depended on guarding prerogative from interpretive challenge" (186); courtesy literature produced a "corpus of strategic gestures" (27) that functioned as commodities, weapons, tools, and in a Burkean sense, "equipment for living" (4). But these commodified gestures make courtesy literature the structuralist master key to social practices of conflict and class struggle at a court situated in the milieu of an early modern bourgeois revolution. Whigham's historical master narrative of two-tiered class struggle—male aristocratic elites challenged by men aspiring to elite class status—produces a static model of aritocratically controlled competition held in tension by rituals of rivalry between the ambitious and the privileged, an orderly binary division which also produces "weird phenomenological mixtures of arrogance and paranoia" in the literature.[35] That symptomatic mixture, however, points beyond the binary structure of aristocratic privilege confronting ambitious assault and toward a fluidity and negotiability of status which resonates with the social-economic conditions in which competition and ambition cross and confuse boundaries. Whigham's specular approach to cultural history and rhetoric views the past as a mirror that yields comprehensible information, viewed and understood through the lens of a structuralist hermeneutics. The limits of such work are apparent when one notes its relative silence on issues of subjectivity, sexuality, and gender. Power flows in an orderly model of conflict. There is no institutional history of a national masculine subject, and whereas Whigham ironically speaks of gender as the "last Given" in his conclusion (186), in his silence on the gender specificity of his study he himself treats it as precisely that. In taking no account of sexual difference or psychosexual anxiety in both the male ambitious and the male privileged, Whigham not only excludes women or the feminine from his structuralist analysis; he leaves out the issue of men, the specificity of cultural masculinity, and the category of sexuality as well.[36] An overriding concern for tropic formalism and the "corpus of strategic gestures" (27) thus leaves us a disembodied structure that never engages questions of the subject of early modern power conflicts. Yet it is here, at the moment of opening the question of the gendered subject, of power and civility, that my own conceptual itinerary—one that yields a conceptual vocabulary for this book while it follows my own reading of the historical processes it interrogates— begins.

Whigham generously acknowledges the influence of Foucault in his study of courtesy literature, but there are telling points of difference between Whigham's use of Foucault and Foucault himself. In "The Subject and Power" Foucault speaks of dominant power's "dividing practices," the normative binary distinctions such as "the mad and the sane, the sick and healthy, the criminals and the 'good boys,' " made and perpetuated in institutions of knowledge.[37] Against such norming practices he poses a move "toward a new economy of power relations" (210) "which would begin with forms of resistance" (211) and place at its center the questions Why *doesn't* power work? Why doesn't it work monolithically and why is there resistance to it? Why doesn't power respect the boundaries of the binary scheme: power and powerlessness? And if it doesn't really work, why do oppressive power structures persist? A close reading of its historical effects—as in the area of early

modern conduct formation—shows power to be far more porous and
negotiable, working continuously against the resistance of other power
forms. Foucault calls for a conceptualization of power as a relationship,
not as the one-sided application of force by the dominant group against
an utterly powerless other. His discussion also calls for recognizing what
we might call the functional dysfunctionalism of power, for neither over-
estimating the efficacy or openly unchallenged status of dominant
power, on the one hand, nor underestimating its effects, on the other.[38]

Asking "How is Power Exercised?" Foucault elaborates. The term
"power" designates for him a consensual (if in its effects unequal) relationship between partners (217), "relationships of communication." It
is "not a function of consent"; rather, power elicits consent, results in
a "modification of actions" and "not a renunciation of freedom." As
theorized by Foucault, power subjectifies—makes subject, subjects persons to—but at the same time preserves (in some indeterminate but
potential form) a certain freedom of the subject: the subject must
"freely" consent, or resist. For power to work, both consent and the
withholding of consent must be possible, the outcome a never wholly
predictable or finally concluded negotiation. Power, then, has a certain
porosity, and it is this porosity that can be observed in the early modern
regimes of conduct.[39]

For the communicative relationship of power, Foucault suggests "the
term conduct": the concept metaphor of power relationships and the
verb that describes the dynamic of relationships of leading, orchestrat-
ing, communicating between the parties in power relationships. Although Foucault does not discuss conduct literature of the Reformation
period, he speaks of the Reformation as a historical turning point that
established "pastoral power" (213) as subjectifying (that is, as making
subject to). The applicability of his conceptualization of power at work
in texts of self-governance and conduct is readily suggested. Thus, for
example, the modifications of affect, behavior, and attitude produced in
early modern regimes of conduct would not necessarily mean an end
of the subject's resistance to civilizing constraints, nor would it result
in an institutionalized petrification of disciplinary practices. Historical
change attests to resistance and resilience. We could still speak of the
ability of the body to confound the discourses that construct it. We
could still trace regimes of conduct to the point at which their efficacy

becomes problematic and porous. A reading of the *Grobianus* texts would support such confounding hypotheses.

Gender-specific texts of self-governance, directed at male subjects and making women an essential and auxiliary other, appear as open-ended and symptomatic texts of power, subjectification, discipline: *régimes du savoir-faire*. Furthermore, Foucault adds something to Elias's thesis on the gradual lowering of the threshold of shame and embarrassment in the civilizing process. The self-wrought coercions that come into play in the subject of civility rely on an education in or a conducting to indecency.[40] We need better information on the terrain of indecency, need to think about what it is the subject of civility says yes to. What painful pleasure is involved in an education in indecency? What indecent ironies come into play? What desire emerges from civility's compulsively repetitive concern with the indecent?

In speaking of subjectification Foucault also recalls the internalization of which Pierre Bourdieu also speaks in "Structures and the Habitus." The process Foucault calls "subjectification" involves the transformation and subjugation of the physical, the inscription of the body in culture.[41] It is what Bourdieu describes as "embodiment": "But it is in the dialectical relationship between the body and a space structured according to the mythico-ritual oppositions that one finds the form par excellence of the structural apprenticeship which leads to the embodying of the structures of the world, that is, the appropriating by the world of a body thus enabled to appropriate the world" (95). Bourdieu's notion of embodiment as a vanishing education process, a "habitus" that trains the subject and reproduces its lessons like "conductorless orchestration," is useful in describing the consequences of attention to behavior in the Renaissance literature of manners, which seeks to form civil subjects by em-bodying them with correct physical techniques and civilized/civilizing attitudes. In Bourdieu's Kabyle society no less than in sixteenth-century Europe, this dual process of subjectification and subjugation has embedded in it the issue of sexual difference. When we deal with the formation of a civil subject in Renaissance texts, we need always to remember that the civil subject is a gendered subject, implicitly if not explicitly male, and its successful constitution is achieved through victory over the ungovernable signs which the civil subject seeks to dominate and to eliminate. In the sex/gender system of the early modern period, the civil subject must assert supreme identity by containment and erasure of whatever in the cultural semiotic scheme is identified as the feminine—a project remarkable in both its futility and its historical efficacy.[42] Without the construction of the feminine, the act of masculine signification is aborted. Yet the process of subjectification in the formation of cultural manhood already contains and must retain precisely that which it claims to exclude.

The discourse on manners and civil incorporation in the sixteenth century remains a special historically poignant case of embodiment. The literature of civility in this period of transition renders the habitus remarkably transparent and reveals the operations of the civilizing machinery before it is successfully internalized and rendered opaque in a second nature of the civil subject. Bourdieu notes:

> If all societies . . . that seek to produce a new man through a process of "deculturation" and "reculturation" set such store on the seemingly most insignificant details of dress, bearing, physical and verbal manners, the reason is that, treating the body as a memory, they entrust to it in abbreviated and practical, i.e. mnemonic, form the fundamental principles of the arbitrary content of the culture. The principles em-bodied in this way are placed beyond the grasp of consciousness, and hence cannot be touched by voluntary, deliberate transformation, cannot even be made explicit; nothing seems more ineffable, more incommunicable, more inimitable, and, therefore, more precious, than the values given body, made body by the transubstantiation achieved by the hidden persuasion of an implicit pedagogy, capable of instilling a whole cosmology, an ethic, a metaphysic, a political philosophy, through injunctions as insignificant as "stand up straight" or "don't hold your knife in your left hand." . . . The whole trick of pedagogic reason lies precisely in the way it extorts the essential while seeming to demand the insignificant. (94)

In addressing the need for cultural anthropology to question the insufficiency of its own structuralist models, Bourdieu reintroduces the "habitus" (a term taken from Mauss) as a more nuanced and encompassing theory of human behaviors.[43] The question remains, however, whether the habitus, in describing processes of internalization and forgetting in which the subject becomes the moving object of "infernal

circularities," is the instrumental term of an improved and refined structuralist approach, more inclusive because it can account for the apparently unpredictable and make it predictable, or the effective critique of
structuralism. The question of the historical role of Bourdieu's habitus
or the alterations to habitus in historical change, as, for example, in the
transitional conditions of the sixteenth century, remains vexing.

It is true that the conduct literature of the sixteenth century—the
works of Erasmus and Castiglione, as well as the *Grobianus* texts—
marks a new institutionalization of habitus, accoutering the early modern subject with regimes of strong and self-perpetuating internal controls, but these regimes and the habitus they mark are the products of
and contributors to historical change. I would not subscribe to mecha-
nistic notions of the transition from an organic, unalienated, use-
economy Middle Ages to an anticipatory protocapitalist Renaissance
period; nevertheless, the texts of conduct literature stand as evidence
of cumulative and dramatic historical change.[44] Yet in discussing that
change, the goal is not better social history or the closed construction
of history at all but rather by working through contextualization to locate
and highlight the indeterminate psychic excess of the early subject of
that history. The effects and symptoms can be located in conduct literature and in the *Grobianus* texts, but questions, rather than answers,
seem to result from finding them; for example, despite the clear indi-
cations in literary and cultural texts of the period that a civilizing process
is inscribing the body in regimes of restraint, how well does the process
work in producing both consent and resistance? How embodied, how
thoroughly and culturally inscribed are the bodies of the civilizing process?

Elias speaks of feelings of shame, embarrassment, a lowered threshold of shame that heightens the sense of delicacy; those categories have
been profoundly influential, regularly taken up in subsequent discussions of Renaissance culture such as Gail Kern Paster's *Body Embarrassed*. Paster sees Elias's civilizing enculturation as introducing shame
to subject formation, to a study of Renaissance "humoralism"; she sees
an early modern preoccupation with "an internal hierarchy of fluids and
functions within the body which is fully assimilable to external hierar-
chies of class and gender" (19). Her illuminating discussions of such
social-scientific analogies and evidence of them in Jonsonian and

Shakespearean drama offer compelling feminist readings of the works. Her argument buttresses and applies Elias's ideas to present a clear and unquestioned development of sociopsychic restraint and repressive effects. It thus tends to work in a way that seems more concerned with effects (shame) than with causes (for instance, discourses on indecency).[45]

Interestingly, Paster sees affinities between Elias's historical and sociological narrative of the civilizing process and Jacques Lacan's psychoanalytic account of the mirror stage, noting in that psychoanalytic *locus classicus* evidence of "the conceptual moment within the life of the subject that begins to instantiate centuries-long civilizing processes" (18).[46] Although for Lacan the mirror stage predates "the social dialectic," she finds that it "does locate shame socially, in the gaze of a desirable other, and thus brings it within the dynamic agencies of theater" (18). Certainly for Lacan, the mirror stage is both a very early alienating moment of separation from the maternal and a recognition of an Other in an experience of disjuncture between an ideal image and the baby's physical limits which anticipates future socialization, where specular relationships prevail in forming the symbolically structured subject. The "drama" of alienation and disjuncture Lacan describes, "experienced as a temporal dialectic that decisively projects the formation of the individual into history," is for Paster a drama of shame.[47] The baby's jubilation at the sight of the ideal image, contrasted with frustration and disappointment when "he" cannot match the perfect image of the mirror, the moment of triumphant specular gazing contrasted to his lack of coordination, locates a place at which social shaming may make its early marks. But to see a genesis of shaming regimes at work in the mirror stage would seem to bestow on shame a cultural authority and make it a powerful structure, even give it the status of a primary process.[48]

If we can view the early modern concern with behavior and conduct as a kind of Lacanian cultural mirror stage, an early or (what Lacan calls) "primordial" entry in the symbolic of civility, recognizing that the reflection on conduct, the process of conduct pedagogy involves the kind of specular activity we see in Castiglione's *Courtier*, it will not be the explanatory end of the story. It may be that something else enters interstitially into the construction of the space of internalization in the

civilizing process, intervenes in the operations of conduct. That motivating "something else" can be called into service to produce the aversive conditioning essential to conduct books, and while remaining
essential to those structures, it is also what remains in excess of structures of civil behavior.

I suggest that we approach that "something else" through the visual
regimes that belong to the operations of conduct (that is, the practice
of imagining how you look to others), as a way to think further about
conduct and subject formation. We then add another conceptual layer,
take the last step in this methodological itinerary, and look to Julia
Kristeva's important work on horror, dread, and abjection. The major
Kristevan statement on these supposedly untheorizable areas is most
fully set forth in *Powers of Horror*, but in her brief but provocative
thought-piece on cinema, "Ellipsis on Dread and Specular Seduction,"
we can see how Kristeva takes on the motivating "something else" of
aversive conditioning: "What I see has nothing to do with the specular
which fascinates me. The glance by which I identify an object, a face,
my own, another's, delivers my identity which reassures me: for it delivers me from *frayages*, nameless dread, noises preceding the name,
the image. . . . For speculation socializes me and reassures others as to
my good intentions in both meanings and morals.[49] Kristeva both alludes
to and confronts Lacan on the mirror stage, for she conceives of specularity as a much less docile phenomenon. In discussing the category
of the specular in cinematic horror ("Represented horror is the specular
par excellence" [238]), Kristeva splits the specular into the symbolic
(what I see, what yields meaning and reassurance) and the "fascinating"
(the unaccounted-for remainder and the power it generates) and offers
a working definition of horror as the site at which (or the moment in
which) the symbolic confronts the (fascinating) scene it is dedicated to
contain. Containment is contractually guaranteed by the workings of
symbolic law that, in the final instance, legislates signification through
the image—"Specular fascination captures terror and restores it to the
symbolic order" (241)—but only after it deals with the excess ("supple-
mental informations" or "lektonic traces" [237]) of which fascination
obliges it to take note.[50]

Kristeva's concern, however, is not only with what a Lacanian structure of subject development leaves out but with what stands in excess

of, in resistance to that specular relationship.[51] Her interest in horror film and in the category of dread as the "fascinating specular" focuses on the as yet unassimilable and uncategorizable: what appears, interstitially, in the moments before the *régime du savoir* ascends and speaks, names the (previously unnamed) horror.[52] In opening that space, Kristeva uncovers a moment like the shaming moment of the civilizing process, a noise before the name, a moment before a normative reaction overtakes it.

In *Powers of Horror*, Kristeva extends her concern with dread and horror to theorize abjection. For the reader of the *Grobianus* texts, this is familiar territory that also deals with the indecent: excrement, bodily effluence, putrescence. Like Foucault's essays on power and discipline, Kristeva's findings are suggestive for the study of conduct literature and its psychic dynamics. Kristeva carefully attends to the micropolitics of subject formation; she underscores, too, in ways that may have escaped Elias, Bakhtin, Bourdieu, Lévi-Strauss and others, or at least to which they insufficiently attend, how fragile the symbolic law is, how vulnerable its modes of domination are to the resisting powers that are also necessary to its continued existence, even as they are in conduct's micromanagement of the subject.

If, as Kristeva says, there are no "abjects" but simply the space of the abject (from which—in panic?—objects are defined and cast out or kept in, from which the subject marks limits and defines proper objects, averts the catastrophe of symbolic dissolution by naming properly), if the experiences of abjection function as "primers of my culture," it is because abjection provides the lesson material for the aversive conditioning that forms the modern subject in the civilizing process.[53]

We can speak of civility's aversive conditioning as a space of psychic and cultural negotiation, where the subject turns from the abject, acts upon abjection with the action of aversion, turning away from horror and toward the so-called security and stability of symbolically bounded and legislated space. Aversive conditioning is the proving ground for the civilizing process, and it remains a repeatable exercise, although it is expected to recede in memory, to be performed without reflexivity. Conduct then serves as a mnemonic device, a memory discipline that, in inscribing the body, reinscribes instinctual memories as abject lessons.

In Kristeva's treatment of the abject, the body has status as primary text: it is the place of cultural inscription, marked by the action of aversion, of ab-jecting. Without the body as palette, or material, abjection (in some ways the unthinkable) is itself unthinkable: "We may call it a border; abjection is above all ambiguity. Because, while releasing a hold, it does not radically cut off the subject from what threatens it— on the contrary, abjection acknowledges it to be in perpetual danger" (9) of falling out of so-called symbolic security and regressing to semiotic territories of "maternal" space.[54] Kristeva speaks of horror as based on a "mechanism of subjectivity," with "literature . . . its privileged signifier" (208). Her concerns are local, historically specific; but it is also possible to apply her discussion of the abject to early modern conduct literature, to see, as linked in the civilizing process, abjection and aversion.

If it is the activity of the symbolic to lay down the law, then the obedience it demands and elicits is motivated from the far less legible categories of abjection and horror. The action of aversion is the consequence of acting upon abjection: a-version, the turning away and creating a version, and a manageable version, of the abject, abjection accoutered with symbolic stakes.

This managing of the abject is the goal of the aversive conditioning engendered in the lessons of conduct literature. Conduct literature produces disgust as the action that translates abjection into the action of aversion. Aversion is the action dictated by the symbolic, but even in turning away, it keeps pointing back toward the abject. It often takes, as in the case of the *Grobianus* texts, the form of dividing practices: woman—peasant—animal; nonmale—nongentleman—non-human; effeminate—common; vulgar—bestial. It can also produce strange maxims of decency and indecency, records of the abject in action: shit, vomit, farts, scabs, ulcerated sores are the worthless horror of unregulated flows. Effluence is not affluence.

When Elias speaks of the curve of civilization and of "progressive sensitization," the lowering of thresholds of shame and embarrassment, he locates a historical moment of transition from a period of fewer controls and anxieties to one—linked always to modern state formation—in which control and anxiety become cultural-historical markers. Domesticating and instrumentalizing the abject are the project of the aversive conditioning of the civilizing process; calling it into service to produce docile, well-mannered bodies is its goal. Yet it is perhaps an indecent irony that the process, however historically enduring, leaves the indeterminate specter of the abject to elude the symbolic whose boundaries it constructs.

An ironic conduct book that praises and recommends the worst possible manners as a means of instilling horror of the body, *Grobianus* focuses relentlessly on the body as the site of social catastrophe. The work employs an ironic-didactic method of aversive conditioning which constantly calls upon the reader to reconstruct decent behavior by actively inverting and at the same time retaining the image of the worst possible scenario, the catastrophe of abjection and horror which must be kept in mind in order to be averted. My itinerary of literary texts will show that at the center of the contradictions of the text stand twin horrors: a horror of the material body and a horror of the inscrutable forces of the modern economy: "materialism." The horror of body, to be controlled by keeping the image of horror ever present, creates and maintains repressive self-consciousness, which renders one marketable or, as Dekker expresses it so well, allows one to "publish" one's "suit": of fashionable clothes, of the unclothed body, of the body in pretentiously fashionable clothes economically beyond the means of the wearer.

These texts reflect back upon a tradition, earlier represented in the pivotal work of Erasmus, whose turning point they mark—one by irony, the other by parody—yet whose project they realize and, as metatexts, read. Together, they contribute to a self-reflexive discourse on identity formation, on the circulation of the body, on manners and conduct books themselves as commodities, on behavior as cultural capital, in the period of early modernity.

While grobianist texts such as these present readers with a way of viewing critically the ends—the goals—of conduct and the civilizing process, they also arguably (since historically the genre continues and undergoes feminization, further bourgeoisification, and trivialization) mark the exhaustion of the form of humanist conduct literature and give the game away on conduct technologies. In marking the end and the exhaustion of a cultural and pedagogical institution, of course, grobianist conduct books do not actually close the doors on that institution.

In a similar way, we could even speak of seeing in grobian literature a view of masculine identity formation as dysfunctional, a failed—but enduring—project.

In revealing the cultural extortion and deception that Bourdieu addresses in "Structures and the Habitus," the disciplining and subjectifying processes of Foucault, the instrumentalization of horror and the abject, perhaps no other text of its kind presents the contributions and contradictions of the conduct book genre and the Renaissance preoccupation with conduct better than *Grobianus*; yet its status remains securely noncanonical, reflecting the problematic "naturalness" of canonization itself. Linked to this textual history, however, is the way in which the work loses popular status among a public that no longer "needs" to see the civilizing machinery at work, or rather, needs not to see and seeks to have its pedagogical operations melt into the horizon of second nature and genderless universality. In providing a way to denaturalize those disciplining operations and offering a perspective on the mechanisms of conduct which have been previously ignored, this work could (but probably won't) be the final word on conduct and the study of conduct and courtesy literature.

I have begun by proposing a revised lineage of conduct literature and by introducing the itinerary of methods that inform this project on historical and formal shifts in the conduct book tradition in which I locate the socially and psychically embedded self-contradictory logic of the conduct enterprise and its consequences for the gendered early modern subject. Chapter 1 positions the indecent and obstreperous grobian and the *Grobianus* texts in a history of a period marked by a cultural-masculine anxiety shared by aristocratic and rising bourgeois classes, located in a milieu in which status and standards are more fluid than fixed, fertile ground for conduct books and the rise of specular regimes. It offers a contextual reading of *Grobianus* as marking a culminating moment in the Renaissance conduct genre. Chapter 2 looks to Erasmus's *De civilitate morum puerilium* (a direct influence on Dedekind's *Grobianus*) and *Colloquia familiaria* as exemplary of the conduct problematic, to study the effects of that fluidity and malleability. Erasmus also addresses the questions of power and gender which find their continuation in the *Grobianus* texts. The formal reading of Dedekind's

*Grobianus* in Chapter 3 sees it as reversing Erasmus's high-humanist lessons in decency but also repeating them with a vengeance. It looks at the ironic-didactic strategy in *Grobianus* as offering a labor theory of conduct as well as a homeopathic treatment of indecency. In Chapter 4, which focuses on Dedekind's chapter of advice to women as a dangerous supplement that underscores the self-contradictory logic of conduct rhetoric, these strategies and their problems are seen as intolerably stressed. Chapter 5 investigates the work's strategy of reform in the arena of vernacular discipline, concentrating particularly on Scheidt's adaptation of *Grobianus* and his added negative focus on the materialism of the indecent body and the social world of indecent, materially corrupted values. Whereas both Reformation disciplinarians dedicate themselves to molding a national masculine subject, Scheidt parts ways with Hans Sachs in handling the theme of materialism, for Sachs's poems on etiquette represent a body at odds with the material world that requires its docility and discipline, and Scheidt represents both the body and the material-commercial world as conspiring against civility. Chapter 6 completes the chronological trajectory of the *Grobianus* texts by taking it into the territory of the English gull, where John Davies' *Gullinge Sonnets* introduce the figure in indecently bad sonnets and Dekker's *Guls Horne-booke* marks the reluctantly transmitted continuity of *Grobianus*. Dekker adapts Dedekind's text for English conditions, making an English gull from the German grobian and echoing Scheidt's critique of materialism in a work that "translates" didacticism into satiric entertainment and reflects on the commodification of the conduct book.

I am interested in using the *Grobianus* texts and the topic of indecency to pry open issues of early modernity: questions of bodily regimes, of cultural gendering, the making of a masculine subject of humanism. I read *Grobianus* more intertextually than locally, as more a European than as a German phenomenon, though the specifically German Reformation contribution is a necessary part of the early modern cultural portrait. Dekker's seventeenth-century English adaptation, for example, rejects the Grobianus figure and assimilates the text to the national particulars of the English gull, but his text owes a significant intertextual debt to *Grobianus*, in many ways is its English sequel. Other Renaissance texts and authors find their way into this book, but I would like to use the *Grobianus* texts to contribute to a conversation on the canon rather than to lean heavily on or to make canonical texts either terminus or taboo.[55]

This book is about the end of conduct and the obscure and marginal Renaissance conduct texts that make it possible to speak of the end of conduct. What could be meant by the end of conduct, and who could imagine such a thing? The deceptively easy answer to the first part of that question is that the end of conduct, its goal, is simply the formation of the civil subject. In pursuing that goal, however, the *Grobianus* texts disclose the mechanisms that render the ends contradictory. What the mechanisms entail, in other words, is more complicated, less determinate or "simple." *Grobianus* is a specifically German phenomenon, but it would be a mistake to see it as unrelated to other European or English events. It is, to be sure, the negative complement to the better-known (even if, in most cases, only a little better known) texts of European Renaissance "courtesy" literature, those of Castiglione, Thomas Elyot, Erasmus, Stefano Guazzo, and Giovanni della Casa—above all, to the canonical. But it is still a necessary complement or companion.

Of course, I would not claim that there ever, historically, was an end or that there is at present an end to conduct. Nor do I foresee a time when what Bourdieu calls the structural apprenticeship of embodiment will, like the capitalist state, wither away. But what I would claim is that it is in the little-known "classical" texts of grobian literature that the end of conduct is to be seen.

The study of early modern conduct literature might be described as the study of minor texts and major problems. Minor texts because, outside of Castiglione's *Courtier* (and perhaps their later incorporation into the eighteenth-century novel of manners), they have not attained canonical status, although serious study might raise still more questions about canonization or contribute to the noncanonical readings of canonical works calllled for in recent discussions of Renaissance texts. Yet these texts address topics of pressing importance to the modern reader of cultural practices: the fate of the body in the civilizing process, crises of cultural masculinity in emerging bourgeois society, the consequences of such crises for European women and men and "discovered" populations, and configurations of power at both micrological and institutional levels which reproduce and enforce the kind of marginalization that the noncanonical is itself a product of and subject to.

Working with an eye toward theory as well as history, I mean to use the *Grobianus* texts to address an important omission in the Renaissance scholarship, to treat conduct and courtesy literature as they have not been treated before. In that sense, my project takes some cues from *Grobianus* itself, stands in a close (if somewhat ironic) relationship to the phenomenon that is my object of study. Like the authors of the *Grobianus* texts, I take the categories of conduct and indecency very seriously. While my critical goals could not be more distant from theirs, they (as much as contemporary theorists) have shown me the intimate links between conduct and the indecent.

Critical readings of what we might view as the repressive and symptomatic operations of early modern conduct literature make clearer the relationship of such literature to its cultural-political milieu. To know what constitutes masculine subject formation—the privileged as well as the tormented object of most of this literature's lessons—and how the early modern text of identity is itself a text in excess of itself, is to render the residues of its naturalized operations in the present more visible, perhaps more changeable in the future. *Grobianus*, we could say, is both subtext and intertext of the more canonical and high-cultural artifacts of the West's civilizing process. It is a work that is absolutely derivative of and absolutely reflexive about the civilizing process. If we can speak of the debts of the modern subject to the legacy of humanist lessons of civility and conduct, then whatever the "worth" of the *Grobianus* texts themselves, their cultural legacy and the cultural debts to them are underestimated; although the texts can be said to mark the end of conduct, those debts are as yet undischarged. I would not claim to discharge them, for that is not possible; my aim is to make them more dischargeable.

My task, therefore, is not simply textual criticism but the reading of social texts, in which a reading of *Grobianus* means a reading of social formation and cultural embodiment. In carrying out this task, I find myself reflecting not only on the historical process but on my investment in historical reading as a form of rewriting of the past which stems from an investment in the present and future. It would not be too ironic to acknowledge at this point that, in the course of writing this text, I have located not only the Grobiana in *Grobianus* but, at unpredictable moments, the grobian within. Having discharged the obligation to confess that, and in the hope that my readers will soon have some self-reflexive good humor of their own, I conclude my Introduction by saying that, while it seems justified to speak of the end of conduct, I do not think this work will be the final word on conduct. But who can imagine the end of conduct?

# 1 / Reading *Grobianus*: The Crisis of the Body in the Sixteenth Century

Now I do not want to go into great detail as regards matters that are already very familiar, such as that your courtier should not profess to be a great eater or drinker, or indulge in bad habits, or be disgusting and dissolute in his manner of life, and act like a peasant who stinks of the soil a mile off. For a man of this sort can never hope to become a good courtier and indeed can be given no occupation other than looking after the farm animals.

—Castiglione, *Book of the Courtier*

Thingis somtyme alowed is now repriued.

—Caxton, *The Boke of Courtesy*

During the sixteenth century in western Europe the instincts and passions of men and women fought the battle of the civilizing process. The outcome of this struggle, situated in the context of other historical struggles of that century, was not total victory for the controls of civility, not some devastating defeat of instinctual freedoms. Rather, it altered attitudes toward the human body, changed the structuring of the human subject, introduced new and historically specific modes of social interaction. The intense examination and reconsideration of human behavior, the dedication to techniques of the body, worked to construct a model of the subject. As the early modern text of identity was composed, the consequences for historical women and men and for notions of gender and sexuality, class and race were differentiated and grave. This civil war of the subject also left embattled residues, indeterminate and unstable, as its incorporated and internalized legacy, even as it established enduring and adaptable models of the national-masculine subject.

In *The Dialectic of Enlightenment* Max Horkheimer and T. W. Adorno called for remembering a once hidden and repressed second history of the subject and the body: "Europe has two histories: a well-known, written history and an underground history. The latter consists in the fate of the human instincts and passions which are displaced and distorted by civilization."[1] Looking to the consequences of such displacement and distortion in German fascist society, the two exiled critical theorists apparently had in mind Freud's *Civilization and Its Discontents*, published in 1931, and its discussion of repression on a social level, its very early attempt to speculate on the possibility of mass neurosis and the connections between micropolitical subjectification and macropolitical structures.[2] Since Horkheimer and Adorno's call for attention to a neglected historical record, social history, histories of *mentalités*, of passions and interests, have restored visibility to that once underground and unwritten historical record that now complicates the master narratives of Western civilization.[3]

In examining the place of indecency in the discourses of civility and in the culturally constituted body of the early modern subject through a reading of the *Grobianus* texts, I hope to contribute to this critical history. I begin by following a cultural-historical itinerary through a period of transition and social mobility which takes us to the point of an opening excess. The discourse on indecency, the shaming disciplines that produce aversive conditioning in the subject of civility, are found in that cultural space, the excess of the body constructed by the discourses of civility, the excess that thwarts and nourishes the process of civilization. It appears in class conflict and problematic class identity: early modern bourgeoisification, confronting the aristocratic models it seeks to appropriate and emulate, yields a picture of historical conflict in which a gap, an anxiety-ridden space opens up. The history that generates that space produces the grobian, and the grobian is positioned uneasily in that historical space, where I locate and read *Grobianus*.

*Grobianus* evokes and elicits horror of the body, produces visceral disgust and revulsion in a way that contributes to control of the body by a newly cultivated mind. The figure of Grobianus is civility's antisubject, or rather, its antesubject. As the outsider and the precondition for the civilizing process, he waits in the wings, providing the cues for the civil subject, well scripted because well schooled in his abject lessons. In playing his role, he reflects on the history of manners that produces him and performs a twisted but recognizable version of that history. He repeats that history with a difference, perhaps even with a vengeance. *Grobianus* takes the form of instructions that invite the reader to visualize them in concrete social dramas, imagine them carried out in a narrative that characterizes the grobian in everyday life.

But of what actions does such behavior consist? What does the good "grobian" look like? In book 1 of Dedekind's *Grobianus*, the reader (who is male) is advised upon rising, no earlier than noon, to take his clothes and dress by the household hearth, ignoring any women who may be present. Those who object to his aggressive nakedness should be told to look elsewhere:

> Sique tuis quisquam factis offenditur, illum
> Cernere si talem nolit, abire iube.
> (1.1.77–78)

> If any man object to thee that manners thou dost lacke,
> Bid him, if he mislike that sight, be gone and shew his backe.
> (1.1.67–68)

The main grobian precept for behavior is always to assert the primacy of the body, an asocial, ruthlessly self-interested body, and to gratify its unreflected desires, unbounded by any conflict of superego and instinct:

> Quisque tibi cedat, nec tu concesseris ulli,
> Conditione tua es liber, et esse velis.
> (1.1.79–80)

> Let every man give place to thee, thy selfe give place to none.
> What man? Why Nature made thee free, then boldely holde
>     thine owne.
> (1.1.69–70)

The grobian expresses his nature-bestowed "freedom" by means of appetite, effluence, and excretion; he scorns all bodily controls and restraints. His is a chaotically active, tyrannical body that wages an aggressive, unrelenting campaign against social order. Society, in turn, is represented as threatened by and vulnerable to the grobian's violent assaults. The speaker of *Grobianus* teaches his students to cultivate the loud mouth, the sneeze and cough (always into the face of a neighbor), large gestures from flailing arms to a grin that distorts the face from ear to ear, and various physical eruptions, both spontaneous and willfully or conspiratorially cultivated. Predictably unpredictable, a student of grobianism constantly spills into the social space, invades it to loot and take what he wants to consume, as at the table when he takes the best food from the platters or tricks others out of it. He takes over social space with loud noises, unpleasant smells, aggressive, distorted looks; he occupies and dominates the space of social visibility with vomit and excrement, destroying the pleasures or appetites of other social members. These remain silent, barely visible, compelled to witness all, even as the grobian unseats and inverts presumably shared precepts and values with his aggressive bodily excess.

In book 1 the young grobian student serving in the house of his father or master does as little as possible and that little as carelessly as he can. A disobedient son, an unserving servant, an insubordinate inferior, he terrorizes house guests, serves them grudgingly with a disheveled appearance and filthy hands, and in every action and attitude inverts and perverts the hierarchy of social positions. In book 2, as an adult and a guest himself, he carefully calculates every opportunity that hospitality presents him and does not hesitate to protest his slightest disappointment. In returning the hospitality, however, as a host he takes all measures to ensure that no guest will want to accept another invitation from him. Walking the public streets after an evening of freeloading, gluttonous eating, and drunkenness, he freely urinates, vomits, and awakens the sleeping citizenry as he makes his way home to berate his servants and beat his wife. With the excuse that the possibilities for grobian precepts are endless, book 3 presents still more of these routines, adding, for the sake of an inclusiveness that could never be fully delivered, a chapter of advice to the female "equivalent" of the grobian.

In an age of manner books addressed to adolescents entering the maturity of civilized life, Grobianus clings by choice to preadolescence, imitating a child without a social superego.[4] A Grobianus acts in the name of single-minded—certainly not mindless—regression. He is an enthusiastically committed two-year-old, instinct in action, whose naive malice Dedekind's ebullient and myopic speaker advocates and tutors.

In the perpetual activity of all his orifices and appendages—squirming, defecating, farting, belching, vomiting, running at the nose, and running off at the mouth—Grobianus is a figure of totalizing physicality who perverts, dominates, even demolishes the entire social environment. He acts with the force of nature as projected from the code of civility and gathers the energy of that projection. A high priest of the goddess rusticity—"alma Rusticitas, nostro dea maxima saeclo"—he represents a phantasmal world in which intellect is the abused captive of instinct, Ulysses is in the hands of Circe, Apollo is the prisoner of Rusticitas. He is nature running amok, the catastrophe that civilization is built as a dam against, a destroyer of philosophy, religion, common hygienic sense, and what the civilized world would—thanks, in part, to grobianism—come to call "simple" decency. He is the realization of the nostalgic desire for the age of Saturn, the invasion from Schlaraffenland or Cocaygne and popular utopian myths, the concretization of fantasies and popular desires, a reality thrown back against the dreamers, a nightmare come true. He is the raging body that speaks the necessity of manners and control, civility's abject in action.

The text's strategy of didactic irony opposes grobian actions to intellectual appeal and visceral disgust. The speaker makes necessarily futile efforts to legitimate grobian actions, often by the specious use of authority, of classical and humanist writers, biblical and traditional proverbs, and scientific (hygienic) opinions, but mainly by the reactions the speaker falsely and ironically claims they will provoke. The efforts necessary to cultivate these legitimating responses create contradictions in an otherwise rather simple set of reversed precepts. Simple or unrefined behavior alone is not enough to repel and educate readers, to lead them toward civil restraint. Simple behavior alone is not worthy of attack; the real enemy is simplicity itself.

In *Grobianus* the attitude toward the body as an unmistakable link to nature is thrown into confusion. It is not that the authors are uncertain about what is right; they have a notion of a straight and narrow path of virtuous civility that leads to a haven from the chaotic disorder of the grobians. Yet by embedding their notion of decency in the text, to be gleaned from their ironic method, they give their projection of uncivil forces, dependent on revulsion and bodily shame, a powerful position. They build social fear by exploring and elaborating on a new uncertainty, providing only the coherence of the concrete, repulsive images of foul, grobian manners. Irony, too, serves that timely uncertainty.

In *The Civilizing Process*, Norbert Elias notes the gradual lowering of the threshold of shame and embarrassment in the early modern period, a growing sensitization to the body as a site of danger. That civilizing process comes about through ever more internalized appeals, dependent on shame and aversion and grounded, I would emphasize, in a specular regime involving outward display, inward restraint, the internalized presence of an evaluating observer. Elias found sociogenic fear on the move in the sixteenth century: "People mold themselves and others more deliberately than in the Middle Ages."[5] Yet the psychic stakes are far greater, the sociopsychic issues more serious than Elias acknowledges, when we consider the substance of such civilizing deliberations and for whom "people mold themselves," that is, who it is who owns the gaze that regards and evaluates the early modern subjects of civility. The specular regime comes with the nurturing horror of abjection; it highlights the role of indecency not only for producing shame and embarrassment, as Elias and his followers have shown, but for containing an archive of the body, the excess that points to the ability of the body, momentarily at least, to confound the discourses that construct it.

We can get a sense of that specular mechanism in Castiglione's description of *sprezzatura*, where the speaker, Cesare Gonzaga, describes a

> universal rule which seems to apply more than any other in all human actions or words: namely, . . . to practise in all things a certain nonchalance which conceals all artistry and makes whatever one says or does seem uncontrived and effortless. . . . We can truthfully say that true art is what does not seem to be art; and the most important thing is to conceal it, because if it is revealed this discredits a man completely and ruins his reputation. . . . So you see that to reveal intense application and skill robs everything of grace. . . . We see in

many of the men and women who are with us now, that graceful and
nonchalant spontaneity [*sprezzatura*] because of which they seem to
paying little, if any, attention to the way they speak or laugh or hold
themselves, so that those who are watching them imagine that they
couldn't and wouldn't ever know how to make a mistake. (1.26.67–
68)

While Castiglione's *Courtier* is in many respects an utterly conventional Renaissance work, observing principles of imitation, using traditional topoi and tropes, observing classical and Renaissance rhetorical
conventions, *sprezzatura* is also a strange neologism, a positive value
that functions to emphasize the negative, the ever-present possibility of
making a reprehensible mistake. For the ideal courtier, revealing is
robbery; self-regard is concealed as naturalized deception that constructs the perfect courtier. Exemplary self-regard, however, achieves
its artful nonchalance, the arduously and artfully wrought illusion of
artlessness, only by anticipating every conceivable fault or faux pas. The
unmentionable is everywhere on the brink of being mentioned. The
work that aestheticizes politics, morality, power, and their constitutive
coercions begins with the autoscopic regime of *sprezzatura*. Its scopic
agenda is not different from the one we find, less mystified, in *Grobianus*. The overarching ironies of Castiglione's text, with their own indecent elements laboriously disavowed, offer us a bridge to the indecent
ironies of the *Grobianus* texts.

The history of manners has been effectively addressed by Norbert Elias
in work that remains indispensable for scholars of hidden histories. Elias
revises the conventional progressive-evolutionary historiography that
sees a gradual, inexorable, schematic process of refinement in the
achievements of Western civilization. To his credit, he takes neither an
affirmative nor an accusatory stance on the civilizing process; in presenting material critical of the conventional view, that is, he does not
fall back on a repressive hypothesis.[6] He not only places manners and
sociopsychic developments in the context of political-historical change
but links macropolitical changes themselves—the transition from feudal
to bourgeois society, the rise of the early modern state—to the psychic
structures of the subject of civility. He locates the civilizing process in

the constellation of those relationships. For Elias, *Grobianus* plays no minor role in developing the curve of civilization; its reverse precepts, in his view, work with a shaming efficacy.[7]

*Grobianus* harks back to a long historical process for which, following the somewhat deviant path discussed in the Introduction, it could be considered a culminating, as well as a genealogizing moment.[8] For reading *Grobianus* takes us not to some high place in a progressive-evolutionary narrative but rather into a history of instability, unassimilable resistance, and excess, to a place where things slip past shaming efficacy.

========

The conventional view of *Grobianus* in traditional German scholarship makes the text a symptom of a period of national cultural poverty. Dedekind, it is usually assumed, witnessed extraordinarily boorish behavior at the universities in Marburg and Wittenberg. From his spontaneous and self-evident revulsion at the sad state of German culture in the first half of the sixteenth century, the "grobian age,"[9] he sought a corrective. Thus, for example, Adolf Hauffen comments that grobian literature developed "under the influence of the coarsening of all aspects of life, which went hand in hand with the decline of medieval culture," and *Grobianus* was published "at precisely that moment when the depraved inclinations of the grobian masses had exhausted the patience of refined people." Gustav Milchsack attributes the long-lived popularity of the work to the long duration of boorishness in the German population which came to an end only in the eighteenth century.[10]

Projected anachronistically from a particular bourgeois historical imaginary, the grobian-age hypothesis grapples with a disorderly episode that it is willing to nominate—in an act of historical abjection—while resolutely maintaining silence on the other events that break with an idealized medieval past and disrupt the smooth historical progression of evolutionary accounts: the Reformation, the Peasant Revolution of 1525, the rise of an urban economy. The sixteenth century, in this scheme, represents a regression from the medieval-aristocratic refinement, of the twelfth century, the age of *Minnesang* and epic, which only the eighteenth century overcomes. When a question of class intrudes, however, the position also reveals a deep distrust of its own lineage of early bourgeois culture as disorderly and coarse, miraculously overcome when bourgeois culture assimilates some aristocratic values and refines itself to the point of producing the familiar cultural giants of eighteenth-century Germany: Lessing, Goethe, Schiller, Kant.

The theory of the grobian age, somewhat like the *Grobianus* texts, is a revisionary reading and most certainly, in its combined repudiation of and prurient investment in "indecency," a grobianizing one. But in many ways it also redramatizes the very conflicts and cultural disavowals that symptomatically mark early modern bourgeois cultural formations. In the sixteenth-century reflection on status, identity, and behavior, a look to an aristocratic past and an attempt to emulate models of the nobility are important, if unfulfilled, aspirations.

During the Middle Ages, religious and secular-aristocratic life was highly organized and stratified. The rules necessary for the administration and maintenance of monastic orders throughout the Continent covered everyday behavior and manners as integral to the disciplines and pleasures of worship and communal life. These ascetic regulations produced a rigid daily routine that affirmed membership in the community: order reproduced the monastic order.[11] In the secular sphere, by contrast, aristocratic life was hierarchically structured by a chain of mutual obligations, pantomimed and symbolized, for example, in the rituals of obeisance to the liege lord. Loyalty was the chief value in peace and in war; hospitality, generosity, and politeness were gestures of peace in an environment otherwise structured by violence. If manners displayed relations of subservience and domination, they also dramatized shared obligations, however unequal or unequally fulfilled. In the feudal order, the vassal deferred to a lord who was mutually bound to protect his loyal inferiors. The actions consisted of concrete gestures as well, coherent and comprehensible all the way down the social chain. They were, for the most part, orally, visually, gesturally transmitted, or recorded in epic verse.[12] The product of an oral tradition, the older precepts for behavior both secular-chivalric and clerical-monastic were based on an aristocratic culture tied to an agricultural mode of production and hereditary lineage, with land and power in the hands of a warrior and ecclesiastic aristocracy.

Such values came with historical contradictions. Loyalty, feudal order, hereditary power—all stood as ways of preventing conflict which preserved conflict. The point is not to idealize this feudal system and its ideology; nevertheless, we can say that its rules of behavior placed faith in concrete, visual actions and binary distinctions that were lost to early modern codification and bourgeoisification, even as men of the early modern period looked back to imitate feudal coherence.

⸻

As Norbert Elias and Stephen Greenblatt have remarked, early modern European culture conducted an examination of personal behavior which, while derived from classical precedents and models, was historically unique. Elias conceives of a "threshold of socially instilled pleasure and fear" moving on a curve of civilization which accompanied the transition from the medieval court to the formation of the state.[13] For Greenblatt, the phenomenon of self-fashioning, although imbricated in social processes and power structures and bearing often serious historical effects, is chiefly theatrical and aesthetic in character, a cultural trope.[14] But we can also see that this closer scrutiny of human behavior and the forms that scrutiny took were linked to historically specific early modern conditions: aristocratic tradition in conflict with the rise of exchange society. While political rule remained aristocratic, a rising middle class and urban patriciate took larger and more visible roles in economic, political, and cultural activity in a more mobile, urban society. Altered hereditary aristocratic structures contributed to the gradually rising value of diplomatic, intellectual, and administrative skills, on the one hand, and, on the other, to the declining status of the feudal warrior aristocracy. Read critically, for example, Castiglione's emphatic valorization of "the profession of arms" and his accompanying disdain for merchants, for men "who smell of the soil," and for effeminacy are symptomatic of a certain cultural siege mentality.[15] They point toward the historical circumstance of the mercenary army, the importance of trade, the mobility of other classes that compete, too, for a standard of manliness and in competing render the boundaries of gender more fluid and negotiable.[16]

In a way, the very familiar passage on *sprezzatura* I have quoted illustrates well what Elias has called the "courtization" of the warrior aristocracy.[17] But the changes that lay siege to the Castle of Urbino are far-reaching. Count Lodovico's insistence on the profession of arms is stated at a time when the *condottieri* of mercenary armies put one kind of pressure on warrior-aristocratic values, while the increased reliance of courts on administrative and diplomatic personnel applied yet another.[18] The courtier's behavior must distinguish him from all that the company at Urbino labors to disavow: he is not a merchant who sells goods for money and profit but one who very carefully promotes (sells) himself in his appeal; he is not a woman but one who occupies a feminized position; and he is not a peasant (who stinks of the soil) but one whose way of life, the structure of the court itself, is still based on an agricultural economy and labor force that it exploits and, when growing markets dictate, impoverishes and displaces. His authenticity consists of nothing more or less than a convincing performance, *sprezzatura*, which in the setting of the text, is ironically presided over by the ailing and sexually disabled duke of Urbino, so conspicuously absent from the company, but for whose benefit the four-day colloquium is held.[19] Even the temporal frame of the text is the contaminated and idealized memory that is Castiglione's nostalgia for a past always already lost and colored by death. He explains his decision to publish the work, parts of which had, without his knowledge or authorization, already appeared: "I began to re-read it; and the moment I looked at it, my memories being stirred by the heading itself, I experienced no little sorrow, which intensified as I read farther and as I recalled that most of those introduced in the conversations were already dead" (32).

A fluid field of competing authorities and standards feeds the crisis that constructs early modern masculinity. Despite the setting in the Castle of Urbino and the class specificity of Castiglione's suave precepts, the work is haunted by its own inability to delineate, much less legislate, difference: of class, as well as gender. Advising the prince—the chief duty of the perfect courtier—means performing the actions of a hired servant and places the courtier in a culturally "feminized" position.[20] Even cosmeticizing his professional work with dissimulation will not cover up the crisis. Cosmetics and the masquerade belong to the cultural work of women.[21]

Altered hereditary aristocratic structures changed the composition and importance of the royal court (in England) and contributed to the gradually rising value of diplomatic, intellectual, and administrative skills, on the one hand, and, on the other, to the declining status of the feudal warrior aristocracy. In Shakespeare's 1 *Henry IV*, for example, Hotspur denounces Henry as the "politic king," "forgetful" of his feudal-aristocratic obligations to those who fought to restore his patrimony (dramatized in *Richard II*). More opportunistic and ambitious than loyal to his aristocratic allies, Henry dramatizes the historical-ethical divide; in that respect he is Shakespeare's reflection on the early modern monarch. Whereas Hal bests Hotspur valorously on the battlefield and shows, apparently, that honor is not a "mere escutcheon," he also defends the king's diplomacy and "policy," the same "policy" represented by the courtier sent by Henry to claim Hotspur's prisoners, who so offends Hotspur's standard of warrior-aristocratic manliness in act 1. Hal's historical hybridization thus continues the new legacy of political maneuvering as a man seasoned in battle—the genuine article of the warrior aristocracy—and worthy heir to the throne, puts into question a standard of manliness.[22] In his eventual succession to the throne he can stands as a ruling model of manhood who is both politic and polite: he displaces violence, allows it to congeal in human interiority, a psychological battlefield where mind games prevail.

Hal seems to echo the quick-witted woman so admired by Lodovico in *The Courtier*, who mocks a humorless fighting man whose immoderately invested warrior identity keeps him from partaking of courtly entertainments.[23] In *1 Henry IV*, Hal deftly caricatures the slash-and-burn warrior-aristocrat hard-wired in Hotspur's character: "I am not yet of Percy's mind, the Hotspur of the North; he that kills me some six or seven dozen of Scots at a breakfast, washes his hands, and says to his wife, 'Fie upon this quiet life! I want work'" (2.4.97–100).[24] As his caricaturing skills show his wit prevailing over Hotspur's grim warrior monomania, so Hal's martial skills will enable him to best "the king of honor" on the field of battle. But his prevailing as politic warrior also works to place the standard of masculinity in a destabilized position, a position familiar to a mid- to late sixteenth-century setting.

In the case of Erasmus, in works such as *The Colloquies* and *Good Manners in Boys* the weakening or even collapse of the distinction between hereditary nobility and bourgeoisifying statecraft is still more evident and vexed. Fluidity is the field here, providing Erasmus with the opportunity to call up classical (Ciceronian, Quintilian, etc.) models for molding and shaping the malleable subject who moves in a more manipulable but less reliable world. As an opportunity, however, it also opened vistas of uncertainty that could take the appearance of a kind of horror show. Whereas Elias saw a continuum of civilizing, incremental change, here what seems important is that historical opening onto vistas of horror, those moments when an uncontainable, historically generated anxiety pushes against familiar evolutionary frameworks of historical or sociological understanding.

Challenges to the feudal order came early and, Elias emphasizes, developed gradually. Growing urban settlements, trade and banking, dislocations brought about in the wake of the Crusades introduced practices that replaced the autonomy and exclusivity of the feudal system: codification of laws, rules of dress—in short, manners.[25] The growth of the towns resulted in increasing use of records, more and more written legislation where custom had once been sufficient authority. The sumptuary laws of the later Middle Ages were belated attempts to retain the old distinctions of class and culture of dress when the traditional hierarchy had already met its replacement. Creating money wealth and mobilizing itself in trade, banking, manufacturing, the new urban bourgeoisie was gradually and tacitly claiming space and power for itself.[26]

Before the twelfth century the main conduct text for England and Europe was the *Disticha Catonis*, dating from the fourth century A.D., attributed to an unknown author given the name of Cato. It consists of abstract maxims, rather than practical or technical lessons in behavior.[27] The other "text" for secular etiquette could be found in custom and oral precepts, or what Elias calls "communal statements from an oral tradition by which commonly held values were passed on in history."[28] It is the modifications to these sources which reveal the historical transformation and the social consequences.

In the twelfth century conditions for the warrior-aristocratic elite begin to change as the Crusades came to an end and trade and urbanization grew gradually. As monastic schools begin to educate children of the aristocracy and, beyond that circle, the merchant bourgeoisie, new ways of defining behavior developed.[29] The elite consensus of the few participants in aristocratic and religious society was increasingly called into question, their principles transformed from rituals of initiation to more technified procedures. The alteration of the code in the hands of the emerging urban bourgeoisie translated aristocratic cultural forms into an emerging cultural voice, sought to appropriate the form without having the ability to duplicate the experience.

As Elias's account has established, between the twelfth and sixteenth centuries in Europe, written etiquette manuals increasingly codified forms and techniques of personal behavior. The audience included clerical students who learned manners as they learned their Latin, members of the courts, and with the advent of print technology and the Reformation, the working members of the court administrations, a literate merchant bourgeoisie, and urban-dwelling tradespeople. The efforts made in the thirteenth century to collect and preserve the traditional aristocratic behavioral precepts in written form were already symptomatic of the older order's demise. Codification and recorded compilation of rules would take the place of what had formerly been entrusted to memory and repeated through gesture as a part of everyday life. In Germany, furthermore, the written courtly etiquette (*Hofzucht*) dammed the flood of "modernizing" forces but revealed its penetrability as well. Its assertions that certain actions constitute nobility sounded a need for affirmation, to identify one situated aristocratic class against another that remains unnamed and invisible.

For Germany, Paul Merker identifies five types of these "table disciplines" or *Tischzuchten*, developed chronologically over four centuries: the clerical-pedagogical behavior manuals of the monastery schools; the *Hofzucht*, or courtly etiquette; the bourgeois *Tischzucht*; the humanist *Tischzucht*; and finally, what should be but is anything but an oxymoron, the grobian etiquette *grobianischer Tischzucht*.[30] According to Merker the first two types are classical manner books; of the other three, which merely modify the traditional models, only the humanist etiquettes prove worthy imitators and successors. The bourgeois *Tischzucht* and the grobian *Tischzucht* are but degraded travesties.[31]

In both court and city, early modern consolidation and regulation pushed toward restraint, toward defining status and boundaries. In speaking of the growing integration and interdependence of early modern society, Elias sees city and courts developing around powerful central figures, prototypes for the absolute monarchies that came to constitute the early modern state of the seventeenth century.[32] Without disregarding Elias's historical trajectory, however, we might study more closely the sixteenth-century encounters, when both court and city sought to distinguish themselves in what was a competitive relationship and to encode competition through increased emphasis on consideration and sensitivity to what in personal behavior might offend.[33] Significantly, in this point of transition, if the former court attempted to hold onto what it was, the urban bourgeoisie tried to codify and justify a less certain identity. In this respect, the modified precepts of the humanist and bourgeois etiquettes specifying what one does—and especially, what one does not do—expose what one is not yet and would like to become. One could speak here of a virtual bourgeois identity in a shifting ground of historical reality. It is in the space of uncertainty that the bourgeois and humanist regimes of conduct flourished, in that space of uncertainty that the texts of conduct and courtesy were written.

Presumably at least, aristocratic manners were not practiced with an eye toward social competition or advancement; they served as the visible sign of a determined and legitimate place in a presumably unchallenged social order. Manners demonstrated ruling-class leadership, domination based on land, title, and physical force. One who offered hospitality in peace could offer hostility in war as well. Even with the rise of the cities, preservation of social place could be reenacted nostalgically in the courts, through the traditional social rituals that recalled a past of cultural and political hegemony. While, as Castiglione shows, that nostalgia was a contaminated memory, it was still accessible to the aristocratic imaginary.[34] As courtly society ceded space and power to urban-bourgeois society, however, terms and identities changed. Though the rules of civility were modeled directly on courtly manners, several features distinguished chivalric precepts or the older courtly etiquettes from the new etiquette of civility. Although both resulted in formalization, according to Elias, in chivalry practicing correct behavior reconfirmed a culturally established aristocratic identity with the concept of courtesy.[35]

Early modern civil manners—for Thorstein Veblen, the "ceremonial code of decorous usages"—documented a way of life, represented as yet unattained aspirations or wishes, contained (by ritualized actions) anxieties and fears of what Claude Lévi-Strauss called the unregulated.[36] With a reflexive element not seen in chivalric culture, they negotiated uneasily between an ideal self-image and a phantasmal unknown with the capacity to loom horrifically. They showed the cultural fashioning of the bourgeois class coming to power and seeking to appropriate a tradition of manners and the identity and legitimacy that went with it.

There is a distance far greater than temporal between medieval-courtly precepts and early modern rules of conduct. Elias sees medieval precepts as straightforward: "You should follow honorable men and vent your wrath on the wicked." "When your companions anger you, my son, see that you are not so hot-tempered that you regret it afterward." "A man of refinement should not slurp with his spoon when in company; this the way people at court behave who often indulge in unrefined conduct."[37] Such pronouncements are far removed from Erasmus's attention to a more nuanced testimony of bodily comportment: "the eyes should be calm, respectful, and steady; not grim, which is a mark of truculence; not shameless, the hallmark of insolence; . . . not too narrowed, a sign of bad temper; nor bold and inquisitive, which indicates impertinence; but such as reflects a mind composed, respectful, and friendly. For it is no chance of saying of the ancient sages that the seat of the soul is in the eyes" (*De civ.*, 274). For that matter, Castiglione's caution to the aspiring courtier to avoid obviously self-promoting behavior—"You know that in war what really spurs men on to bold deeds is the desire for glory, whereas anyone who acts for gain or from any other motive not only fails to accomplish anything worth while but deserves to be called a miserable merchant rather than a gentleman" (1.42.89)—is historically pointed. Erasmus's attention to internalizing discipline to incorporate body consciousness and Castiglione's evocation of the terror and taboo of unmentionable mercenary or mentionable merchant status signal early modern instability and uncertainty.

The transition from medieval to civil manners manifested a problematic bourgeois self-image, locations for conflict and crisis in a changing world.[38] In a mobile, exchange society, the literature of conduct manifested stress in a preoccupation with sexual difference, with standards of manliness, with controlling the position and the behavior of women as a prerequisite for masculine security.[39] Veblen suggests some causes of a bourgeois crisis of patriarchal authority in the transition from a traditional, preindustrial division of labor, in which martial exploits characterized elite masculine "production" and drudge work was left to women, to a capitalist division of labor, in which "virtually the whole range of industrial employments, accounting, selling, trading, management, is an outgrowth of what is classed as women's work in the primitive barbarian community."[40] Certainly the late medieval misogynist literature shows a remarkable hostility toward women, projecting grotesque female figures from a beleaguered masculine identity seen, perhaps at its horrific worst, in a text such as the *Malleus maleficarum*.[41] In Germanic lands, at least, the bourgeoisie of the sixteenth century directed an aggressive humor at the rural peasantry as well. H. G. Koenigsberger and George Mosse, for example, see in Breughel's paintings of drunken peasant revels, commissioned by bourgeois patrons, "a gratifying and sophisticated, if essentially futile, comment on the changed terms of trade between town and country."[42]

Merker mentions a wealthier peasant class of the late Middle Ages which mimics the refinements of the aristocracy by copying its external behavior.[43] The prodigal peasant son in Werner der Gärtner's *Meier Helmbrecht*, who leaves his father's comfortable rural home with ambitions for a life away from the soil and sometime later returns cross-dressed in aristocratic clothing, would be a powerful example of aspiring mimicry.[44] In that thirteenth-century text, the conflict between the son's transgressive aspirations and his father's protestations is resolved in a punitive spectacle during which the son is violently humiliated and killed off.[45] The text produces not only a family tragedy but also a reassuring and compensatory experience for its aristocratic readers. Yet it also records transgressive desires that will reappear.

When, very much in the manner of the upstart peasants of Merker's descriptions, the bourgeoisie mimicked noble manners, no such restabilization or compensatory satisfaction in seeing offenders punished was to be found.[46] The new commands of civility emphasized the role of external appearance, emphasized individual actions and techniques, and they tended to forbid more. At stake was making a certain impression, not doing something else lest you look like or be thought a fool or a peasant. When aristocratic precepts emphasized the opposition between "aristocratic manners" and "a peasant lifestyle," the appeal was less reflexive than formally reassuring, referencing what amounted to a visible contrast the law could enforce.[47] For the bourgeoisie, for whom identity was much more ambiguous, the contrasts were not so strong, the threats internal. Conduct produced an internalized punitive spectacle that was constitutive, rather than cathartic.

Written, for the most part, by humanist authors, these manuals of self-production drew upon classical models and prescribed new modes of social interaction. They described in new rules and techniques the appropriate behavior from rising in the morning until retiring at night, and focused particularly on the exact comportment of the body and behavior at the table. With their detailed and mechanized descriptions of hygiene, social intercourse, appearance, and "management" of body functions and movements, the works are technical manuals, blueprints for building a machine.[48] As Norbert Elias has noted, they stand as symptoms of anxiety about behavior and express a need for refinement and standardization, a new self-consciousness and sense of shame. Elias places early modern codified manners in the context of change and a growing "question of sociogenic fear."[49]

The new manner books were directed at creating and manipulating an unnamed cultural-ethical identity, a self-image in process and on trial. In line with the pedagogy of the urban universities, with the humanist emphasis on rhetoric, "They wish to form life, rather than to comprehend it."[50] In their focus on the male adolescent as the proper object of their teaching (though the audience is not limited to youths), they represent an emerging civil formation in a vulnerable state of immaturity and percarious liminality, in need of reform to make it over the threshold.[51]

Situated in a milieu of emerging exchange economy and religious reformation, the conduct model that emerged was aimed at producing a disciplined, self-denying, accumulating, distinctly gendered subject. Urban and bourgeois, he prized material gain as access to power and the means to happiness, while his quotidian life required delayed gratification of instinctual needs to succeed. As members in a fraternity of civilization's discontents to which Freud later dedicated his speculative labors, this emerging class of urban dwellers pursued a way of life that posed obstacles to its own ideals.[52] If the new activities in the realm of economic exchange meant greater opportunities and freedoms, they were also imbued by constitutive contradictions that marked a new and vexed masculine habitus.

Although it would be anachronistic to speak of anything but a protoindustrial bourgeoisie for this early modern period, even in the sixteenth century early types of manufacture (textiles, brewing and distilling, mining) and commodity production flourished, and the stage was set for more advanced developments. Dislocations in the countryside caused by plague, natural disaster, and economic reversals sent peasants to the mines and to the towns to create an urban labor pool.[53] Despite their conflicts over regulation of the trades and governance of the cities, the merchant bourgeoisie and the guild artisans had in common a way of life devoted to labor, accumulation of money wealth, and upward social mobility which distinguished them from both the landed aristocracy and the stably situated rural peasantry. Simultaneously dependent on the laboring classes and on the political power of the aristocracy and religious authority, the new bourgeoisie could by means of the market's economic instruments manipulate but not yet challenge traditional authority in its own name.[54] It could not in any determining way act politically upon its economic power, any more than it reflected on the sources of its wealth: appropriation of others' labor in early forms of manufacture, accumulation by exchange, or selling time in the form of interest on borrowed money or credit. It was a secondary and derivative mode of life, haunted by impossible aspirations.

To the ironic structure of the early modern psyche, then, was added the overarching structural irony of the society and economy of early capitalism: the private appropriation of socially created wealth. Yet contradictions, indecent ironies such as these were endemic to its character and buried in the rationality of a work ethic that glorified honest work and self-determination. The domination of agricultural and laboring populations and the conquest of external nature were unthinkable without practices of self-domination and the institutionalization of a second nature of civility.[55]

This class grew strong from dislocations of society in the period of transition at the end of the Middle Ages; it was formed in part from a peasantry made homeless and impoverished or making itself more mobile by increasing its wealth or moving into urban trade, by alterations and upheavals in rural economies; it prospered from the needs of the aristocracy for commodities, services, and credit.[56] Its fortunes grew in the fluctuations of the exchange economy. Using the technology of printing and the skills of its educated members, the urban bourgeoisie spoke from within the culture of dislocation which developed in the transition from the late Middle Ages to the Renaissance. Of the many forms its voices took in sermons, pamphlets and handbooks, satirical, didactic and polemical works, the literature of conduct was a distinctive manifestation among the tracts of self-help and self-fashioning.[57]

Whereas most scholars take pains to separate humanist-bourgeois from grobian etiquettes, Aloys Bömer includes *Grobianus* as the last of the humanist etiquettes.[58] Published some twenty years after Erasmus's work, it transformed the *Tischzucht* and attitudes about the body. With the publication of Dedekind's *Grobianus*, and especially with Scheidt's vernacularization of the work, the embourgeoisement of manners became complete; manners, disclosed as a study of indecency, were institutionalized; indecency was tacitly canonized.

Dedekind's and Scheidt's ironic satire is part of this effort but it also rewrites the altered code of social and personal behavior. *Grobianus* is a particularly derivative and hybrid work. In addition to its debts to classical satirists and Lucian's irony, it borrows and reverses material from Ovid's *Ars amatoria*, in which amatory arts and social graces and pursuits are suggestively linked. It recalls the ironic encomia, those humanist treatises and rhetorical exercises in praise of trivial or "unworthy" topics.[59] In the type of behavior presented and in its title, derived from Sebastian Brant's ironic saint and other literary treatments of boorishness, it recalls folk-book characters such as Eulenspiegel and Markolf.[60] It borrows anecdotes from this popular literature as ironic exempla, linked through allusions to the less reputable gods of the ancient past, Ceres, Bacchus, and Sylvanus. Its rowdy scenes and themes of drunkenness and gluttony recall the German Lenten plays and farces (*Fastnachtspiele, Schwänke*) and contemporary and medieval Latin and vernacular drinking literature. The derivative composition, conventionally imitative, also reflects the mixture of models in the bourgeois class-fashioning project: it appropriates ancient authority to make cultural capital of a classical heritage, partakes of high-humanist ironic genres, imports stock roles from popular literature. It mixes high and low forms in an ironic didacticism that preaches and repels.

If the lessons are meant to be the same as those of other conduct books, the effort at reformation becomes a re-forming as well, and not only the form but the substance of the lesson is altered. In the process, we are left with bourgeois manners, which seek, on the one hand, to represent the nonexistent nobility of the middle class by aping ancient aristocratic hospitality rituals and social gestures and, on the other, to place a maximum amount of distance between the bourgeois class and its peasant origins by evoking revulsion for the entire physical realm. Bourgeois manners become a fictive narrative, a drama that would disavow the existence of the very platform upon which it stands: the stage of the body.

To be sure, both Dedekind and Scheidt are sincere in their intent to reform "bad" manners. In structure and in content, their handbook does not really differ from its predecessors. It covers the same material, the same actions, in the traditional order; none of the conventions, which reach back to the twelfth century in written records, is missing. Even the method of parody and reversal, of mock codification had a lengthy and respectable past by the mid-sixteenth century, for table disciplines, particularly in Germany, had already introduced elements of humor, irony, and parody.[61] But the *Grobianus* texts not only contain in reverse form all the conventional precepts of social behavior; indeed, they assume knowledge of traditional etiquettes for their humorous effects. They also include descriptions in which, as Hauffen puts it, "it is not decency that is taught, but rather indecency that is shockingly depicted."[62]

Dedekind and Scheidt developed and refined Erasmus's powers of observation as well. Whereas Erasmus's text reveals his ability to observe and to view appearances, movements, and gestures as external evidence for internal substance, these authors, working with indecency, work even more deliberately toward psychological manipulation of their audiences. They aspire to teach decent social behavior by recommending its exact opposite and portraying it so vividly and so unattractively—all the while holding it up as the model—that the reader of the text will be anxious not to be seen doing such things. In concluding *Grobianus*, Dedekind explains that he has personally witnessed much of what he writes about, and his work depends for its effect on the readers' ability to evaluate the scenes, to place themselves in the images conjured up and see themselves performing the unmannerly actions described. Not only are they expected to make the intellectual leap required by the irony and reverse psychology, and thus to reverse things, in the manner of the older parodies; in addition, by hypothetically watching themselves perform actions that are the opposite of what they should be doing, they are to retain the repulsive images in anxiety-laden fantasies. Such possibilities contribute an interesting addition to the virtual identity of the new bourgeois standard.

Interestingly enough, Karl Marx offers what is perhaps the earliest and most trenchant critique of the historical phenomenon of grobianism. In "Moralising Criticism and Critical Morality," a polemical newspaper piece written against Karl Heinzen, an anti-communist opponent, Marx first makes an analogy between the transitional period of the sixteenth century and the "era of revolution" in the mid-nineteenth century:

> Shortly before and during the period of the Reformation there developed amongst the Germans a type of literature whose very name is striking—grobian literature. In our own day we are approaching an era of revolution analogous to that of the sixteenth century. Small wonder that among the Germans grobian literature is emerging once more. Interest in historical development easily overcomes the aesthetic revulsion which this kind of writing provokes even in a person of quite unrefined taste and which it provoked back in the fifteenth and sixteenth centuries.[63]

Suggesting the chief characteristic of grobian literature—it provokes revulsion "even in a person of quite unrefined taste"—Marx goes on at length, describing grobianism while never losing sight of the object of his own contemporary attack: Karl Heinzen and the republicans as nineteenth-century "grobianists" who attempt to suppress economic-social analysis by raising the specter of revolution and making bogeys of materialist thinkers such as Marx and Engels. In making grobianism the model for the mechanism of specular revulsion in jingoist republicanism, Marx reads both texts astutely:

> Flat, bombastic, bragging, thrasonical, putting on a great show of rude vigour in attack, yet hysterically sensitive to the same quality in others; ... constantly preaching morality and constantly offending against it; sentiment and turpitude most absurdly conjoined; concerned only with the point at issue, yet always missing the point; using with equal arrogance petty-bourgeois scholarly semi-erudition against popular

wisdom, and so-called "sound common sense" against science; discharging itself in ungovernable breadth with a certain complacent levity; clothing a philistine message in a plebeian form; wrestling with the literary language to give it, so to speak, a purely corporeal character; willingly pointing at the writer's body in the background, which is itching in every fibre to give a few exhibitions of its strength, to display its broad shoulders and publicly to stretch its limbs; proclaiming a healthy mind in a healthy body; unconsciously infected by the sixteenth century's most abstruse controversies and by its fever of the body; . . . Solomon and Marcolph, Don Quixote and Sancho Panza, a visionary and philistine in one person; a loutish form of indignation, a form of indignant loutishness; and suspended like an enveloping cloud over it all, the self-satisfied philistine's consciousness of his own virtue—such was the grobian literature of the sixteenth century. . . . To Herr Heinzen belongs the credit of being one of the re-creators of grobian literature.[64]

The analogy of Heinzen's moralistic jingoism with early modern German grobianism is important. Grobianism also sought moral reform in the name of an emerging nationalist consciousness, demanded national embodiment at the expense of the bodily material. Marx's critique unmasks one rather pernicious consequence of sixteenth-century protonationalism. At the same time it is interesting to note in his remarks Marx's own suspicion of the body and the pleasures of the body—perhaps as well the self-satisfied pleasures of the suspicion of the body—the suggestion of Marx's own grobianism and civil inscription by the odd cultural legacy of grobian texts.

Elias uses the term "Grobian reversal" to describe the technique of reverse precepts, of teaching by negative example. Merker and Perry Thornton list the grobian *Tischzucht* as one type of etiquette book. Though it derives from the older *Tischzucht* parody, grobian literature is ironic-didactic literature that formulaically reverses precepts and deploys repulsive images. The *Deutsches Wörterbuch* defines *Grobian* as a "person of disruptive, unrespectable behavior," a coarse fellow, often equated with a peasant or rustic, someone who lacks or offends against what are considered to be good manners, particularly in reference to behavior at the table.[65] The adjective *grob* connotes coarse and antisocial behavior: "rough, rude, unfriendly." In its position in a cultural constellation, however, grobianism exceeds handbook or dictionary definitions.

By the time Dedekind wrote *Grobianus*, he was able to draw on a certain cultural mythology-in-progress. The name Grobianus first came into use late in the fifteenth century as unflattering jargon for a peasant, part of a tradition of medieval peasant satire. Thus Thomas Zeninger's *Vocabularis theutonicus*, a vernacular glossary published in 1482, offers Grobianus as the German equivalent of the Latin *rusticus* or "peasant, clown, boor."[66] The sixteenth-century neologism *Grobian* was not Dedekind's invention, nor was Dedekind the first author to put it to literary use. Sebastian Brant introduced "a new Saint Grobian" in chapter 72 of *Das Narrenschiff* (1494). Brant uses this figure, which crosses the secular and religious realms, as part of the tradition of pre-Reformation clerical satire. A short text of 1538, *Grobianus Tischzucht bin ich genannt*, known as the "Kleiner Grobianus," by W.S. (authorship sometimes attributed to a Wilhelm Salzmann) takes the form of a mock-rule of a religious order of grobians. Likely in reaction to anticlerical satire, the Catholic polemicist Thomas Murner put a Herr Grobian in his *Schelmenzunft* (1512).[67]

We know that the properly improper name Grobianus is already a hybrid monstrosity, Civility's monstrous and indispensable double, but complete social etymology of the word remains lost to us. We will never empirically reconstruct the moment when the vernacular *Grobian* underwent its Latinized renascence as Grobianus. It is Dedekind who takes the grobian of the folk book and puts him through the Reformation humanist finishing school. Latinization of the German comes rather easily: *grob* Jan, *grober* Hans, *grob* Johannes, Grobianus—genre, genealogy, gender: Grobianus. Although we cannot retrieve the event, it is possible to fantasize an etymological scene in which a boy, or boys, studying his, or their, Latin in a humanist Latin school of the early sixteenth century, playfully adds this humanistically refunctioned popular name to his (their) study of Latin language and civil conduct. In a way, it multiplies students' pleasures (or autoscopic *Schadenfreude*?) by allowing them both to learn and to mock Latin and the regimes of conduct which come with the language lessons. But the originator need not have been young. The name may have come as an insult from the

Latin teacher, perhaps singling out a boy of humble origins, attaching the hybrid appellation to remark on his status and aspirations while making him the object of his disciplining efforts. (I do not exclude the possibility that the hypothetical boy came from loftier origins.) Ascham's advice to pedagogues to teach "gently" and eschew corporal punishment in favor of referring the student to an evaluating classical authority— "Tully would have placed this word here, not there; would have used this case, this number, this person, this degree, this gender," etc.— would by no means proscribe such psychological coercion; indeed, control by means of mental discipline and manipulation would be the teacher's goal.[68] Dedekind was no more than twenty-five when *Grobianus* was first published; Scheidt was a schoolmaster when he adapted and translated the work.[69] Their shared attraction to the tasks of composition and adaptation suggests an appeal for students and pedagogues as well.

In his monograph on Scheidt's pupil and literary successor, Johann Fischart, Christoph Mühlemann sees in both Dedekind's and Scheidt's work "a deep satisfaction in the coarse and indecent," and Barbara Könneker remarks on their civil prurience, "If one takes Dedekind and Scheidt at their words, one cannot fail to notice that despite the display of indignation, they paint the world of Grobianus with apparent contentment. It is the same contentment with which Rabelais narrated the grobian childhood of Gargantua or had him report on the newly developed technology of 'ass-wiping'; the same, too, that Marguerite de Navarre confronts us with in the casual depiction of latrine scenes in *The Heptameron*."[70] While it may be a question of historicizing Renaissance humor, it is also possible to see in the ambivalence of grobian humor an element, at least, of an aggressive and compensatory refunctioning of humanist training, even, we might speculate, a (proto-Nietzschean) guiltless, shameless, malicious joy.[71]

Whereas Dedekind and Scheidt are no literary giants, scholars such as Wilhelm Scherer offer a certain grudging admiration—always mixed with disgust—of "the author's inventive handling of the filthiest material."[72] Where the complicated reactions and pleasures come to a halt and just how many subject positions the subject of civility might occupy are what Chapter 3 considers in its more formal reading of Dedekind's text. Before that reading, however, it is useful to examine Erasmus's work, so influential for Dedekind, as reflecting the historical changes in conduct.

In *De civilitate morum puerilium* (*On Good Manners in Boys*), Erasmus also offers a specular regime as the foundational lesson for his pupils, instilling or inscribing in them lessons of reflexivity which will make them always conscious of the visual signs they broadcast to the observers who judge them. For him the specular regime is grounded in a politics of malleability which responds to a crisis of authority and subject status, as well as sexual difference. At a time when social mobility stood in a competitive relationship to nobility, the fluidity of relations and identities produced unsettling anxieties about distinctions that could not be guaranteed. Elias refers to the early modern tendency to emphasize observation, the increased visual awareness of external surroundings and others' actions. But awareness does not stop at or even center on external observations; it points toward self-consciousness and a movement of internalization as well. For both Castiglione and Erasmus, the subject is truly and (in a Kristevan sense) ironically a subject-in-process/on trial, who molds himself for a sternly, rigorously evaluative gaze. Yet in this scheme of civil scopophilia, the question Who is watching? can only be answered, You are. If it's to work, the subject of civility must both generate and incorporate the gaze of the other. You never relax your vigilance because you don't want to make that fatal, mortifying mistake; in order to avoid it, you have to see yourself—as the grobian—doing it.

## 2 / Malleable Material, Models of Power: Woman in Erasmus's "Marriage Group" and *Good Manners in Boys*

Dic, Eutrapele: uter infirmior, qui cedit
alteri, an cui ceditur?

Tell me, Eutrapelus, which is weaker, the one who submits or the one
to whom submission is made?

—Erasmus, *The Colloquies*

Renaissance studies in English literature have often looked to the figure of Elizabeth I as an unsettling force in sixteenth-century England, using investigations of her style of rule and the structure of the court to develop theories of early modern power and subject formation. In two notable examples, Stephen Greenblatt[1] and Louis Montrose[2] argue that, as monarch and as woman, Elizabeth exploited and provoked psychological anxieties in her male subjects, anxieties of male selfhood which reflected the political tensions of a society in transition, and that those tensions are dramatized, contained, and preserved in works such as Spenser's *Faerie Queene* and Shakespeare's *A Midsummer Night's Dream*.

Yet Erasmus's writings on pedagogy and his more popular *Colloquies*, taken as pedagogical writing as well, reveal on the European Continent, too, and certainly earlier in the century, signs of a kind of psychopolitical crisis of masculine identity and authority among members of a rising intellectual bourgeoisie attempting to negotiate positions of authority in a power structure still largely determined by the hereditary nobility and the institution of the church. That Erasmus enjoyed considerable influence among English readers of Latin and that the pedagogical writings, as well as many of the *Colloquies*, were available in English translation before Elizabeth came to the throne should, at the very least, serve to complicate regiocentric interpretations.[3] Here we cannot speak of the provocation of a female monarch; yet, as in the case of Elizabeth I, this crisis of the subject also contains sexual-political tensions and to a great extent revolves around questions of gender.

The suggestion here is that Erasmus's discourse on civility and the fashioning of secular male selfhood, far from constituting the (Burckhardtian) rebirth of individualism and the transcendent self, discloses an insistent concern for beleaguered masculine identity.[4] As a topic frequently embedded in or echoed in early modern discourses on the self, women became a cause of concern not because, as in Montrose's regiocentric discussion of Elizabethan England, "authority is everywhere invested in men—everywhere, that is, except at the top" (61)— but because the conflict between hereditary and intellectual or bourgeois claims to power reveals sexual anxiety in shifting notions of subordination and superiority and calls attention to women as designated subordinates who might threaten—because in their ascribed and increasingly codified roles they reflect—the uneasy dynamics of power. In this ambivalent negotiation, too, it does not seem surprising that women and conflicts of the sexual-political order would become (open or embedded) topics of concern in humanist writings.[5] Some authors, such as Castiglione in *Il Cortegiano*, might make relations between men and women a convenient vehicle with which to introduce the entertaining and commonplace battle of the sexes topos; others, of a more particularly peace-loving character, might treat gender relations as still another project for their conciliatory efforts.[6] In any event, both strategies disclose evidence of projected threats to early modern manhood, and although my concern is to place Erasmus's conciliatory commitments under scrutiny, with neither strategy successfully contains the threatening questions it raises.

The question here is, what is the function of woman in humanist discourses of early modern civility, devoted, as they are, to the formation of cultural masculinity? In order to provide some answer to it, I would like to focus on Erasmus as that irenic personality who, against a historical backdrop of conflict and instability, concerned himself with the formation of civil subjects as the precondition for a project of establishing social, domestic, and religious harmony. Toward this end I have chosen those selections from Erasmus's *Colloquia familiaria* which treat women's behavior, the "Marriage Group." These pleasant and useful conversations develop a theory of power and a model of reconceptualized cultural manhood in the early modern period, and their concerns carry over into one of Erasmus's more influential pedagogical works, *De civilitate morum puerilium* (*On Good Manners in Boys* [1530]).

Interestingly enough, like *De civilitate*, these dialogues (and protonovels of manners), composed between 1496 and 1529 to teach his male readers a double lesson in Latin grammar and moral precepts, present Erasmus grappling with two important issues and relating them to a mutable text of identity in the early modern civil subject: the dangerous problems of women's power and the instability of adolescence as the treacherous, liminal period when the boy appropriates his sexual identity as the prerequisite for entering the civic realm.[7] In the stabilizing gestures Erasmus makes to deal with the problem of power in the spheres of courtship and marriage, the "Marriage Group" anticipates Erasmus's model of the male bourgeois student of civility, who in learning to govern himself sets the best example for his superiors to follow in governing themselves and their subjects. But read with *De civilitate*, these dialogues evidence a profoundly personal investment as well. These also bear an interesting relationship to Erasmus's own strategies for exercising and manipulating power—as teacher, humanist, and intellectual deeply involved in a personal politics of conciliation, living in a changing and often threatening world, which did not hesitate to oversee and scrutinize his success (and that of other humanists as well), to question his texts for their potentially disruptive meanings. In this unstable environment, Erasmus's dedication to the topic of manners reveals an interest in inscribing identity formation with the structures of power.

In posing the question of the function of woman, I want to depart from traditional studies of images of women or studies of notable Renaissance women and suggest that although Erasmus's work on pedagogy and civility is concerned primarily with boys, there may be some displacement or substitution at work, some maneuvering that would signal us to ask some probing and productive questions about the position of women and the structuring of feminine and masculine identity in discursive practices of the Renaissance period.[8] That is, Erasmus may both explicitly exclude and dismissively close women off from his pedagogical theories, while his texts themselves reveal that he implicitly includes woman or a version of woman (woman as constructed by discourse or a "woman function"—for example, effeminacy, weakness, insufficient reason or control, signifiers of feminine gender, but to a far greater degree, signifiers of a failing of masculinity) in the construction of the young male student, and the texts themselves may provide us with important disclosures of this double action as a strategy absolutely essential to his pedagogical project. In other words, if we are looking at a new discourse on identity in early modern society in order to establish a critical interpretation of power and the role of the subject in larger social and political structures, we shall want not only to observe domestic relations as indicative of a kind of social structure but also to look at pedagogical practices and grammar lessons as making use of sexual relations and gendered references. Rather than identify the domestic and pedagogical realms as two distinct cultural spheres, we may find an overarching concern with the structuring of identity and power in which youths and women play a determining role.[9] A careful reading here may allow us to look beyond the myths of the monumental figure in Erasmus studies and focus a critical eye on his pivotal and symptomatic contributions to conflicted areas of early modernity. In being critically appreciative of the ambiguities and consequences of gender discourse, by scrutinizing the text of power in the early modern formation of cultural masculinity, we may learn "in excess" of Erasmian pedagogy and discover some things, both historical and theoretical, about the social construction of men and women.

Erasmus maintains a privileged position in humanist studies, enjoying an unparalleled and seldom challenged status as a sympathetic figure of early modern cultural history. J. K. McConica's essay on the central importance of peace and consensus in Erasmus's writings, on the dread of conflict that caused him to declare that he "would endure anything rather than provoke dissention," has had its equivalence in a kind of irenic contract between Erasmus scholars and their object of study.[10] Efforts to work beyond hagiography and to apply a critical eye to this influential figure have only recently begun to appear; up to the 1980s, the more critical remarks remained limited to psychopathological and clinical analyses.[11] For the most part, that is, despite the exertions of German pathologists, the "bones" of Erasmus remain undisturbed, the terms of the contract respected. The continuing investment in Erasmus as the peace-mongering spokesman for Christian humanism is clearly linked to the humanist project itself, which manages to project Erasmus as model from its aspirations to retain an essentialist and pacifically affirmative humanist framework in the face of critical and posthumanist challenges.[12]

Discussions of Erasmus's position on women extend, organically, from these humanist investments and projections. J. K. Sowards's essay "Erasmus and the Education of Women" is typical here.[13] On the minus side, Sowards notes the absence of women from the pedagogical writings, such as *De civilitate*, where "feminine civility is never mentioned" (78). He identifies Erasmus's conformity to civic humanism's notion of education as preparation for the *vita activa*, to which women are systemically denied access. Furthermore, women are directed, in humanist writings such as those of Erasmus and Vives, toward domestic duties, their education intended to make them better companions to their husbands and better mothers of their offspring. Yet though Soward does not see in Erasmus "a powerful advocate for the education of women," he claims him as "one of the most important champions of women's rights in his century" (77), and uses the (by now) familiar arguments of structural functionalism and historical relativism to perpetuate a circular and apologetic logic: Erasmus was progressive for his times, but his ideas were culturally determined, circumscribed by historical conditions.[14]

If we take a more contemporary, more theoretical direction, there is an underlying and clearly poststructuralist premise operating here, which is developed in pathbreaking work by the feminist cinema scholar Teresa de Lauretis and the theoretical context out of which she writes (semiotics, psychoanalysis, neo-Marxism) and to which she responds critically.[15] "Woman" is constructed, appropriated and reproduced by the early modern civilizing process (as is man); we are speaking here not of a transcendental human subject but of the cultural construction of masculinity and femininity. Gender, then, like "the subject," appears as an "aggregate of effects," a "text" written by discursive negotiations —albeit one with concrete consequences. We can use the tools of discourse analysis and critical theory to go beyond traditional progressive-evolutionary notions of history and civilization—as the forces that continue to marginalize the questions of women's history— while not succumbing to any essentialist or compensatory positions in which categories of gender (or the notion of gender itself) remain still privileged and unscrutinized. On the one hand, then, when we look at woman in early modernity, we must say, with Lacan and French feminists, that there is no woman here but rather a discourse on women, a representation, expressing ideological investments in the form of what we might call "woman effects."

But on the other hand, poststructuralist critiques of the unified subject and theories of woman's textuality and representation are not the end of the story. As de Lauretis suggests, rather than remain arrested at the level of textuality, we must also insist on concern for the things that happen to bodies, the material consequences of those discourses on gender which construct, maintain, enforce cultural masculinity and cultural femininity: "The discrepancy, the tension, and the constant slippage between Woman as representation, as the object and very condition of representation, and, on the other hand, women as historical beings, subjects of 'real relations,' are motivated and sustained by a logical contradiction in our culture and an irreconcilable one: women are both inside and outside gender, at once within and without representation" (10). With this caveat in mind, we can address the function of woman for Erasmus as an author whose pedagogical writings, devoted to constructing the male subject of humanism, contributed to the discursive formation of woman and thus to the material effects of such gendering discursive practices on historical subjects—women and men—as well.[16]

To examine the role of women in Erasmus, without arresting the investigation with a thesis of historical circumstance, is to introduce feminist questions. Here awareness of Erasmus's discriminatory attitudes toward women becomes a site not of accusation but rather of investigations of early modern subject and gender formation. Though

women are seldom explicitly addressed in his pedagogical works, there
are implicit references to women; women function as an essential negative to be overcome by civilizing labors and education, a constructed
threat—and the uncanny echo from the machinery of changing power
relations—that motivates male students to inscribe themselves in cultural masculine structures of civility.

Many of Erasmus's *Colloquies* take up manners, behavior, relations with
superiors, but two of these from the eight dialogues that are known as
the "Marriage Group," "Courtship" ("Proci et puellae") and "Marriage"
("Coniugium"), particularly speak to the issues of my discussion and
create a strange model of substitute power,[17] power to create the conditions of your own subordination. Both have as their dramatic and
narrative settings crises in sexual and power relations centered around
the heterosexual couple. In the 1523 dialogue "Courtship," Pamphilus,
a suitor who describes himself as "a lifeless corpse" ("unum cadauer
vides exanime" [88/2]) accuses Maria, the object of his affection—and
also, as she is quick to point out, the product of his psychic projections—of "slaying" men by not sufficiently returning his interest and
agreeing to marry him: "You slay men for sport as the god does. Except
that you're more pitiless than Mars: you kill even a lover" ("Quia que-
madmodum illi deo pro ludo est homines interficere, ita et tibi. Nisi
quod tu Marte crudelior occidis etiam amantem" [88/2]). Erasmus constructs a male suitor who is no less conscious of the phallic symbolic
order than Maria, and the dialogue achieves much of its liveliness from
their consistently sustained double entendre (much to the delight, one
must assume, of the young Latin students) in which each character is
more than willing to mistake the sign for the thing. When she protests
that she is "a girl, not a stone" ("puella sum, non lapis" [89/29]), he
seizes upon the trope and calls her "harder than adamant" ("sed ada-
mante durior" [89/29]). The danger of her usurping and subverting sexual power is underlined when, having exhausted the argument, and
clearly showing that she has the intellectual upper hand, Maria places
her own earned position in question and asks the outwitted Pamphilus,
"Do I really have so much power?" ("Egon' rem tantam possum?" [91/
281]) Whether as plea or acknowledgment (or as an attempt to contain
the threat of what might happen if she retained that position), he replies

that she "can bring a dead man back to life" ("potes vel mortuum ad vitam reuocare" [91/281]).

In the argument over virginity and marriage which ensues, an argument she must lose in order to win, Maria demonstrates that her wisdom extends to the field of cultural anthropology. She understands virginity as the withholding of power from the man, a way of deferring the moment of full initiation into the symbolic contract (motherhood), but knows its position in a cultural context as well. That is, in a society where women circulate as objects of exchange and where the market of the libidinal economy may be manipulated by withholding sexual gratification or through mediated desire, virginity's power can have value only as temporary withholding: timing counts for everything. She begins to give ground gradually and cautiously, until it is Pamphilus who sees revival appearing, like the magical enactment of his will and without the agency of a magician, on the horizon. Thus after intellectually outmaneuvering an impatient lover for most of the dialogue, she follows the circular model of the ideal woman—smart enough to pose danger, smart enough to contain it—and assures him (with irony that takes one's breath away) that he has "tractable material. See that you form and fashion me" ("Habebis sequacem materiam, tu vide vt me formes fingasque" [9/28]).

In "Marriage" a troubled young wife named (most appropriately to Erasmus's purposes) Xantippe learns how to get her husband to stop abusing her by cultivating subordination instead of defiance. The advice is summed up, significantly, in the name of the friend giving it—Eulalia ("sweet speaking"). In the ideal figure of Eulalia, Erasmus offers the exemplar of a woman intelligent enough and sublimely skilled in navigating the dualities and double binds of gendered power structures, to educate her husband to rule her well. She demonstrates, at a later stage of a sexual—and civil-political—relationship, the wisdom and strategic pliancy of the young woman in "Courtship" and recommends to Xantippe the techniques of behavioral modification, rewarding good conduct and ignoring the bad. A character constructed to work hard to protect the mystification of power in marital politics, to accommodate herself to the structural demands of this elementary sociopolitical unit, she offers as advice: "Mark the good in him, rather, and by this means take him where he can be held" ("Illa potius contemplare, quae bona

sunt in illo, et hac ansa praehende illum, qua teneri potest" [125/310]).
Whereas in the colloquy "The Godly Feast" husbands are held responsible for controlling the conduct of their wives (just as rulers would be
accountable for controlling their subjects or for maintaining a structure
of power at court), here the wife confronts a far more complicated
situation.[18] She is responsible for instructing her superior to rule her in
the best way, obliging her to demonstrate superior understanding and
truly sophisticated techniques of self-control and psychic doubling, to
have the power to instruct, on the one hand, matched by the control
to invert that power into her own subordination, on the other.[19] Unlike
the male administrative underling or the court intellectual, for whom
inverted power will be exchanged for social mobility and professional
success (favor, patronage), what Eulalia seems to derive from this master-slave dialectic in the way of satisfaction or compensatory experience
(aside from the act of instructing other women to follow her lesson)
amounts to a kind of pleasure at giving a virtuoso performance in which,
much like Castiglione's *sprezzatura*, the art appears spontaneous. Sat-
isfied she is. When she informs Xantippe that divorce is no longer permitted and Xantippe exclaims, "May heaven punish whoever robbed us
of this right!" she invokes the authority of Christianity. Alluding to Circe
and offering as compensation an appropriated, much civilized form of
witchcraft, she sets an assignment in self-authorization: "You determine
whether you have a husband or a swine." At every stage of the conversation where Xantippe rages against the injustice of the domestic structure and storms the walls of the civil-symbolic edifice, Eulalia comes
forward confidently to domesticate and, like the man-made Athena who
placates the Erinyes in Aeschylus's ancient civic drama of the world-
historical defeat of the female, to "defeminate."[20]

Like Sowards and many others, Jacques Chomarat argues that Erasmus speaks for the dignity of women (looking to the model women of
his acquaintance, such as Margaret Roper, or the daughters of Willibald
Pirkheimer and Thomas Blaurer), and Craig Thompson sees the "Marriage Group" colloquies as significant contributions to Renaissance
"feminism."[21] In marriage, according to Erasmus, subordination of the
woman does not signify her inferiority; he exempts the relationship of
husband and wife from the taint of any notion of power or domination.

Instead, faithfully following Pauline thought, he holds that the marriage represents a natural fulfillment of a divinely ordained law.[22] Interestingly, however, Chomorat also sees in this domestic arrangement— which plays on illusions of power so often exploited in ideologies of separate spheres, real versus virtual power, and the position of women in the home—the defense strategy of the humanist himself in religious controversy (897), a situation in which the humanist might come across as a strident, irrational, and power-hungry Xantippe in need of "eulalic," taming gestures. The "eulalic" model suggests that if you can fashion your behavior, you can control the behavior of others. But that does not mean such power, unless demonically inverted in the manner of a Iago or a Lady Macbeth, will extend beyond the devious and indirect, that it could ever become more than a power that folds upon itself in a decisive moment of self-subordination. We do not have to know much political science to see that what is at work here reaches beyond the primary social arrangements of the marital sphere and into larger social units, but also, on a third level, that it suggests a particularly personal investment on the part of Erasmus, whose published defense of the *Colloquies* sought to placate critical church authorities by trying to assure them that the pieces supported institutional goals and doctrinal structures in every way.[23]

But there is much that we can read in Erasmus's relationship to power which strongly suggests that his treatment of women has more to it than merely a conventional mouthing of Pauline doctrine, that in the overlapping of the domestic and pedagogical spheres, Erasmus's constructed woman may function to conflate issues of sexuality and class in a way that could conveniently also serve to contain and pacify anxieties stemming from social change and negotiations of power.

Nowhere is this possibility more evident than in "The New Mother" ("Puerpera"), the third colloquy of the "Marriage Group." Written in 1525–1526, the time of the most violent Reformation struggles and the Peasant Wars in Germany, the text opens in a setting both remarkable and elaborately constructed. Against a background of dismembered order, the context of domestic and national violence, there emerges the icon of organic wholeness, the mother suckling her infant. Organicized order is at stake here. When introduced in the text, Fabulla, the new mother, has hired a nurse and is not breast-feeding her infant. Through a debate with her older male friend, Eutrapelus, the icon must be (re)constructed as a symbolic restoration of order in the larger sphere.

Menacing images of disorder appear throughout the dialogue. Eutrapelus greets Fabulla with an anecdote about Polygamus, a man (appropriately named) who "recently buried his tenth wife. When I asked him what the news was, 'In this house,' says he, 'a woman's body was cut in two.' 'For what crime?' 'If the common gossip is true,' says he, 'a wife tried to skin her husband,' and off he went with a laugh" (269). Fabulla's recent pregnancy and the deceased woman's severed body reappear as motifs for Eutrapelus's report on the violence and disorder of the times: "The commons are bent on anarchy; the Church is shaken to its very foundations by menacing factions; on every side the seamless coat of Jesus is torn to shreds. . . . Confession totters; vows reel; pontifical ordinances crumble away; . . . Antichrist is awaited; the whole earth is pregnant with I know not what calamity" (269–70).

In this scheme of calamitous versus fortunate pregnancies, monstrous versus blessed births, mutilated and whole bodies, Fabulla attempts to defend and legitimate the position she has fashioned for herself. Against the objections of Eutrapelus, she sees no need to question the custom of hiring a wet nurse and indeed seems to make use of a good humanist education, which enables her to lay out the humanist mind-body dualism and insert her maternal concerns within its values, values that would have her express greater concern for her son's intellectual and moral development, for his mature future, than for his infantile present: "Congratulate me on a safe delivery if you like, Eutrapelus; on a happy one when you see my offspring prove himself an honest man" (269). Eutrapelus praises her for her correct foresight but works to make clear that Fabulla is also "out of order," her values disordered and disordering. In one sense Fabulla's concern already indicates what will soon undermine her confident combining of knowledge and maternal authority: she sees the immature child still in utero, which is what the household signifies. But it is this most maternal site that betrays her error in thinking that her speech corresponds to language or that she has access to it. In attempting to assert what can only be a paradoxical hybrid of paternal and humanist authority, she takes on the attitude toward education which belongs to a later stage of the child's development and more properly to another guardian: the father. Fabulla thus reveals the flaw in her otherwise exemplary reasoning: the tendency to cross boundaries and to cross-dress in roles that could never belong to a new mother. This transgression and confusion reflect the disunity of the conflicted historical context, not the timelessness of the maternal signifier, and mark her downfall in the argument.

Eutrapelus accuses her of "transfer[ring] more than half the name of mother" (727) by conceding to the custom of a hired nurse, of alienating natural functions by employing a woman whose interest is in money, not nurture or education. The child, he argues, needs the mother's "good and serviceable bodily organs" (282) and the mother provides hers, but no one should mistake this action as in any way analogous to the alienation or instrumentalization involved in the action of the wet nurse. The mother is urged to answer the call of nature ("listen to your own body" [282]), for "of their own accord" her breasts speak the organic principle of unity in which, as in the cases of husband and wife, ruler and ruled, sexual division of duties does not mean alienation of duties. To keep the peace, to maintain organic unity against dismembering and alienating forces, there should be no usurping.[24] Thus chastised and instructed, Fabulla gives every indication of her intention and ability both to adhere to the rules of the micropolitical game and to be an articulate spokesperson for its enforcement and perpetuation. Yet Fabulla's dualism is countered with dualism. As mother, the woman nourishes the body of her (male) child until she transfers "nurturing" responsibilities to the father, who (when the child reaches age seven) looks to education and "harder lessons, which are the father's responsibility rather than the mother's" (23). It is the mother, grounded in the maternal body, who nurtures the infant's body as the "instrument of the mind," until formal and manly education takes over. No amount of organic imagery can cover up the division of labor, and the structure of divided authority this colloquy discloses.

I have chosen *On Good Manners in Boys* as an example of a work that gathers together Erasmus's pedagogical and social interests in a grammar and rhetoric of civility. Perhaps more than the earlier and more eloquently styled *De pueris instituendis* (1509, but not published until 1529), *Good Manners in Boys* has an explicit or more developed concern with the instabilities of social mobility. Yet it could also be claimed that even *De pueris instituendis* makes evident the conciliatory agenda for *Good Manners in Boys*.

In his preface of 1529 to *De pueris*, Erasmus refers to a "method of education" which "is especially appropriate for children of rulers; they, more than anyone else, need a sound education." To his dedicatee, Prince William of Cleves, whose own tutor (Konrad Heresbach) has encouraged Erasmus to compose the treatise in the first place, Erasmus has final encouragement: "Persevere in your glorious struggle, so that your instructor may illumine your lofty position with his teaching and you may surround his learning with the radiant aura of your good fortune and position."[25] The teacher as the motivating light, destined to be encompassed and outshone by aristocratic aura, recalls the recurring figuration of power and cultivated subordination from Erasmus's colloquies on domestic relations, in which a wife like Eulalia educates her spouse to eclipse her manipulative efforts with the aura of masculine domination.

In *Good Manners in Boys*, Erasmus highlights the class distinctions between nobility and mobile, aspiring other classes in his attempt to create a notion of manners as universal civil discourse. His work, written for the family of his patron in Freiburg and dedicated to the young Prince of Burgundy, takes care to distinguish both the two levels of audience and the two kinds of needs, at the same time that it indicates the common interest in the goals of power and ambition. Playing with the insecurities of noble and common members of his audience alike, he calls his noble reader into service: "For it will be a considerable additional spur to all the young to observe that children of illustrious descent are dedicated to learning right from their earliest years, and are competing in the same race as themselves."[26] Obviously, the participants may not all be in the fast lane of this race, but Erasmus plays a power game with nobility—and himself shows the political utility of learning—when he plays with the commonplace argument on *vera nobilitas* by ambiguously describing technical-legal and ethical—or second nature—nobility: "Now everyone who cultivates the mind in liberal studies must be taken to be noble. Let others paint lions, eagles, bulls, and leopards on their escutcheons; those who can display 'devices' [*insigne*] of the intellect commensurate with their grasp of the liberal arts

have a truer nobility."[27] Indeed, the ten-year-old prince may have no
need of Erasmus's instruction in this "meager" philosophy;[28] but the
author's concern is with signs less self-evident, signs of a meritocracy
of learning in which the student acquires nobility in a new-fashioned
way: he earns it and, I might add, inscribes the signs on his body. The
devices (strategies) Erasmus focuses on are techniques of the body,
techniques that constitute the devices (signs) of "nobility" as acquired
goodness. Thus Erasmus presents his readers with the knowledge of
both the signifier of nobility and production of nobility through good
manners.

Here Erasmus begins to replace the idea of noble birth with a new
notion of acculturation: the accumulation of formal knowledge and social techniques of the body and of the labor necessary to acquire them,
as a substitute for, even something to be regarded above, social station.
Yet in redefining "nobility" to make place in the social order for the
nonnoble (but innately noble), Erasmus speaks to the constructed need
of both groups to reevalute manners in a changing world in which the
chivalric ideals of a medieval warrior aristocracy no longer apply as
before, in which the administrative and intellectual talents of a rising
bourgeois class are recognized but do not yet constitute a power. The
old presumption—that the noble are good—takes a new turn. Now,
because well-behaved, commoners can be nobler: learning manners is
en-nobling. Nevertheless, Erasmus later cautions readers not to think
that just because someone—of whatever class—should err in his behavior he is not *bonus* (noble). Erasmus's apparent magnanimity and
flexibility seem aimed at sparing the spontaneous gaffes of the upwardly
mobile, as well as, importantly, the hereditary aristocracy who may be
less obsessed with outward signs of refinement than their more anxious
competitors. The ambiguity here becomes a deliberate attempt to balance the aristocratic model with a reconciliation and unification of noble
and bourgeois standards, but the result is the creation of a standard
that, with its notions of fair labor, exchange, merit, mobility, acquisition,
we must finally call bourgeois.[29] Such a civilizing model constructs a
relationship that, mirroring the domestic relationship of wife to husband, challenges no standard of superiority and subordination, yet retains the anxiety that it is singularly dedicated to contain and control.
In the model of civil behavior and its detailed techniques of bodily

control and psychic repression, the unsettling textual resolution of patriarchal crisis sees the middle class ruling over the instincts, itself, its sons, and placing a "good" ruler, shaped, molded like this boy addressed in Erasmus's text by bourgeois humanist standards and served by competent administrators and stewards. With such a standard ruling both groups, good manners also become a kind of substitute experience of power, the initiation to which is constituted by accumulating hygienic and mechanical techniques based on a perception formed by and forming modern cultural manhood. They, too, learn to maneuver their masters to rule them benevolently, to treat them well, as "wives."

Yet how complicated a negotiation this is, for lest the arguments for what must be intended to be two distinct spheres—domestic order, civil order—resonate too closely, Erasmus, in the scheme of gestural stereotyping which follows, retains the horror of "effeminacy" as boundary: "The eyes should be calm . . . not grim, which is a mark of truculence; not shameless, the hallmark of insolence; not darting and rolling, a feature of insanity; nor furtive, like those of suspects and plotters of treachery. . . . Puffing out the cheeks is a sign of arrogance, while deflating them is a sign of mental despair: the former is the characteristic of Cain, the latter of Judas the betrayer."[30] We find that many of these "devices" have to do with striking the right balance between the extremes of bestiality and effeminacy.

> The gait should be neither mincing nor headlong, the former being a sign of effeminacy, the latter of rage. . . . It is boorish to go about with one's hair uncombed: it should be neat, but not as elaborate as a girl's coiffure. (274–75)

> Attention must be paid to the care of the teeth, but to whiten them with fine powder is for girls, while brushing with salt or alum harms the gums. To brush them with urine is a custom of the Spaniards. (276)

> To drag long trains after one is ridiculous in women, reprehensible in men. . . . It was once held to be somewhat effeminate not to wear a belt, but nowadays nobody is faulted for this, because with the invention of underwear, shirts, and hose, the private parts are concealed even if the tunic fly open. (279)

Perhaps the strongest insistence on gender boundaries appears in *De pueris*, where Erasmus—some would say in an uncharacteristically harsh manner—invokes strict Pauline thought in condemning female teachers in schools, including them with his horror stories of the most sadistic male teachers and referring to the "tyranny of women" as a form of "unnatural domination."[31] The key term here is "molding" or "fashioning," the explicit goal of the humanist education, explicitly identified in *De civilitate*: "We are concerned in moulding a boy" (275). But the duties of molding are both gendered and gendering. In "Puerpera" Erasmus's Eutrapelus instructs Fabulla that gently nurturing the child is appropriate for the first years of life, but in *De pueris* Erasmus singles out for especially strong condemnation those women who coddle the child excessively or for too long in his life (331), and ranks them on a scale with the danger of "constant exposure to beatings" (331). He warns as well against the indecent molding of nursemaids (308) and female servants. His caution takes in not only physical and sexual fondling but comparably indecent intellectual "fondling": ballads, "wives' " tales, and gossip (338). When the boy is seven, as we have already learned, the father appropriates the molding duties, as befits his parental role: "To be a true father, you must take absolute control of your son's entire being" (299–300).

Like other humanists, Erasmus supported the education of girls and saw it as a lifelong project, but like Vives and Luther, he also insisted on steering the female student toward the domestic and marital sphere.[32] That an educated girl would be better prepared for raising children and for meeting the expectations of her husband for suitable and stimulating companionship is familiar to readers of Erasmus; but the strategy of confining girls to distinctly gendered (and thus gendering) spheres also allows Erasmus to create a more comfortable distance between the oxymoronic kind of superior subordination he constructs for his civilizing project, his pedagogical goals, and their analogies to sexual politics. Although *De civilitate* reflects the deep commitment of Erasmus and of humanism in general to grounding the social changes surrounding them in a thoroughly patriarchal value structure, a regulatory domain in which virility is defined by its strong opposition to "effeminacy" and by the ability to contain "thy other self" through self-governance, the effort creates the circular mechanism of self-governance as preparation for a system in which the subordinate exercises the power to educate his superior to rule him well.

A brief comparison with Thomas Elyot's *Book Named the Governor*, an English pedagogical-political handbook published in 1531, highlights the distinctiveness of Erasmus's *De civilitate*.[33] Elyot follows classical precepts on beginning the study of Latin when the boy is seven, and removing the child "from all company of women" to prevent sexual threats (19); but his notions of class are significantly more rigid.[34] Even in insisting that nobility is not only lineage, he retains the traditional view that birth is the determining prerequisite (105). Most important, Elyot's "magistrates" are trained to serve the "sovereign governor" not as illuminating inspirations but as "inferiors" who receive orders and execute them, following Aristotle, as appendages ("his eyes, ears, hands, and legs") of the sovereign (13).

In contrast to such rigid distinctions, in which women are written out, Erasmus's concern for enlightened pacification—the construction of a realm modeled on the happy home—is echoed here and points to complicated strategies for containing the conflicts of an irenic personality. We might also observe that constructing and maintaining the mystification of the public/private distinction—private control, public submission; private governance of the individual subject, public subjugation—allow questions of authority always to collapse back onto the figure of the officially ruling authority, privileged to recognize no alienating separation of these realms, to invoke its own traditional, more organic legitimacy. (One could also suggest, looking back to Montrose's concerns, that in a monarchy, such as Elizabeth I's, where public and private distinctions are deliberately blurred, perhaps the attraction to and popularity of monarchical forms lies precisely in the vicarious enjoyment of such privileged integration.) Erasmus's lessons in civility are haunted by familiarity: *de te fabul[l]a narratur*. The scheme of tutoring and nurturing one's superiors retains intimate connections to notions of feminine decorum and duty, and discloses the uneasy presence of the socially constructed feminine, threatening to erupt from its place within the new cultural manhood.

That threat is spelled out most clearly in the colloquy "The Abbot and the Learned Lady" ("Abbaatis et eruditae"), in which Atronius, a clerical straw man erected to represent the sordid state of learning in the Church, confronts the intellectual skills of Magdalia, who ably and eloquently defends learned women from his empty and unreflected opinions. When she warns him of the consequences of his ignorant pleasure seeking—"If you're not careful, the net result will be that we'll preside in the theological schools, preach in the churches, and wear your miters" (223)—and invokes the names of historical learned women (the Pirkheimer daughters, Margaret Roper) as evidence of a more broadly based movement, potentially threatening to male power unless it can prove its competence. Natalie Zemon Davis reads this colloquy as evidence of Erasmus's singular sensitivity to the resentment of the marginalized,[35] but read in the context of other colloquies on power and sexuality, we might also see here Erasmus's own urgent plea to retain control. In response to Magdalia's threat Atronius protests, "God forbid!" and Magdalia replies with specific instructions: "No, it will be up to you to forbid. But if you keep on as you've begun, geese may do the preaching sooner than put up with you tongue-tied pastors. The world's a stage that's topsy-turvy now, as you see. Every man must play his part or—exit" (223). "See that you form and fashion me." Geese may preach or women may enter theological schools in a world that can be set right only when superiors get the right instructions from their subordinates.

Andrew Maclean praises the essay collection *Rewriting the Renaissance* because it "obliges the specialist to reconsider Renaissance literary and historical texts in light of women's position."[36] He identifies the need to restore "her story to history" and calls for the recovery from obscurity of marginal female figures. To be sure, the need to open Renaissance studies to noncanonical texts, to produce noncanonical readings of canonical texts, to broaden the object of study to include the full range of historical participants, the full range of questions, is more pressing than ever. Yet this "let's add women" approach (which often arrests itself at the level of a belated sense of guilt) constitutes a circular process that only collapses back on patriarchal authority. Feminist concerns, I would assert, should not be introduced simply as a site of accusation; rather, they should be seen as an opportunity for self-reflexive scrutiny. Women, I might now suggest, have no "real" position from which to speak and to counter conventional historical and literary historical approaches. To claim that they do risks reinscribing gender ideology, reproducing the very mechanism, the "technology of gender," which works to exclude women from historical inquiry. Speak they must, then, to challenge imperatives of silence; yet there is another consideration here, still more important: Woman, marginalized or mystified or demonized, was never excluded from Renaissance humanist writings. On the contrary, as the repository of an ideology of identity constructing the sex-gender system of a patriarchal society, woman is everywhere in these texts, constructed to motivate the civilizing process, to further the projects of civic and Christian humanism. As the case of Erasmus shows, especially in humanist discussions of civility, woman has an essential function, projected as the horror of effeminacy, which must be contained. In that structural and functionally efficacious horror lies also that which, as de Lauretis states, exceeds representation: "For gender, like the real, is not only the effect of representation but also its excess, what remains outside discourse as a potential trauma which can rupture or destabilize, if not contained, any representation" (3). Erasmus's underlings, who illuminate their rulers only to have their light surpassed by the aura of aristocratic power, who nurture and cultivate subordination, who attempt to contain even as they preserve the Woman function, show the signs of that unsettling, perhaps promising excess.

# 3 / Reading *Grobianus*: The Subject at Work in the "laborinth" of Simplicity

Symple condicyons of a persone that is not taught,
Y wille ye eschew, for euermore they be nowght.
—John Russell, *Book of Nurture*

I have followed an itinerary, both conceptual and historical, that has brought us from questions of courtesy and conduct to the place of the indecent as what stands in excess of the discourses of civility. I have also situated the *Grobianus* texts historically in overlapping contexts of early modern discourses of conduct, class, gender, and power. We have seen a version of this rich cultural problematic in Erasmus's key texts on civility (*On Good Manners in Boys*) and social grammar (*The Colloquies*), written for and circulated among boys and men at a time when the malleable material of gendering and bourgeois empowering produced and reproduced specular anxieties constitutive of the masculine subject of civililty. Positioned in this context of historical transition and its sociopsychic tensions, *Grobianus*, I have argued, makes a strong case against the legitimating claims that the civilizing process has a progressive-evolutionary history or that it produces a triumphant civil subject of *régimes du savoir-faire*, and it suggests that such claims will be undone by their own constitutive unmentionables: anxiety, abjection, and disgust.

In the "laborious" reading of Dedekind's *Grobianus* which follows, I investigate this cultural constellation still further by examining the workings of his humanist didactic irony: its attempt to rewrite humanist conduct in a way more effective and subjectifying than its predecessors; the politics of a didactic irony that is necessarily more than simple reversal; its attempt to appropriate "simplicity" anachronistically by rejecting a rustic-agrarian past and by having cultured simplicity both supersede and precede it; and its homeopathic method of civilizing reform. My concern for laborious reading comes not only from Dedekind's dedicatory instructions to his youthful reader, urging him to apply himself to careful and arduous reading of the text ("Hunc, studiose puer, vigili perdisce labore"), but especially from R.F.'s canny and perhaps uncanny *translatio* of Dedekind's introductory remarks on the daunting project—producing the civil subject that has eluded other humanists—that lies ahead:

> Non facilis labor est, mores formare decoros.
> Saepe gravis magnis res fuit illa viris.
> Auxilio superum tamen has et numine fretus,
> Difficiles magno pectore inibo vias.
>
> (1.31–34)

T'is no small thing in perfect sort good manners thus to frame,
Great men, good schollers, have beene oft times troubled with
   the same.
Yet by the helpe of all those gods and goddesses Ile try
To passe the tedious laborinth of this simplicitie.

(1.27–30)

Whatever his intention may have been, the unknown translator puns on Dedekind's text with the early modern English laborinth (= labyrinth). In rendering "vias difficiles" as "tedious laborinth," R.F.'s *paranomasia* respects Dedekind's neo-Latin concern with the labor of producing a shaming discipline ("Non facilis labor est, mores formare decoros") in what he considers a new way. Dedekind means it to achieve the salutary effects withheld from those illustrious predecessors whose serious, decent appeals have left the world's indecency untouched. The way to civility is indeed difficult work; it entails revulsion at every stage, iteratively and tediously performed in the subject as it is repeated in the text. But it is the labor of aversive conditioning which would allow the subject of civility to proceed, with difficulty, toward the goal of becom-

ing the abjecting civil subject. Perhaps we don't need Dedekind's didactic irony to tell us so, but it is only when we make the laborious
journey into Dedekind's work of reverse precepts that we see it and
read it, retrospectively, back into the tradition.

Like Erasmus's boy, who works by internalizing cultural anxiety and
rehearsing the teetering act of masculine identity to cover himself in
the insignia and signifiers of civil and "ennobling" status, Dedekind's
grobian reader takes upon himself the essential drudge work of the
countless small acts of aversion. This twisted path will demonstrate
Bourdieu's notion of the way, both intricate and difficult, the habitus
works to produce the outward effect of conductorless orchestration:
extracting the essential while seeming to demand something merely
trivial. In this case, at least, the demand is for something so (seemingly)
trivial that it is indeed tedious, so essential, moreover, that it has become a central pedagogical investment for humanist reformers of manners, molders of early modern men. In producing his ironic-didactic
lesson, Dedekind not only echoes Erasmus and repeats his labors; he
rewrites conduct in a way that a laborious reading will show to be both
transforming and revealing of the way conduct texts and civilizing subject formation work.

Dedekind's grobian speaker offers his ironic precepts much in the manner of Ovid's speaker in *Ars amatoria* and emulates the confident voice
of that "praeceptor amoris." That influential classical text on love arts
and social graces was well known to sixteenth-century humanists; Dedekind uses its method of offering advice in direct address to the reader,
even imitating (mutatis mutandis) some of its episodes. Nonetheless,
although there is a certain amount of homage to Ovid in recommending
behavior that clearly will not win anyone's love,[1] it is Erasmus who
provides the structuring authority for the didactic trajectory of *Grobianus*, and Dedekind looks often to him often. On the one hand, Erasmus ("Roterodamus") is the only modern authority (though an "old
sage" for R.F.) among the classical figures—Plato, Aristotle, Tully—to
whom Dedekind alludes in the preface:

> Utile formandis puerorum moribus, istis
> Temporibus scripsit Roterodamus opus.

Quae tamen utilitas hoc digna labore secuta est?
Consilium vitae quis melioris init?
(Praefatio, 35–38)

So did old learned "Roterodam" set foorth a booke of price,
From which for manners straitest rule all youth might take advise,
And yet what profite did he get by that most worthy booke?
Or who did on it, as he ought, for better counsell looke?
(Preface of the Author, 31–34)

On the other hand, more often throughout the work it is not the earnest
and presumably nonironizing speaker of the preface but rather the
ironic and clearly unreliable grobian speaker—a counterauthority—who
aggressively invokes Erasmian authority:

Neglectus iuvenem cultus decet, inquit Erasmus:
Quis dubitet tantum dicere vera virum?
Hunc igitur credens vestitum neglige, nec te
Qui cultus deceant respice, quive minus.
(1.2.325–28)

Old sage "Erasmus" counsaile tis: Regarde not thine attire.
(The precept of so grave a man who will not much admire?)
Doe as he bids thee then, regarde not how thy garments sit,
Whether they be too little, or too bigge, or very fit.
(1.2.266–69)

What can be said of a humanist authority who can so easily be co-opted
by the boorish? Why would it be so easy to undermine the civilizing
values Erasmus treated with such attention to pedagogical efficacy? It
is Erasmus's goal of molding a civil subject which Dedekind, like other
humanists, promotes; yet contemporary bad manners elude the tutelary
embrace of Erasmus's systematic wisdom.[2] Confronted with the pan-
demic of *simplicitas* Dedekind sees infecting contemporary life—the
medical puns and tropes appear throughout the text—he finds some
flaw in the Erasmian humanism he so admires: it doesn't measure up
to conditions. Scandalously, no one heeds the advice of such a wise
philosopher; Dedekind sets out to achieve Erasmus's goals of inculcat-
ing the value and instituting the regimes of self-discipline and bodily

restraint by other means. When he puts the words of Erasmus into the
speaker's mouth, he uses those means, another kind of labor, to structure another "system" of aversive conditioning.

Of course, the issue in the passage just quoted is not limited simply
to ill-fitting garments; rather, it leads to the question of whether one
should wear a long gown that collects dirt (of all kinds) from the street
or one so short that it indecently exposes the body. Both recommen-
dations present indecent extremes embellished with indecent ambitions:

> Et toga longa pedes tibi demittatur ad imos,
>   Hoc erit antiquae simplicitatis opus.
> Et tua sic verret post te vestigia, ne quis
>   Quo sis progressus, cernere possit iter.
> Latus et extrema limbus tibi vestis in ora
>   Collecto plateae stercore firmus erit.
> Viderit hoc aliquis spacio distante remotus,
>   Te bene praetextam credet habere togam,
> Panniculos mittunt Bombicum munera Seres,
>   Hinc procul in Scythia munera nata plaga:
> His credere tuas solitus praetexere vestes,
>   Infima si lato plena sit ora luto.
> Sin minus ista iuvant, (quoniam nova tempora mores
>   Insolitos secum ferre subinde solent)
> Veste brevi induitor, quae vix tegat undique lumbos,
>   Quae tibi detectas non vetet esse nates.
> Hoc gaudent cultu qui Martia castra sequuntur,
>   Quique modo nomen nobilitatis habent.
> Et tibi ut aut miles, vel nobilis esse puteris,
>   Cura sit ut semper veste tegare brevi.
>
>                                   (1.2.303–22)

A long gowne weare, which all the ground may sweepe as thou doost
    go,
For so no man the place whereon thou troddest well can know.
The dirt which on thy hem thou getst, as thou doost walke along
Will make the lowe welt of thy Gowne seeme to be very strong.
And if a man espy the durt, when he is farre remote,
Hee'le thinke you weare a very rich embroydred garded cote.
Cloth, made by silke-wormes paineful Art, from "Scythia" land doth
    come,

Some strangers give to deerest friends, to others they sell some.
A man would think that with this cloth your gowne were garded thick,
If on the hemme a great way off, he should see dry durt sticke.
Or if you like not these longe gownes (as oftentimes we see
As many men, so many mindes and manners there will be)
Weare a short coate, which scarce will keepe your buttockes out of
   sight,
Like Noblemen, and those which doe reioyce in martiall fight.
                                                      (1.2.252–65)

Dedekind's dialogue with Erasmian authority relies in part on simply repeating the precepts of traditional conduct literature, putting Erasmus's own words and thoughts in the mouth of the grobian speaker. The autospecular concern for how one looks to others ("Viderit hoc aliquis spacio distante remotus, / Te bene praetextam credet habere togam," "And if a man espy the durt, when he is farre remote, / Hee'le thinke you weare a very rich embroydred garded cote"), the noble signifiers that can be appropriated, however comically or grotesquely, by the grobian subject are familiar to readers of Erasmus's *De civilitate*, where, ironically enough, they have encountered them almost word for word:

> Neglectior cultus decet adolescentes, sed citra immunditiam. Indecore quidam interularum ac tunicarum oras adspergine lotii pingunt, aut sinum brachialiaque indecoro tectorio incrustant, non gypso, sed narium et oris pituita. Sunt quibus vestis in alterum latus defluit, aliis in tergum ad renes usque, nec desunt quibus hoc videatur elegans. (1037)

> A degree of negligence in dress suits young men provided it does not lapse into slovenliness. Disgustingly, some people decorate the hems of their shirts and tunics with drops of urine or encrust their shirt-fronts and sleeves with a repulsive plastering, not unfortunately of plaster, but of snot and phlegm. Some wear their clothing lopsided, while others have it hitched up in back as far as the kidneys—some people even think this is elegant! (279)

The grobian speaker's vulgar concern for noble status (the "toga praetexta" is worn by Roman magistrates), for those who "hitch up" their coats to look like noble men ("miles, vel nobis esse puteris"), rather than Erasmus's emphasis on *vera nobilitas*, may suggest a point of difference; yet both authors are preoccupied with the external, visible signifiers of status, with appropriating noble status for a bourgeois standard that relies on ocular activity as well as ocular proof. One hardly need mention, too, that in selectively and opportunistically citing or shamelessly plagiarizing Erasmus, in taking Erasmus at his word, the advice offered betrays, ironically or altogether logically, the very fastidious preoccupation with attire which Erasmus strongly advised against. The "final" or topping irony, however, is that Erasmus's detailed advice on appearance, his unvarnished descriptions of bad behavior, and his emphasis on an evaluating spectatorship in *De civilitate* also produce that very preoccupation.[3]

Dedekind's work continues the Erasmian scheme of *De civilitate*, with its emphasis on discrete techniques of the body and self-instrumentalizing anatomization (do this, not that, with this part of your body, in this setting, for this effect, and lest it produce this negative effect), with the emphasis on observation and internalization on which Erasmus relies. To be sure, *Grobianus* achieves many of its humorous—and therefore also serious—effects by startling and incongruous references to the conventional markers of civil training. It is in many ways an academic exercise that works optimally only if the reader has already been—or, in the case of young readers, is simultaneously—an initiate at the academy that taught him his Latin, his Ovid, Lucian, Juvenal, and Horace, and his techniques of the body. The text allows him to revisit the scene of bodily and linguistic discipline and turn it upside down, only (in the final instance?) to reassemble it in a redoubled civilizing manner. The result may be that it further develops the attitude about manners and reveals still more about transforming, civilizing values by assimilating humor and entertainment to the project of civil self-discipline. But there is also a subsuming ironic stroke that informs the structure of the work. That is to say, while Erasmus is the structuring authority, he is (as in the advice to disregard one's attire) revisited ironically:

> Ethica concedant veterum morosa sophorum,
> Cedat Aristotele, cumque Platone Cato.

Concedat Cicero Latius: concedat Erasmus,
Et quotquot morum de gravitate docent.
Hic liber exactam dat morum simplicitatem,
Eque nova nuper prodiit ille schola.
Hunc, studiose puer, vigili perdisce labore,
Qui cupis ornatus moribus esse bonis.
(Title page dedication)

Give place time-scourging "Aristotle", vice-controuling Plato,
Yeeld learned Tully, deepe Erasmus, and fault-finding Cato:
And you which by your tedious works, though to your mickle paine,
Did teach behaviours perfect meanes, and manners to attaine.
This Booke, which from a new found Schoole of late time did arise,
Behaviours pure simplicitie within it doth comprise:
Then yong and olde that doe desire nurture and education,
Peruse this Booke each day and houre with great deliberation.
(Title page dedication)

The title of R.F.'s English translation—*The Schoole of Slovenrie, or Cato turnd Wrong Side Outward*—faithfully transmits Dedekind's method of reversing precepts. That the book guarantees the delivery of simplicity ("exactam," "pure simplicitie") to the reader who works to read it, however, complicates simple reversal and reveals the ironic method as work with a double meaning: there are the good simplicity and the bad; Dedekind uses the indecent one (the one that's the wrong side outward) to present the other. The diligent work of the reader, taking a good dose of Dedekind's method, is needed to uncover the double meanings and set things straight. Yet even to the hard worker, Dedekind's irony may yield meanings other than simple reversal and point toward significations that are other than or more than "simple" inversion.

As Norman Knox has pointed out for English literature, the word *irony* was rarely used before the eighteenth century, and Dedekind's motto, "IRON CHLEVASTES" (scoffing or mocking deceiver), is a notable example of its use by continental humanists.[4] The *eiron* was a traditional figure in Greek comedy, whose sly mockery and self-deprecation worked to unmask and expose the *alazon* or pretender. Both are imposters, but whereas the *alazon* pretends to be more than he is, the

*eiron* pretends to be less and uses dissimulation to defeat his antago-
nist.[5] Plato's Socrates could be considered the supreme *eiron*, exposing
opponents through his self-effacing pretense of ignorance and modesty.
Aristotle refers to *eirony* in rhetoric as the way to praise by blame or
blame by praise, effecting a reversal whose deception surprises. But
Dedekind would have other inspirations for masterful pretense. In addition to the classical models offered by Lucian, Juvenal, and Ovid,
there was Erasmus and the figure of Folly in *The Praise of Folly*.

In *The Word "Irony" and Its Context, 1500–1750*, Knox lists three
definitions for irony in English literature between 1500 and 1755.) Most
often it meant praising by blame or blaming by praise, but it could also
express saying the opposite of what one means or speaking by contraries, or it could be used for saying something other than what one
means.[6] In offering reverse precepts and grounding the advice by promising public approval for disgusting actions, Dedekind and Scheidt may
have had the first two definitions in mind. *Grobianus* owes a good deal
to the humanist ironic *encomium;* the text takes pains to praise boorishness and boorish actions; and the authors take pains to point out
their intentions to teach by contrary example. It is the third characteristic, however, with its classical source in Quintilian, which is semioti-
cally rich and most problematic not only for the didactic project of the
work but for regimes of conduct themselves.

According to Linda Hutcheon in *Irony's Edge: The Theory and Politics of Irony*, it is the "other than" of irony which constitutes its defining
"edge" and indicates the differential character of a mode that comes
from relational and. political context.[7] Hutcheon responds in part to
Wayne Booth, who sees irony as an "astonishing communal achievement," whose "complexities are, after all, shared: the whole thing cannot
work at all unless both parties to the exchange have confidence that
they are moving together in identical patterns."[8] Although his faith in
consensus seems questionable, especially for bourgeois-authored conduct texts and the historically specific kind of irony found in the *Grobianus* texts, Hutcheon shares Booth's recognition of irony as effecting
an act of communication. She sees irony as "situational," rather than
formal (3), and "functioning in [the] context . . . of a social and political
scene" (4). As a communicative act, the ironic utterance lays out a
relationship of power: the relations of power in relations of communi-

cation. Where Booth sees community building, inclusion, and essentially victimless humor and pleasure, however, Hutcheon understands power relationships very much as Foucault formulated them, namely, as indeterminate and unstable, marked by a defining edge that cuts between.[9] Irony "operates not only between meanings (said, unsaid) but between people (ironists, interpreters, targets)" (58). Thus irony is "relational" ("the result of the bringing—even the rubbing—together of the said and the unsaid, each of which takes on meaning only in relation to the other"), "inclusive" (its both/and refuses reversal or binary limits), and "differential" ("the unsaid is other than, different from the said") (59), and works with a remarkably mobilizing semantic strength. The edge that cuts between includes (that is, cannot exclude) the said and the unsaid, and differentiates; it not only subverts the ironist's intentions ("Nothing is ever guaranteed at the politicized scene of irony" [15]) but gives irony the capacity to operate and oscillate with a deauthorizing power and a political capacity.[10]

Even if we did not have the heart to scrutinize Booth's good-hearted assumptions of community, *Grobianus* rather demolishes them.[11] On the one hand, the text works from a snide sense of complicity: the reader, already initiated into the autoscopic conduct rites of civility, knows what Dedekind knows, knows that Dedekind knows that he knows, and enjoys the humorous reversals. On the other hand, in the autospecular regimes of placing readers in situations of imagining their own indecent actions, *Grobianus* contributes toward building a specific, still more exclusionary audience in which inclusion (having fun) means self-victimization (having horror) or, at the very least, keeping the subject of civility on the hook.

As we know from Erasmian examples, though, civility too has a defining edge. In Erasmus's *Good Manners in Boys* and in the *Colloquies*, subject formation relies on an ultimately unreliable malleability: the very flexibility and malleability that enable the pedagogue (in loco parentis) to mold the subject confuses the lines of power relationships and point to an inability to secure both status and sexual difference. Here in *Grobianus* the issue of malleability is taken to new lengths, extended to the ironic-didactic method of the text, which counts on the reader's successful negotiation of ironic reversals; now, as Dedekind's first

English translator (perhaps unwittingly) puns, we are in a "laborinth" of simplicity, tasked with the labor of negotiating ironic precepts.

In building upon the work of its illustrious but (retrospectively) ineffectual predecessor, Dedekind's *Grobianus* produces a labor theory of conduct which grapples with a double notion of simplicity. It attempts to secure the distinction between simplicity as unadorned and indecent nature (*natura naturans*) and a somewhat oxymoronic cultured simplicity (*natura naturata*), a simplicity that both supersedes and presumably antedates the former. Such a distinction would secure other distinctions (of class, gender, normativity) and restore the world to its imagined and culturally projected originary simple and virtuous state.[12] The projected enemy is Simplicity, the cause of "rustic," boorish manners, the rallying cry of those who look longingly back to a golden age uncorrupted by the complexities of urban life (and self-restrained social behavior) and follow the rule of the goddess Rusticitas, "nostro dea maxima saeclo" (chief goddess of our century), as Dedekind describes her. Yet Dedekind's text reveals that the world of simplicity is lost precisely because it was never there to begin with. Confronted with such a civil-ideological double bind, no wonder that the way for the subject of civility is difficult.

Like Erasmus and Castiglione, Dedekind relies on the autospecular regime by which the subject of civility contains and preserves a horror of the body, but in continuing Erasmian pedagogy, Dedekind goes beyond Erasmus in cultivating restrained behavior. Erasmus, too, puts his readers through subjective labors. They learn Latin grammar, rhetoric, manners, bodily comportment as bodily rhetoric. Dedekind requires more intensive labor from the readers who follow his ironic-didactic method of teaching conduct. If the successfully socialized subject of civility is the man or boy who is disciplined to keep the worst-case scenario ever in mind—the things impossible to mention, the things we cannot think about without the greatest disgust, those things that stand as the affect record of phantasmal projection—then Dedekind more directly confronts what that part of the civil imaginary so fearfully contains but also ferociously preserves. In *Grobianus* an effort is made to be absolutely inclusive about the worst things, to summon and body forth all the abjects of civility.

We have already been introduced to Grobianus's visual "qualities" in
the text's advice on personal hygiene: an unwashed body, with long,
unkempt hair and dirty yellow teeth, attired in a filthy gown that is
indecently either too long or too short. Two passages farther into the
text make that introduction seem mild indeed by comparison. The first
is from book 1, chapter 2, "De ientaculo, & modestia oculorum, frontis,
narium, item de garrulitate, sternutatione, obscoenitate, tussi, ructu, &
de incessu, & habitu in plateis" ("The breakefast, the modestie of the
eyes, the forehead and the nosthrilles: also of pratling, sneezing, baw-
dinesse, belching and going, and behaviour in the streetes"):

> Illa tibi gratis tanta ornamenta parantur,
>     Quae puto non parvum sunt paritura decus,
> Cuncta tibi rerum bona contulit ipsa creatrix
>     Natura, ut vita prospicit illa tuae.
> Sed modus est rebus servandus in omnibus, ergo
>     Hanc tibi mensuram qua modereris habe.
> Mucor ubi patulo stillans influxerit ori,
>     Tunc emungendi tempus adesse scias.
> Ad cubito facies, et te civilior alter
>     Non erit: hanc laudem solus habere potes.
>                                         (1.2.181–90)

Nature, the maker of all things, to decke thy life the more,
Hath lent thee of such ornament a most aboundant store.
Wherefore, as in all things besides, so in this, keep this meane:
When store of snot is in thy mouth, thy nose then make thou cleane.
Do this but closely now and then, and sure I thinke, than thee
No man deserveth greater praise for his civilitie.
                                         (1.2.152–57)

The second takes the reader to the table in book 1, chapter 4, "Qui
mores in mensa servandi, ante apposita cibaria" ("Concerning the behaviour at the Table, before meate be set on"):

> Interea varias tere tempora longa per artes,
>     Ocia sunt pigris insidiosa viris.
> Si mala te scabies dulci prurigine vexat,
>     Qua liceat causam, fallere tempus, habes.

Scalpe frequens digitis (nihil est iucundius illo)
    Ulcera, quae multa putrida tabe fluunt.
Aut velut exciso quondam sub monte Metallum
    Quaeritur in venis terra benigna tuis:
Sic scabiem immisso varie rimabere cultro
    Doctus et occultos ingrediere poros.
Inde nec absterso cultro data prandia sumes,
    Nec digitos gelidae flumine lotus aquae.
                                                    (1.4.553–64)

Meane time be casting with thyselfe, which way the time to spend,
Beaware on idlenes, on which all vices do attend.
Hath the scabd dogge with tickling itching all thy bodie bit,
Thou maist have meanes to spend thy time by over-looking it.
Scratch off the scabs with busie fingers, that is verie good,
For so of putrefaction thou maist let out a flood.
Or as our Metall-mongers do, with their industrious paines,
By digging mountaines, rob the earth of her rich mettall vaines,
So with thy knife from out thy body scabs thou maist dig store,
And seeke diseases which do lacke in every hidden pore.
Then with your unwasht knife to cut your meate can breede no hurt,
Nor wash your hands, you know that water cannot scowre off durt.
                                                    (1.4.454–65)


Not all the advice in *Grobianus* is so graphically disgusting, but it would be fair to describe these passages as representative of what is most pedagogically compelling and sensationalistically indecent—most grobian—in the text, and to suggest as well that all the advice and examples point toward this indecent extreme or exist on a continuum of indecency in which these passages are found simply farther along, not elsewhere.[13] They also illustrate the representative techniques of indecent representation: morbidly tedious length, specious reasoning, bad syllogisms; a mixture of classical rhetoric and aggressive tasteless-ness that is intellectually trying as well as viscerally disgusting. The in-decency to which Castiglione and Erasmus allude as unmentionable is what Dedekind foregrounds, hoping to provoke a visceral response: laborious and disgusting work. But the passages also contain compli-cations rather than simply harsh simplifications of the civil lessons

Dedekind would reinforce—through ironic reversal or inversion—in his contribution to aversive conditioning.

=====

There's a sickness—(rustic, perverted) simplicity—against which Erasmus's good intentions are ineffectual, for which the ironist Dedekind would provide the cure, restoring (civil) simplicity. Dedekind presents himself as a homeopathic physician who will treat the patient by small doses of the poison that contaminates him.

Here again Dedekind crosses paths with Castiglione's idealizing text and takes up a game that very early *The Courtier* claims to abort after Cesare Gonzaga proposes it:

> Thus they say that in Apulia when someone is bitten by a tarantula many musical instruments are played and various tunes are tried until the humour which is causing the sickness all of a sudden responds to the sound with which it has a certain affinity and so agitates the sick man that he is shaken back into good health. In the same way, whenever we have suspected some hidden strain of folly, we have stimulated it so cunningly and with so many different inducements and in so many various ways that eventually we have discovered its nature; then, having recognized the humour for what it was, we have agitated it so thoroughly that it has always been brought to the culmination of open madness. And in this, as you know we have enjoyed some marvellous entertainments. . . . So I suggest that our game this evening should be to discuss this subject and that each one of us should answer the question: "If I had to be openly mad, what kind of folly would I be thought likely to display, and in what connexion, going by the sparks of folly which I give out every day?"; and let the same be said of all the others, following the usual order of our games, and let each of us seek to base his decision on some genuine signs and evidence. Thus each of us shall benefit from this game in finding out his faults and being able to guard against them all the better. (1.8.47)

Castiglione's participants are wildly amused at Cesare's suggestion for this confessional and purgative entertainment—it "provoked a great deal of laughter, and for a while no one could stop talking"—but they continue their deliberations until Count Lodovico comes to the topic of perfection and initiates the four-day discussion of the courtier (1.14).

Whereas Castiglione handles the small crisis of subversion with cathartic humor, Dedekind favors homeopathic methods.

In *De civilitate* Erasmus degrades the status of the conduct book to "crassissima philosophiae pars"; Dedekind's goes farther. First, he seems similarly to devalue the conduct book and to second Erasmus's evaluation when he refers in his preface to the work of past authorities on the subject of decent behavior:

> Atque ita iam nemo sequitur meliora docentem
> Ingenioque libet vivere cuique suo.
> Sic homines vanum docti sumpsere laborem,
> Nilque tot egregiis obtinuere libris.
> (Praefatio, 77–80)

> So that he which doth nowadaies precepts of manners give,
> May preach and teach, but all in vaine, men as they list will live.
> And so, good men which in this subiect have great studie spent,
> Have lost their labor, for to follow them no man is bent.
> (Preface, 67–70)

The tradition, from Cato to Erasmus, is thus reduced to the bootless labor of good men who mean well, to futile work and misplaced efforts. Dedekind seizes on more productive means, relying on subjective labor in constructing the subject of civility through grobianism and the work of civil irony. Through the actions recommended in the text, the serious lesson—the stable, nonironic context of civil standards and proper behavior—must be produced by the reader. That internalization is characteristic of early modern conduct literature, but in coarsening the lesson and intensifying the labor, *Grobianus* both extends and undermines Erasmus.

Both Dedekind and Scheidt, the vernacularizer of *Grobianus*, rely on organic and medical tropes to justify their methods. Dedekind, in his prefacing letter, uses the metaphor of disease—"Cum mala sint nimium tempora nostra" (22), "bad mens ill conditions do so the times infect" (18)—and figures himself as a physician administering an antidote to a poisoned patient by an unusual method when all other conventional treatments have failed:

> Nonne vides, dubio medicus succurrere morbo
>   Cum nequit, et superat pharmaca sana malum
> Ut varias animum solertem vertat in artes,
>   Aegrotum docta curet ut ille manu.
> .   .   .   .   .   .   .   .   .   .   .   .
> Ergo suam vertens mox in contraria mentem,
>   Antidoto morbum frigus habente petit:
> Et misero quam non licuit sperare salutem,
>   Hac demum felix arte sine arte tulit.
>                  (Praefatio, 117–120, 131–34)

You see the good Phisitian, whenas he cannot cure
By medicines might a sicknes great, sprung from a bod'impure.
How many waies he seekes to ease his patients grievous smart,
By seeking learned physickes aide, by labour or by Art.
.   .   .   .   .   .   .   .   .   .   .   .   .   .   .   .
At length he comes to contraries and alters quite the case,
From hote to colde, he gives him antidotes in Cordials place.
And thus to him he doth restore his unexspected health,
Which he before could not procure by physicke, friends, nor wealth.
                                   (105–8; 117–20)

Just as a small dose of the same poison shocks the patient back to health,
so Dedekind will administer some bad advice to already diseased minds:

> Quae fuerant facienda veto, fugiendaque mando,
>   Ut doceam gestus foeda per acta bonos.
>                                   (137–38)

All that which good men ought to practise, I forbid them flat,
All that which country clownage counteth currant, I bid that.
That so, whereas throughout my book I still forbid the good,
The contrarie I mean, the bad I would have understood.
                                   (123–26)

The curing shock will be a mixture of recognition and shame:

> Forsitan haec aliquis iocularia scripta revolvens,
>   His speculum vitae cernet inesse suae.

Et tacita culpa, nulloque monente rubescet,
Et fugiet posthac turpe quod esse videt.
                    (139–42)

Perhaps while some with greedie minde my iesting rimes doth view,
He shall behold of his owne life a looking-glasse most true,
And blushing, of his owne accord, when no man doth hem see,
Will spie his faults, and mend them all, and give some thanks to mee.
                    (127–130)


Unlike the *Tischzucht* parodies, which simply and formulaically re-verse the rules, the method of correction or "cure" in *Grobianus* is not simply "contraries" and goes beyond the kind of irony described by Booth as a "powerful shock of negative recognition" or D. C. Muecke's "simple corrective irony"; it requires substituting for the traditional ex-ternal authority of ancient sources an internal and specular authority; it comes through the autoproduction of shock and shame.[14] Irony, humor, even grobians had appeared in didactic literature before *Grobianus*, but Dedekind's predecessors such as Brant or Murner offered their lessons as sermons, given as external appeals or commands. Here the irony becomes organicized, "natural," a homeopathic cure, and the way of reading itself becomes linked to the second nature of civil values. Com-ing from Dedekind's pharmacy, the dose laboriously administered pu-rifies by means of controlled infection; thus inoculated, the body maintains its centrality as the ultimate organic-civil object; the outcome is catachretic organic-civil bourgeois subjectification.[15]

Since so much of *Grobianus* is located and relocated at the table, where the descriptions of food and eating provide such rich material for unappetizing descriptions and repellent advice, it will be instructive to look at sections of book 2 which advise the grobian student on his behavior as a dinner guest. In chapter 1, "Quomodo ab alio invitatus se ad coenam praeparet" ("How to prepare himselfe being invited of an other"), he is instructed at length to demand in the most petulant man-ner a detailed list of what will be served. This list is fastidiously con-sulted and checked off in chapter 2, "De moribus in edendo" ("Of behaviour in eating"), where the reader is informed that it is good to come to the table with a dog and instructions are given on what to do if you burn your mouth with hot food and why it is good to let food from your mouth get into the wine cup. Chapter 3, "De moribus in mensa post primum missum" (Behaviour at the table after the first course"), presents an even more labored table scene of gluttony and excessive drinking. Chapter 4, "Alia praecepta de modestia edendi et bibendi" ("As concerning other precepts of modestie in eating and drinking"), prescribes drastically gluttonous eating, justifying it with a reference to the speech therapy of Demosthenes and recommending that the reader also roar with his mouth full, preferably into the face of a neighbor. Chapter 5, "De voracitate, risu, vomitu in mensa et aliis civilitatibus" ("Of devouring, laughing, vomiting at the table, and other such like civilities to be observed"), carries gluttony to its explosive consquences and recommends vomiting at the table, followed by more gluttonous consumption. Chapter 6, "De lotione manuum a coena, de mensis secundis, et quid apud virgines deceat" ("Of washing the handes after supper, second courses, and how to behave yourselfe in the company of maides"), repeats the advice in chapter 3 on spectacular post-prandial ablutions performed before women, repeats advice on gluttonous eating, and in addition describes how to harass female guests. The last three chapters give advice on departing and arranging for the next night's meal, going home drunk, and alienating guests.

Preceded by book 1, chapters 2, "De ientaculo sumendo, et compositione totius vultus et corporis" ("Of manner in eating"), 3, "De ministerio mensae" ("Concerning manners after dinner"), 4 "De moribus in mensa ante cibum" ("Behaviour at the table before meate"), and followed by book 3, chapters 5, "Exempla civilitatum in mensa" ("Examples of civilitie at the table"), 6, "Exempla de evacuatione vesicae, vomitu, et aliis morum elegantiis" ("Of emptying the bladder, vomiting, and other such like elegancies of behaviour"), and 7, "Exempla de crepitu, ructu, retentione urinae, et aliis rusticitatibus" ("Of farting, belching, holding his urine, and such like rudenesse"), these projected table scenarios are the heart of the lessons of *Grobianus*. It is not only that their structures and particulars derive from the *Tisch-zucht*, where etiquette lessons revolve around the social setting of the dinner; it is that Dedekind's catastrophic representation of social eating enables him to produce strong sensory effects: the represented smells, sounds, and especially the visual images that drive home lessons in abjection and civil subjectivity.

In chapter 2, for example, the advice to commence the meal by putting as much in your mouth as fast as you can includes a few words on what to do if the food is too hot:

> Ore tuo calidas afflabis fortiter escas,
>     Spiritus ardorem temperat ille cibi,
> Nullus est usus nimis in sufflare modeste,
>     Quas etenim vires lenior aura ferat?
> Flaturus totas vento distendito buccas,
>     Difficilis quaesi sit buccina flanda tibi.
> Hinc, velut Æolius mittit sua flamina carcer,
>     Collecta in calidos flamina mitte cibos.
> Magno cum sonitu prorumpant fortiter aurae,
>     Non secus ac flammas Sicelis Ætna vomit.
>                 (2.2.243–52)

Thy burning meate with cooling breath thou stowtly oughtst to blow:
In little blasts against this heate no comfort can be found,
Then puffe thy cheekes with winde, as if a trumpet thou wouldst
    sound,
From whence, as if the boystrous windes were from their prison
    freed,
Set foorth great blasts against thy meate to helpe thee at thy neede.
With rumbling noyse let store of cooling blasts breake forth their fill,
In like sort as do flames of fire from "Ætnaes" burning hill.
                (2.2.1699–1705)

Again, to intensify the effect and color the spectacle, the speaker includes a dinner partner as witness and victim, assuring the reader that he will add to the speaker's approval:

> O mihi quam placeas, si convertaris ad illum,
>     Qui tibi vicinus cotinguusque sedet.
> Illius in vultum volo te spirare calorem,
>     Et calido totas spargere iure genas.
> Protinus applaudent alii, factumque probabunt,
>     Atque iocum talem saepe videre volent.
>                 (2.2.253–58)

If to thy neighbours face thou turne, I will thee much commend,
And store of breath and pottage to his cheekes be sure to send.

If thus thou doost, all will applaude thee and thy trickes allow,
And often will desire to learne this pretty jeast of you.

(2.2.1706–9)

The section continues with advice to besmirch the wine cup—likely, at
this time, to be shared with others—with crumbs from your mouth,
joining meat and drink by natural authority:

In calicem tenues ex ore emittere micas,
    Nil, agreste licet quis putet esse, nocet.
Nam cur non liceat dapibus confundere potum?
    Illa hominum vitam, sed bene iuncta, fovent.
Ipsa iubet iungi potum natura cibumque
    Et res alterius altera poscit opem.

(2.2.287–92)

Out of your mouth into the cup some little crummes to send,
Though some will say tis clownish, yet it cannot much offend.
I pray, whie is it hurtfull thus to mingle meate with drink?
If they be mingled thorowly, they nourish more, I thinke.
That meate and drinke should thus be ioynd Nature her selfe hath
    said,
For in the world one thing doth still desire anothers aide.

(2.2.1752–57)

The speaker supports his lessons repeatedly, claiming that good health
demands them, nature authorizes them, classical authority supports
them, every witness approves; they are winning social acts. Thus in
chapter 5, after you vomit at the table (because it would endanger your
health to restrain yourself) and impress the other guests with the display
of food they have already eaten and are sure to appreciate again, you
should continue to eat because now your stomach is empty and nature
abhors a vacuum:

Cumque reversus eris, ventrem iam denuo reple,
    Ut nova iam vacuum repleat esca locum.
Non bene ferre potest rerum natura creatrix,
    Corpore, sub coelo, qui vacet esse locum.

(2.5.739–42)

And being set, take care againe to fill thy belly straite,
And in the rowme of all thats gone, thrust in another baite.
Nature her selfe which made all things, cannot indure that wrong,
That any thing thats under heaven, should thus be empty long.

(2.5.2148–51)

By no means should you place your hands in water to wash before or after the meal because cold water may chill your heart. But if you do take a chance on washing your hands, be sure to wash first (most energetically) and wash not only your hands but your face, dirtying the water for the other guests.

As an ironic lesson in the school of simplicity, *Grobianus* seeks to produce the powerful shock of negative recognition of (your own) boorish behavior. As mentioned, part of the task of irony of horror and reversal, however, is to appropriate "simplicity" and anachronistically assimilate it to civility, projecting nature from the code of civility. Tortured, labyrinthine reasoning, unappetizing casuistry, moralizing synesthesia compose the rude simplicity that Dedekind laborously constructs in order to erect over it the civil simplicity that repels, abjects, and yet, most important, preserves it. Thus the work presents notions of simplicity in a relationship of inversion: the rustic, "natural" simplicity of the uncultivated and undisciplined rural society, on the one hand, and the legitimated simplicity of a civilized order, a second nature of urban life, man-made and man-making.[16] Paradoxically, the author presents the primary simplicity of nature running amok as that which perverts ways of behaving which are actually simpler. Hysteron proteron: first-order, uncivilized simplicity is the disease of an otherwise and originally "simple," healthy social order; chronologically and semantically, however, each sphere contaminates the other. Civil irony, the irony of "simple" and straight reversal and inversion, seems to have a edge that cuts both ways. In the text's ironic-didactic scheme, in which the civil imaginary rewrites its history through elision and effacement, boorishness or primary simplicity is the deception conspiratorially aimed at twisting and perverting a naturally ordained social order.

Following Dedekind's homeopathic regimen would produce the recontaminating purification that would also constitute the painful pleasure of the text. Using the horror of (primary) simplicity to produce the second nature (nurture) of civility-as-simplicity is indeed labor intensive; the subjective labor needed to accomplish it is apparently never ending. Even the successful construction of the civil subject—the making of man—produces something that incorporates the failures of which it needs to remind itself in order to be successful: hom(m)eopathy indeed.

Dedekind refers to the difficulties in achieving a safe and civil reception when, in the conclusion to the third edition, he compares his labors to the difficulties of navigating a ship through stormy seas:

> Hoc duce te Bingi tandem superavimus acquor,
> Te lacerae dextram subijciente rati.
> Non ego me vasto temere committere ponto,
> Et maris insani fluctibus ausus eram.
>
> (Conclusio, 1–4)

> This raging sea (most deere friend "Bing") with good successe at last,
> Helpt by thy friendly Pilots hand, my tattred ship hath past.
> If to the waters mercy I had trusted all along,
> I know my ship had long ago with waves beene over-throwne.
>
> (Conclusion, 4425–28)

The conventional trope of navigation and/as didactic writing recalls Sebastian Brant's pre-Reformation social satire *The Ship of Fools*, in which the ship serves as an allegorical vehicle bearing the cargo of social-ethical types—among them, as we know, the newly "canonized" Saint Grobian—who were the objects of Brant's comprehensive social satire. For Dedekind, however, the metaphor of navigating in rough seas aptly describes his labors and his dilemma as moralist and ironist. Dedekind's apologia describes the method of his reformation project and defends it against misunderstanding by his critics.[17] His *scriptum iocularium* must make the lessons humorous and lively; it cannot appear to endorse the indecency it would instruct against. And Dedekind sees his work or "ship" threatened not only by the hostile winds of criticism, likely to condemn his work as pernicious or trivial and useless, but also by the "boistrous waters" ("maris insani") of boorish society in which it set sail.[18] Yet the ship carries a full cargo of the indecent. To create viscerally repulsive images, then, humor itself becomes the discipline: a painful pleasure. It is not the only purpose of the humor to keep readers from taking too much offense at what is being said about them; the humor is linked to discipline and restraint; laughter itself is civilized.

There is a good deal to straighten out in Dedekind's tedious laborinth; the text is not composed of "simple" reversals but constructs grobian arguments as elaborate as they are coarsely embellished, and justifications as self-interested as they are inimical to standards of civility. For example, as in the advice to grow the hair long, the speaker equates "simpler," good old days with a rustic and primitive past and ancient virtue. Then, too, he equates neglect of grooming or lack of self-control with manliness and "civility":

> Est amor in stratas urbis prodire plateas?
> Purgatum capitis tegmen habere cave.
> Qui nimios ambit, muliebria munera, cultus,
> Ridendus merito cuilibet ille venit.
> (1.2.295–98)

> If thou desire at any time to walke into the streete,
> That all thy hat with dirt and dust be sprinkled it is meete.
> He that regardeth cleaneliness, which onely women use,
> At him let all men mocke and scoffe, let all men him
>     abuse.
>
> (1.2.246–49)

Such examples clearly reverse conventional civil precepts, but their ironic effects also depend on the projection of innocent observers, whose gaze not only evaluates but is assaulted by the grobian scene. Those observers become especially important when the speaker links bodily effluence with affluence, filth with wealth, ornament with excrement ("mining" for scabs, yellow teeth as gold, street filth as ennobling fashion accessory, nose "ornamentation"), or display of the body with their approval, appreciation, envy or desire:

> Quin etiam ne se toga cruribus implicet, atque
> Impediat gressus, detineatue tuos:

Disiicienda utrinque manu est, a parte videri
   Corpus ut excellens anteriore queat.
Quaeque tegenda toga fuerant, thorace tegantur
   Et caligis, illud quis neget esse satis?
Talia delectant castas spectacula matres,
   Virgineoque solent illa placere choro.
Scilicet aspiciant quam sis bene iunceus, et quam
   Constringant ventrem vincula firma tuum.
Protinus ergo tui captae accendentur amore,
   Foemineus quavis arte movetur amor.

                              (1.6.743–54)

Or if you weare a gowne, take heede that not your legs it hides,
Lest that it hinder all your pace, your steps, and eke your strides.
Cast it behinde with both your hands, that all men so may see
Your perfect bodie, and your limbs, and foreparts what they bee.
And that which else your gowne would cover, tis enough to hide
It with your doublet, and your breeches, lac'd on every side.
Such sights do please old matrons very well, I tell thee trew,
And these are very welcome sights unto the virgins crew.
For then thei'le marke your slendernes, and all your nimble ioyntes,
And eke how well your bellie is tide with girdle and with pointes.
And then forthwith with love of thee thei'le quite be set on fire,
Which done, each act will more and more inflame their hot desire.

                              (1.6.718–29)


Such justifications ensure a shock of negative recognition and condemnation by the readers; each should recall the reversal of a past
lesson and reject or condemn the reverse reasoning but also acknowledge the possibility of doing such things himself, before he "abjects"
the indecent possibility and reconstructs the boundaries of decency and
civility. Each recognizable erroneous association also brings the reader
face to face with the indecent. Dedekind's homeopathic pharmacy delivers not just the visual evocation, in other words, but an affective
confrontation and a negative mnemonic of humanist lessons.

The harsher lessons of indecency are integrated with other milder
forms, with the result of making indecency the lowest common denom-
inator. Unsubtle facial expressions and grimaces, loud talking and laughter, taking someone's place at table, being an insubordinate or indolent

server become the indecent equivalents of farting, vomiting, defecating, urinating. That leveling to equivalence and to commensurability also raises anxiety to the level that civil propriety demands.

=========

Dedekind's text is framed in epistolary form: it begins with a dedicatory letter to his friend and patron Simon Bing, a former schoolmate at Marburg (witness, we might presume, of at least some of the coarse behavior recorded in the text) and now secretary to Landgraf Philipp von Hessen; the conclusion completes his appeal for Bing's support.[19] The third edition versifies and lengthens the preface and conclusion.

Dedekind's letter explains the device of the textual irony and thus presumably prevents readers from misunderstanding it. No one, he wants to be certain, should get the idea that he actually means to endorse or to condone bad behavior. (Scheidt, in the first of many clarifications of Dedekind's text, includes as the imperative motto of his title page, "Liß wol diß büchlin offt und vil / Und thuo allzeit das widerspil" ["Read this little book often and well / And always do the opposite"].) Stable irony is the plan: simple reversal with nothing to supplement or complicate it.

Dedekind deploys the mirror trope not only for its traditional significance in the speculum tradition but as a means of defending himself and explaining his method:

> Qui tamen in speculo te contemplaberis isto,
>     Verbaque multa tuis moribus apta leges.
> Ne mihi, neve meo precor indignere libello,
>     Iusta nec est irae causa futura tuae.
> Non mihi propositum fuit hic perstringere quemquam,
>     Degeneres mores carpere fervor erat.
> Sin fuerit qui se prae multis esse notatum
>     Credet, et indigne verba iocosa feret:
> Noverit hac ipsa sese ratione mereri,
>     Iam Reus ut possit rusticitatis agi.
>
> (Praefatio, 143–52)

But by the way, thou which within this glasse dost thus behold
Thine owne disordred manners and thy life, be not so bold
As to finde fault with me, thy friend, or with my little booke,

Which upon thee, as upon all, with self-same eyes doth looke.
If any will assume these faults as theirs, at the first view,
Know they that they confesse themselves some of the rusticke
    crew.

(Preface, 131–36)

Dedekind's mirror looks back at an ineffectual tradition. *Grobianus* would build a better mirror, be a more efficacious device. But it will not yield the idealizing moment of a developmental stage but rather recall, retrospectively, the horror and dread of whatever haunts civility in context. If Dedekind's mirror produces an inhibiting decency, it produces it by the difficult way of "retrospecularity."

The odd contradictions of using indecency to promote propriety, using coarse images to refine taste or lies to teach a truth (the truth that lies behind propriety and decency), do not escape Dedekind; classical authority also looked down on such deception.[20] As we have already seen, Dedekind's preface includes references to Greek and Latin moralists, to philosophers from Plato and Aristotle to Cicero and Erasmus, authorities who have vainly attempted to reform human behavior through a direct appeal to reason or intellect (69–79).

Yet it seems he labors under the compulsion to deceive in order to teach. There are, according to Dedekind and Scheidt, two reasons that the direct and intelligent (nonironic) appeals of traditional authority have not worked: first, human nature is itself perverse and resists virtuous action; second, the body holds human reason captive. Thus Dedekind speaks of his contemporaries,

> Nil iuvat aetherea traxisse ab origine mentem,
>     Et ratio turpi victa furore tacet.
> Barbarico vivunt crudarum more ferarum,
>     Quoque vocat ventris caeca libido ruunt.
> Immodice praeter quam corporis exigit usus,
>     Distendunt variis viscera laxa cibis.

(Praefatio, 51–56)

What though their souls were sent from heaven as things
    of peerless price,
Yet thi'le love Reason worse than Follie, Vertue worse than Vice.

They square their actions by the rule of beasts of brutish kinde,
And to their bellies blinde desire they captivate their minde.
Their wide stretcht guts, beyond the use of Nature or of neede,
In every place, at every time, unsatiately they feede.

(Preface, 47–52)

Not only do they act badly; they misbehave to a public audience and seem to expect praise for their disgusting behavior:

Quin etiam tactant sua crimina turpiter, atque
Ob sua laudari facta pudenda volunt.

(61–62)

If, after Gods gifts thus abus'd, they heere at length would end,
Twere well, but they exspect for faults that men should them commend.

(55–56)

And the expectation of public approval appears repeatedly, thus yielding the specular lesson.

Dedekind's and Scheidt's willingness to dissimulate sets *Grobianus* apart from simple *Tischzucht* parody. As Fritz Bergmeier describes it, Dedekind "placed himself as master in the midst of the raw, raucous turmoil, put himself in the midst of drunkenness and gluttony, . . . built a dam against the universal confusion of manners. For what's hateful can hardly appear in sharper relief, what's ridiculous can hardly appear more irredeemable than when one apparently offers it as an ideal, endows it with the very qualities it lacks."[21] In handling the complicity effect, however, the two authors diverge significantly. Whereas Scheidt's speaker is a character identified as the craftsman (*Meister*) Grobianus who boasts not only of his own grobian deeds but of those of members of his household, Dedekind's speaker refers to himself as *magister* but never identifies himself—or anyone—as Grobianus. He addresses the reader in the second person and, almost without exception, does not himself claim to perform the actions he recommends. Although he certainly simulates the effect of reveling in what he is proposing, it is the reader who is to act out the advice.

Although the title page of Dedekind's text bears the motto "IRON

CHLEVASTES" (mocking or scoffing deceiver), the name Grobianus never once appears in the text.[22] Instead, a first-person speaker, the "master" of the subject and teacher in the school of simplicity, talks about simplicity, rusticity, addressing the reader to give lessons and advice:

> Quisquis habes odio rigidi praecepta Magistri,
>   Qui nisi de morum nil gravitate docet:
> Huc propera, et placidis utentem vocibus audi:
>   Non tonat hic aliquis tristia verba Cato.
> Da mihi te docilem crasso sermone loquenti.
>   Nec dubita, parvo tempore doctus eris.
> Discipulus facili superare labore Magistrum,
>   Crede mihi, antiqua simplicitate, potes.
> Et licet haec aliquis rigida de gente sophorum
>   Vituperet, morum quae documenta damus:
> Non tamen illa tibi quicquam nocuisse videbis,
>   Sedula Musae jussa sequere meae.
>
>                                        (1.1.39-50)

> Whose're thou art that hat'st at heart a Masters crabbed charge,
> Which reades a Lecture every day of gravitie at large;
> Harke hither, come and heare this man, a man of quiet speech,
> No thunder-thumping Catonist, you neede him not beseech.
> My speech is brode, be rul'd, and then I'le do the best I can,
> Be rudible, and sure I thinke, you'le prove a learned man.
> Be but a carefull auditor and scholler unto me,
> And then you'le soone excell your Master in simplicitie.
> What though some crabbed wi-tall do not like my precepts well,
> Yet they can never hurte you, if you marke all that I tell.
>
>                                        (1.1.35-44)

R.F.'s colloquial "And sure I thinke," "I tell you true," "I do it not mislike," "And I confesse, for honest men it is a custome fit," embellish and astutely read Dedekind's ironic-didactic project in which the speaker is an unidentified voice of counterauthority. Speaking in the first person underscores the speaker's prominence in the text as *magister* and *praeceptor* while distancing him from the disgusting actions

toward which he cheerfully manipulates the reader's imaginative fac-
ulties. He works to incorporate readers in suggestive coarse scenarios;
the more they are encouraged, the stronger abjection becomes, the
greater their sense of civilizing revulsion. Again we turn to one of the
sensationally indecent passages:

> Saepe etiam illapsus gravis est pulmonibus humor,
>     Crapula quem potuit gignere sive gelu.
> Hunc homines aliqui quando eduxere screantes,
>     Iamque super linguam plurimus ille iacet.
> Turpiter impuro prius ore diuque volutant,
>     Quam spuere, et foedo pure carere, velint.
> Quos tamen accipiant ex illo nescio fructus,
>     Sed mire factum tale decere scio.
> Et scio quod multis moveatur nausea, et illa
>     Sufficiens ratio cur imiteris erit.
> Me quoque si facias illud praesente, profecto,
>     Res mihi nulla quidem gratior esse queat:
> Os tamen ut semper, votis ardentibus optem,
>     Impuro plenum sit tibi pure tuum.
>
>                                        (3.3.321–34)

Sometimes there from the liver comes an humour like to snot
Which either riseth from some cold or surfet lately got.
This divers men with hauks and hems will from their stomacke bring,
And keep it on their tongue, as if it were a pretious thing.
And in their mouth this fleamie stuffe they love to rowle about
A prettie while, before they will beginne to spit it out.
What profite by this beastly tricke they get, I do not know,
But in my iudgement it doth make a very seemely show.
Although if some should see this tricke, their meate they would refuse,
Yet this I thinke a reason is, for which they should it use.
Though ne're so often in my sight this tricke should used bee,
Yet sure it should be counted for a welcome sight to mee.
And as for my part, I could wish, if I might have my minde,
That I at dinner store of snot within your mouth might finde.

                                        (3.3.3080–93)

The speaker who heartily recommends phlegm spitting as a welcome
sight directs the reader to the spectacle of bad manners in which he is

invited to imagine himself in the starring role. But who is the *eiron*? Who scoffs whom? Scoffing manners and society, the speaker ends by reversing his advice, mocking himself; yet there is the reader's role to consider as well. Using direct address, the speaker pretends to be working toward turning the reader into a scholar of simplicity, and the speaker wears an ironic mask, advising "you" this or that. *Grobianus* is well titled; but who is Dedekind's Grobianus? Is this an *eiron* with a double edge?

Hans Rupprich's remark that Dedekind "has fantasy and humor and creates a main character with a three-dimensional personality" is only partially right.[23] The speaker has a personality, but there is no character in Dedekind identified as Grobianus. One reads, in other words, with the impression that there is a character performing these hypothetical actions with their overpowering physical images. (While the text offers short exempla, and covers the daily events of the grobian life, there is no extended action narrative.) Yet, the second-person commands suggest that it is the reader who, by imagining them acted out, is the character. The effect of direct addresss is thus to make the reader into the hypothetical character, to write the reader into the text. Although Dedekind confesses in his concluding letter to Simon Bing that, at least in his youth, he himself was not innocent of certain social sins, the text creates a relationship that in effect inserts the reader into the representations of indecency.[24] The subject position of Grobianus is shared; the reader is just as much a Grobianus as the speaker, so that the answer to the question is much like the answer to the question of who the evaluating observer is in Castiglione's *Courtier*, the absent one for whom the courtier maneuvers between negative possibilities and conceals his carefully calculated performance of artless spontaneity. Who is watching? You are. Who is Grobianus? You are.

If, in the manner of Booth, we treated this text as an example of stable irony and went through his four-part reconstruction, we would end up with an encompassing statement which would go something like the following: Praising "simple" behavior, the text shows this form of simplicity to be incompatible with civility. The two cannot coexist, nor can the "natural" model of reasoning be an authority for appearance, behavior, interaction. Just the opposite is true. Authority, because this text is its counterauthority, must therefore be sought in opposition to it. This authority, these precepts, being orderly where the others produce disorder, are what are intended as "natural" and "simple." That is what adherence to the civil standard would demand. Yet because the ironic strategy itself is linked to the growing complexity of life, to the unstable order of the changing world in which the work was written, it is the standard itself that comes into question.

In this respect, the civilizing attitude shows itself hostile toward the nature it projects as well as toward the body it constrains. But if civility is hostile toward the nature of rural life and the material body, it will at the same time appropriate nature for its arguments and make it an ally of its own processes, just as it will preserve the body in a hygienicized form. The stable irony of simple reversal is thus transformed into a mutually contaminating relationship between simplicity and Simplicity, between civility's claims and things concealed from the civilizers, things disclosed to us in reading the civil irony of *Grobianus*. In this sense, the question we could have asked all along—Is the text really didactic?—evaporates. Even if it is just a scandalizing revisit to the scene of lessons of Latin, male puberty, civility, *Grobianus* reinforces the very things it entertainingly (if not explicitly didactically) revisits. The default mode of the ironic didactic is a disciplining effect, now made even more insidious as entertainment. *Grobianus* becomes the peepshow of civility.

Dedekind's thematization of simplicity in a time of increasing complexity is still another manifestation of the early modern crisis of identity and authority. If the Grobianus was the figure for all that threatened a society in transition, then *Grobianismus*, Dedekind's project of appropriating and canonizing, socializing, and naturalizing simplicity, can be understood as still another manifestation of the crisis of identity and authority, a defensive response that located and tried to contain the threat in the figure of Grobianus. Dedekind's *Grobianus* reveals the tension of a class caught between mimicking aristocratic forms and being unable to free itself from the demands of its material-bodily substance or instincts. When Elias sees in grobian literature a need for a "softening" of manners, he is speaking not of a period of great coarseness or a "grobian age"—as it has been called by the anthropologizing cultural historians who sum up the period—but of an alteration of perceptions in the sixteenth century.

Dedekind has no more and no less trouble teaching cultivated simplicity than Castiglione has in offering instruction in artless spontaneity. For Castiglione, distinguishing between affectation and artlessness depends on calling up a sense of organicity that could never be anything but antithetical to the concealment, cosmeticization, and control of *sprezzatura*. Dedekind's civil and second-nature simplicity will always depend on complex labors.

The urban middle class was caught between two traditional identities: that of the peasantry, with its popular literary tradition in which the body plays a triumphant, unabashedly antiauthoritarian, and subversive role, and that of the aristocracy, with its rituals of power and decorum. Even in appropriating manners from the aristocracy, the middle class could not duplicate the experience of aristocratic cultural and material life, for the middle class had to deal with the inscrutable economic forces that constituted the urban economy, stood behind the new social relationships, and that, in the final instance, could wield greater power than the traditional remnants.

In Dedekind's hands, the mirror would become a neutral instrument that views all with friendly indifference but also reflects and returns repulsive images for which there can be nothing but self-reproach. In the *speculum ironiae*, the text becomes a lengthy exemplum to mirror a civil subject's inhibitions, fears, and anxieties. The anxiety is mitigated by humor and irony; yet the text, unable to exhaust the possibilities and concluding each part with the excuse that the speaker could go on forever, takes care to feed the isolated civil subject the anxiety for every negative possibility.

With Erasmus, one can break wind and cover up with a cough; it is possible to spit and conceal. One is given a sense of what is permitted, what good behavior is, and if one was at odds with the other, at least it did not fail to acknowledge physical necessity and the body along with the civil standard. Here, with this new kind of mirror of negativity and the calling up of an inner voice (what would become Scheidt's vernacular "innerliche einsprechung") of internalized control, there is no covering up because you yourself are the witness to your own perverse and potentially dangerous behavior. Any physical urge or communication of the body to the mind becomes suspect, cause for an increasing sense of anxiety. The mind must be perpetually on guard before such behavior even becomes likely, but the vigilance requires the recognition that there is no purification or simplification; indecent contaminations and complications are always already there.

In Dedekind's pharmacy, medicine and poison work to produce internal scapegoating. The patient-subject takes on the discipline of irony and expels, or abjects, what he recognizes as pollution. Dedekind's homeopathy gives the reader coarse simplicity and draws out of him the revulsion that sets him on the path to the refined simplicity of good manners: the installation and triumph of a second nature. Yet in constructing the painful pleasure of purification, Dedekind sets in motion a fluid and unarrestable process of disciplines and resistances, right readings and subversive ones. Above all, the labor of reading precept reversals reads back on the tradition of the conduct book. The "wrong side outward" is the inside, exposed; when it is righted, the veneer of proper behavior shows itself on the outside, while the indecent inside is internally preserved. Instead of "simply" reversing the ironic reversal, we are left with sedimentations of pleasure and discipline. Where they finally come to rest, whether on the side of institutionalization or subversions, may be arguable. But what the text sets in motion remains as a record of a mobilizing conflict. This ironic oscillation, then, is the program and the result of Dedekind's labor theory of conduct. In making use of Erasmus, Dedekind both repeats and alters the Erasmian program, revealing what was already problematic. The work of irony separates by combining, distinguishes by mingling, complicates by simplifying, acts as a mode of containment by letting loose, and purifies by recontaminating. We are left with irony's edge and the politics of civility.

It is when Dedekind puts a Grobiana in *Grobianus*, however, that the laborinth of simplicity is revealed in its fullest complexity. The limits—and the potential—of irony emerge when Grobiana comes to *Grobianus*.

# 4 / Grobiana in *Grobianus*: The Sexual Politics of Civility

Could I forget that precious half of the republic which produces the happiness of the other and whose gentleness and wisdom maintain peace and good mores? Amiable and virtuous women citizens, it will always be the fate of your sex to govern ours. Happy it is when your chaste power, exercised only within the conjugal union, makes itself felt only for the glory of the state and the public happiness! . . . It is for you to maintain always, by your amiable and innocent dominion and by your insinuating wit, the love of laws in the state and concord among the citizens. . . . Therefore always be what you are, the chaste guardians of mores and the gentle bonds of peace; and continue to assert on every occasion the rights of the heart and of nature for the benefit of duty and virtue.

—Jean-Jacques Rousseau, "Letter to the Republic of Geneva"

Dedekind added a third book to *Grobianus* when he revised and lengthened the work in 1552. Most of the material in this additional section follows the principle of iterability suited to the subject of indecency. One could go on and on with ever more drastic advice, never exhausting the possibilities for misconduct.[1] Much of book 3 simply repeats advice and examples from the previous two books; some of the new material takes the form of crude anecdotes, further collated from Dedekind's sources, such as Heinrich Bebel's *Facetiae*, but the last chapter, "Grobiana," offers something new. It imitates the minor Renaissance genre of advice to women and addresses female readers. "Grobiana" is added, the speaker somewhat disingenuously explains, in response to the just requests of his female audience; it is addressed to young women, or "virgins." For all its brevity, this final chapter reopens the issues of civility, reflects back on the text's ironic-didactic project, and highlights even more powerfully the problem of gender and decency in early modern subject formation.

To begin this chapter on the specific situation and status of women, on the precarious and destabilizing presence of Woman in *Grobianus*, I make a somewhat anachronistic gesture and pose questions to my epigraph, taken from the 1754 letter to the citizens of Geneva, which prefaces Rousseau's *Discourse on Inequality*.[2] What concern or anxiety underlies Rousseau's compulsive afterthought on women? Does he remember women only in order effectively to forget them, as he seems to in *The Social Contract*, where, identifying the family as the first society (and the "only natural one") and the first political unit, he defines it as a father and his children?[3] Perhaps Rousseau really could not forget the Other 50 percent—"that precious half"—of the civil population, but his question discloses a problem with the subject of women's civic role which the remainder of the text attempts to remedy by containment and some apparently paradoxical political configurations. Rousseau's women citizens rule by not ruling. The issue of their power, their potentially governing role, is circumscribed by Rousseau's appropriating act, which operates with an insidious circularity that *makes them what they are*. Rulers whose legitimacy lies only within the patriarchal structure of marriage, speakers who subordinate other discourses of difference to the abstract homogeneity of state and public happiness, women become the repository, the visible sign of Rousseau's urgent wish to see the realm of nature placed in the service of civic values that systematically exclude and marginalize (or infantilize) women, thus making them members of that delinquent stratum which insures the stability and vigilance of those in control.

In taking up the issue of women's behavior, identity, and civic duties, Rousseau's civic discourse of the eighteenth century echoes an important predecessor, the Renaissance discussion of civility. In the sixteenth century, too, one could not forget to address the problem of women; indeed, it was addressed frequently and in a manner that reveals the major investment of the shapers and fashioners of a new civil mentality in containing the threat that woman and problems of sexual difference posed.

Dedekind's "Grobiana" is not really addressed to women, nor is it simply about women; instead, like Erasmus's *Colloquies*, it is about the signifying function the feminine serves in conduct books and the civilizing process. Thus, it is not my intention in discussing "Grobiana" to focus on the marginalization of women in order to highlight their roles as active producers of cultural history, the important efforts to address the difference that women have made for a cultural history of the Renaissance notwithstanding.[4] Rather, by examining the representation and function of woman, I wish to continue to interrogate the "curve of civilization," to study the constitution of the civil subject as the vehicle and product of changes in attitudes in this transitional age. As we have seen in Erasmus's work, in the narrative of the curve of civilization the topic of women is always at least tacitly indicated, contained with only limited success and never stabilized; woman functions as the essential inessential for the constitution of cultural manhood.

The debate on the position of women in early modernity is linked to debates on the Renaissance and the civilizing process.[5] The traditional early modern view of woman oscillated wildly between villification and veneration and assigned women positions in the extreme.[6] Conventional wisdom proclaimed that there was no being who could reach the heights of the virtuous woman or the depths of female depravity, and this view was thoroughly expounded both in learned works published during the lengthy *querelle des femmes* and in popular pamphlets. In the *querelle*, antifeminist writers following classical and patristic examples depicted women as insatiable monsters; feminist defenders such as Christine de Pisan countered with portraits of saints and selfless martyrs.[7] In the pamphlets, women were represented as delinquents and criminals, anarchic threats to patriarchal hierarchy.[8]

Corresponding to what Joan Kelly calls the dual vision of the tradition, women also had a special double role in the myth of the grobian age. On the one hand, they were the object of coarse attacks, the victims of abusive behavior, of accusations that are on the record in the large body of misogynist writings.[9] On the other hand, they are accused of complicity in constructing their own negative image. According to Waldemar Kawerau, "A strong, misogynist strain makes its way into the literature of the sixteenth century; when women are mentioned it is mainly to complain about them, to take cheap shots at or to insult them. Not a hint of the courtly poets' chivalry and their veneration of women.

A large percentage of the weaker sex [*sic*] in the sixteenth century appears to have earned the dislike of men. To an extraordinary measure they flaunted not only extravagance and sensuality but excessive drinking as well."[10] In the nadir of the so-called "grobian age" of the sixteenth century, women were viewed as succumbing to coarsening cultural influences and, unlike the women of medieval aristocracy, unable (or unwilling) to provide the traditional example of refinement and decency, the simultaneously inspirational and disciplinary role traditionally ascribed, by Rousseau and so many others, to the "gentler sex." Even Dedekind's speaker sheds his ironic persona to decry the state of contemporary maidenhood:

> Quis pueros meliora sequi, vitamque priorem
>    Deserere, et mores excoluisse docet?
> Non vir, non mulier, meminisse videntur honoris,
>    Omnia deposito quisque pudore facit.
> Virginibus quondam laudi pudibunda dabantur
>    Lumina, virtuti cum suus esset honos.
> Nec nisi pauca loqui casto sermone solebant,
>    Indicium casti pectoris illud erat.
> Nunc decus est oculos temere quocunque vagari
>    Virginis, et rectas non tenuisse vias.
> Nunc decus est, verbis illas petulantibus uti.
>    Rusticaque est, blando quae nequit ore loqui.
>                                    (1.11.1741–52)

Who teacheth youth to mend their lives, or bids them to forsake
Their former most disordred life, and better courses take?
Nor man, nor woman, nowadaies their credite do respect,
But loving vice most shamelesly, all vertue they neglect.
In times of olde, when men by vertue did to honour rise,
Young maids were much commended for their chaste and
    shamefaste eyes.
They seldom spake, and when they spake, their speech was chaste
    and pure,
Which of a chaste and pure minde was an argument most sure.
Now tis a credite for a wench to have a gadding eye,
And if she cannot keepe her way, shee's praisde immediatly.

Now, tis a credite for a wench to have her tongue to walke,
And she is thought a clownish wench which cannot boldely talke.
(1.11.1456–67)

Norbert Elias notes, of Erasmus's *Good Manners in Boys*, that modern readers tend to be shocked by what now seem unthinkably coarse details in early modern conduct manuals. Yet this period of transition was not an age of crude habits but rather one in which habits came increasingly to be perceived as crude and shameful, was not an age of boorishness but one that produced a standard that created—and used—boorishness. To apply Foucault's remarks on discipline and punishment, this age did not merely identify delinquency; it produced delinquency and did so in a way that makes clear how indispensable such delinquency and indecency were to the construction of an early modern cultural order.[11] The reformation and refinement of manners—as the fashioning of identity and power—at this time signified a crisis of patriarchal authority in what Norbert Elias has described as an accelerated civilizing process, brought about by the rapid development of an urban and middle-class society and the movement of power from the warrior aristocracy to a merchant and protoindustrial bourgeoisie. In addition to the unsettling questions of gender and power for men and the displacements that ensued from them, the position of women was also in transition, especially with the Reformation's increased emphasis on marriage, parenting, and the household. The growing importance of urban life produced reflections on women's changing public and economic roles.[12] Along with the proliferation of handbooks and treatises on manners which focused on the importance of self-governance and bodily restraint came, it is no surprise to find, attention to women's behavior and to notions of female propriety; nor could one do other than expect that women would occupy an important, necessarily subordinate position in the changing order.[13]

We have already seen how the figure of woman functions in Erasmus's *Colloquies* and in his pedagogical works, how it is linked to problems of power, class, and masculine identity. There, where Erasmus writes about women, historical women are tangential to the texts, numerically insignificant in terms of the text's reception and widespread influence. For Erasmus, the figure of woman is incorporated into the text of civility with a heuristic function: studies in feminine power (such as "Courtship," "Marriage," "The New Mother") yield lessons in political subordination for the male student, so that he prepares for service in a class hierarchy and for domination in the domestic sphere of the humanist companionate marriage.

The issue of the incorporation of woman into the text of courtesy is also taken up in Castiglione's *Courtier*, where, like the question of those "things . . . impossible to mention," the woman question interrupts the text and what begins as a decorous incorporation proves indecorous in the end. There are several woman questions in *The Courtier*: What is the relationship of the woman of the court to the courtier? Is there an ideal woman courtier? If so, would she be the exact equivalent of the male? How far, how consistently can one carry this discussion of compared roles? The topic of woman first threatens to disrupt the order of Castiglione's text, when in book 2 it creeps into consideration—almost as a digression—through Federico Fregoso's discussion of the power of impressions. He relates a short narrative of women who, in a geometrically progressing chain of mediated desire, become infatuated with a man they have never met simply by reading another woman's love letters. One woman after another falls in love with the unknown, unseen man by learning, through letter and rumor, of another woman's love for him.

At this point the misogynist straw man Gasparo Pallavicino interrupts what might have become an interesting and anticipatory disquisition on the function of the simulacrum and distracts attention from the topic of impressions with one of his many antifeminist commonplaces about women's inferiority and irrationality. In the course of constructing a defense of women, anticipating the discussion of a female counterpart to the perfect male courtier and retrieving his point about potent impressions, Federico hints once more at those negative possibilities lurking in the background, those "things . . . impossible to mention." His subsequent excuse that "it would be too long and wearisome to attempt to speak of all the faults that can occur" defers the subject of women's ideal conduct to book 3 and the following day. The door has been opened, however, for when the conversation on women begins in ear-

nest, Gasparo and allies readily contribute notions of "all the faults that
can occur," and they reinforce the links between women and disorder,
indecency, and the unspeakable already established by Federico.[14]

For Il Magnifico, taking up the woman question rectifies a weakness
in the text. So much has been said about the courtier "that whosoever
imagines him must consider that the merits of women cannot compare"
(2.98.201). To "redress the balance," then, an evening is to be devoted
to the woman of the court. Yet the discussion, a compendium of the
conventional *topoi* and dubious wisdom from the debate on women in
the Renaissance, is marked by discontinuities and interruptions. Frisio,
for example, protests that "it would be neither pertinent nor opportune
to speak about women, especially as more remains to be said about the
courtier, and we ought not to confuse one thing with another" (3.3.210).
He is concerned with keeping to the topic at hand and not losing focus,
but confusing one thing with another continues to infect the conversation.

When Frisio is countered by Cesare Gonzaga, who argues that it is
necessary that "ladies take part in it and contribute their share of the
grace by which courtiership is adorned and perfected," and Ottaviano
quips, "There you catch a glimpse of the allurement that turns men's
heads" (3.2.208), the indication is that, at least at the beginning, woman
has a status emphatically distinct from and not at all equivalent to the
courtier's. Yet the discussion tries to have it both ways, insisting on both
equivalence and distinction. Such a specular and trivializing introduction—woman contributes as an alluring ornament—given in such a
breeezy tone suggests that for her the autoscopic regime of the courtier
will not be the same, that woman must always be regarded by the men
who possess the gaze, that every virtue must enhance an allure that is
in turn circumscribed by the bedrock virtue of chastity.[15] The mean
achieved by artful moderation in the *sprezzatura* of the courtier becomes for her "a certain difficult mean, composed as it were of contrasting qualities, and . . . certain fixed limits" (3.5.212).

Nothing said in woman's defense, moreover, will work to establish
"the old dream of symmetry" held out as structural promise at the
outset of the discussion.[16] To be sure, such a hope is thwarted precisely
in the defensive posture that seeks equitable inclusion of women within
an unscrutinized masculinist framework. Certainly the progression of

exempla of women's self-destructive sacrifices to the cause of chastity, staples in the conventional defense literature, works to remove the woman of the court ever farther from weighing in with the ideal courtier. Even more poignantly, it leads Cesare Gonzaga to offer an awkward analogy, placing the duchess in the company of virtuous and heroically martyred chaste women. The gesture produces an uncomfortable disclosure of the duchess's situation: for fifteen years she has stoically endured sex martyrdom in her marriage to the sickly and impotent duke of Urbino. That disclosure, although brief, may place the duchess in the company of virtuous women, but it also places the frame of the text in a more spectral and eerie light. The place of the woman of the court vis-à-vis the courtier is here interrupted and circumscribed by a question of masculine and class authority which renders the Castle of Urbino more permeable as the frame for the discussions.

Perhaps most imbalancing to and subversive of the discussion is the question, never asked, of what name to give the lady of the court. *Cortegiano* ("courtier") when feminized is scandalizing: *Cortegiana* is "courtesan," an unchaste figure. The imbalance is a scandal of equivalence that backfires. The woman of the court may not be *cortegiana/* courtesan, but the courtier, in effect, is. It is the courtier, the adviser to the prince, who occupies the woman's role here. He is the cultural ornament (martial arts and all) who legitimates as he aestheticizes political power, who tutors the prince in virtuous actions and inspires the prince by his superior and ideal example: an artful dissembler propping up an illusion. The disavowed courtesan gives the lie to the "perfect" courtier as keeper of the flame of warrior-aristocratic values in the face of the cosmeticized and aestheticizing politics of *sprezzatura*.

At first glance Dedekind, too, seems to introduce Grobiana to bring his text to completion. It is an opportunity too good to pass up, perhaps; if not suggested by a colleague, by the *Ars amatoria* (the entire third book of which is addressed to women), or by knowledge of Scheidt's adaptation, it may well have suggested itself in the process of revising and expanding the text. It is easy to imagine how the topic of women's behavior might readily suggest itself to Dedekind, first, because of the many official and popular debates and opinions concerning women at this time and also because he had already touched on the position of women or the treatment of virgins, wives, and matrons by grobians in

the first edition of the work. Yet, since the work is far less concerned
with the behavior of women than with the place of women in a masculine social order and, for the sake of that order, is most concerned
with purging male readers of any feminine proclivities, the advice to
women is at best limited. Nevertheless, if Dedekind was to promote
seriously a particular standard of civility, then, along with male behavior
toward women, he would want to treat the social role of women themselves. Like Castiglione, Dedekind redresses an imbalance, seeks completion for a text that could continue ad infinitum—certainly ad
nauseum—on the subject of disgusting behavior. As it does for *The
Courtier*, however, the attempt to balance and complete the text by
adding woman backfires. Although the discussion is less sustained than
that in *The Courtier* and is not really addressed to women at all, "Grobiana" proves to be a dangerous supplement.

It was not uncommon, of course, for etiquette manuals to include
some advice for women, and although not as plentiful as instructions to
men, there were texts, such as Juan Vives's *Instruction of a Christian
Woman*, specifically addressed to the behavior of young women.[17]
Whether brief or extensive, these works are notable for the structural
tension between precepts of attraction and control, the insidious femi-
ninized dialectic of allure and discipline. Whereas men and boys are
commanded to make a good impression, women are commanded to
attract sexually, but to take measures to contain and control the attraction as well as to suppress their own sexual expression. As we have seen
in Erasmus's work, the female subject of civility is responsible not only
for her own behavior but for the man for whom she takes on a maternal-
pedagogical role. The texts deal with piety, decency, and the proper
way to attract a man; they stress instruction in obedience and proper
proportion of charm, disciplined allure circumscribed by the overarching value of chastity.[18]

Because of the gendered nature of the civil standard, women are
given a special role in the civilizing process. On the one hand, they are
seen as closer to instinctual life, and thus, "by nature," they pose a
serious threat to civil standards; on the other hand, they are given the
obligation of influencing men to control their instincts, for if they do
not, women assume the responsibility for leading them astray. As mothers and wives they are to cultivate the role of guardian and "nurturer";

thus, women assume some importance as civility's "police," but always in support of a standard, and a civil subject, which is male. *Grobianus's* contribution to humanist etiquettes and to the masculine standard of civility is its distinctive exploitation of the problematic masculine identity that emerges from the standard.

Scheidt's *Grobianus* offers no advice addressed to women but in its preface introduces Grobiana, the master's consort and accomplice and an "experienced spinner of ill bred wenches and lazy maids." In Scheidt's text she herself advises Grobianus to reflect on his mortality, especially the fleeting life of grobians, and to write down his precepts for posterity; like Dedekind's Rusticitas, she is a grobian muse.[19] Scheidt also brings in some grobian maids to accompany Bacchus in the invocation of the prologue, referring to them as "baurenmetzlin" (peasant wenches) with disheveled clothing, feathers and straw clinging suggestively to their backs; their hair uncombed and infested. He sums up the image with the marginal comment: "Das endlichen mägd," a derogatory sexual pun on chastity, aging, and "the eternal feminine." Scheidt also suggests in one of his parenthetical embellishments of Dedekind's text that there may be women, well disposed toward things grobian, who enjoy being harassed on public streets:

> (Man hat jetzt lust zu solchen dingen
> Und sind die töchter heimlich worden
> Und gern im Grobianer orden,
> Und haben selber lust darzuo,
> Dass man grob mit jn reden thuo.)
> (1095–99)

(One likes to do such things nowadays; for the daughters have secretly become grobians and joined the Grobian order. They themselves enjoy being treated coarsely.)

In writing *Grobianus* and adding the "Grobiana" section, Dedekind, like Erasmus, could be seen as contributing to the "improvement" of the position of women, not only by encouraging in men—always by negative example—attitudes of respect and reverence toward women but by integrating delinquent women into the civilizing process by the same ironic-didactic method employed for male readers. Yet "Grobiana," the chapter Dedekind devotes to female behavior, is no docile addition and it exposes problems in the work's ironic-didactic method.

Through the production of shame and socially instilled anxiety, the civil irony of the text presents good manners as the reconstitution of the natural, the triumph of true, civilly sanctioned nature over the presumptive or even usurping nature of rusticity and incontinence. Thus the text projects nature from the code of civility and represents it as freedom from the prison of instinctual demands, a realm represented by the peasants, children, animals, and women who function in the text as ironic exemplars. When we reach Dedekind's chapter on women we realize, in other words, that Grobiana is already in *Grobianus*. Thus, when the author purports to reach out to a female audience already so marginalized, the text's own inscribed gender system introduces difficulties, and the slippage supposedly concealed or controlled in the notion of civil nature—versus what is perversely natural—begins to become both apparent and unruly.

Like Castiglione and other authors of manner books, Dedekind includes "Grobiana" as something difficult to leave out (like Rousseau, could he forget?) and a logical continuation of the text, a gesture made to complete or exhaust the topic of manners which would primarily focus on men. Following common sense he would see a symmetry at work here; yet, like Castiglione's courtly discussants he is unable to treat women in the same manner or as the equivalents to men. Because of the multiplicity of positions in civility's code of cultural masculinity (inspiration, allure, horror, policing, delinquency) and so rendered in the civilizing process, they are not privy or translatable to the civil irony of the work. Taking on the topic of female behavior, claiming to treat it in the same way and for the same didactic purpose as the rest of the text, is a task that disrupts and unravels—again—the coherence of the ironic-didactic reversals.

Consistent with the rest of the work, there is no female character (no Grobiana) in Dedekind's "Grobiana"; the author speaks in the second person singular to a hypothetical character, the imaginary female reader, whose coarse behavior is described to suggest vivid scenes. Some advice is repeated from previous chapters for the instruction of the female grobian; for example, their clothing should be dishevelled and dirty; as in book 2, chapter 2, women are told to carry a puppy to the dinner table so that, should they break wind, they may loudly accuse the dog. Like the male grobians, who are told to hunt down lice in their clothing and and execute them at the dinner table, the women are told to hunt their fleas, in a reference to the Renaissance topos of the war between fleas and women.[20] Whereas the men are advised to adorn themselves with "ornaments" from the nose, women receive the advice to hang garlands of flowers from their noses, in order to look like country maids. Repeating the anecdote about a man who vomits into a bag at table, the speaker narrates a story about a young woman who vomits into a bag containing her prayer books.

The speaker instructs young women to cultivate immodest habits— to let their eyes wander promiscuously and to expose parts of the body (bosom, thighs) for sexual appreciation:

> Lumina permittes quocumque proterva vagari,
>   Omnia quo retro cernere et ante queas.
> Quea sibi nullius est mens conscia criminis, audet
>   Lumina deposito recta levare metu
> Atque hominem quemvis erecta fronte tueri;
>   Quae sibi mens culpae est conscia, spectat humum.
>                                   (3.8.1329–34)

Permit your wandring gadding eyes in every place to bee,
So that before, behinde, on everie side, you all may see.
The minde which nere committed any trespasse, may be bold
Each man, each thing in every corner, freely to behold.
And with a brazen fore-head looke the prowdest in the face,
Let those looke downe which for offence have suffred some disgrace.
                                  (3.8.4186–91)

> Inde manu vestes prudens utraque lavabis,
>   Sordida si multo sit via facta luto,
> Candida quo possint tua crura et utrumque videri
>   (Altius o pudeat tollere velle!) genu.
>                                   (3.8.1335–38)

With both your hands in comely sort hold up your coates you may,
If, as you walke, you chance to enter any dirtie way.

Let both your knees and eke your milke excelling thighes be spide,
But go no further, parts which higher are you ought to hide.
                                        (3.8.4192–95)

    Pectore nudato prodire sinuque patente
      Quam deceat, certe quisque videre potest.
    Lactea colla oculis pateant teretesque papillae:
      Grata puellipetis res erit illa procis.
                                        (3.8.1347–50)

To shew your bosome unto all, and eke your naked breast,
Because it is a very comely sight, I hold it best.
Your tender dugges and snow-white necke must be beheld of all,
Which when some wenching youth espies, in love with you hee'le fall.
                                        (3.8.4204–7)

Gossip, loud talk in public, exposing the body, gaping and staring, im-
modesty, excessive drinking—all these have furnished the foundation
for ironic advice to the male grobian, but the advice tends to be gender-
specific as well. In addition to idle, as opposed to learned, talk, gossip,
slander, and female complaints are also recomended for meeting like-
minded friends on the street:

    Quae tibi cumque venit quondam tibi nota sodalis
      Obvia per mediam foemina facta viam,
    Nil opus est dicta prius acceptaque salute:
      De rebus variis incipe multa loqui.
    Heu, mala multa premunt miseras et magna puellas,
      Omnia quae tenero sunt toleranda gregi!
    Huic gravis est rigidae nimium censura parentis,
      Iurgia terrifico quae tonat usque sono.
    Imperium dominae male sustinet illa superbae
      Subdit et indigno libera colla iugo,
    Heu mihi, quam multas fallax decepit amator
      Promissam veritus nil violare fidem!
    Hinc igitur semper, quae multa queraris, habebis:
      Utere naturae dote, puella, tuae.
    Foemineum omne genus fecit natura disertum,
      Id mulier donum caelitus omnis habet.
                                        (3.8.1355–70)

As thus you walke to take your pleasure in the dirtie streete,
If with a wench which your acquaintance was, you chance to meete,
You neede not with good morrow, nor good day begin to speake,
But bluntly into talke of divers weightie matters breake.
Maides and great mishaps there are, which many men oppresse,
Which they (poore soules) are forc'd to beare with patience
    ne'rethelesse.
Their parents hard and crabbed censure oft they must abide,
With cruell words, and bitter taunts their daughteres oft they chide.
Their curst and crabbed mistris makes them oftentimes to weepe,
When she their tender neckes in choler churlishly doth keepe.
And yong men also do their trustie lovers oft deceave,
When promising to marrie them, alone they do them leave.
Of these, and such like things, to her be sure thy plaint to make,
That use of tongue which Nature gave thee, freely thou maist take.
Your sect hath store of eloquence its weakenes to defend,
That gift to woman-kinde, I thinke, great Jove himselfe did send.

(3.8.4212–27)

The idle and lengthy conversation, complaining about women's woes at the hands of controlling parents and feckless lovers, has a seditious, antiauthoritarian resonance and characterizes the grobiana as quarrelsome and difficult. Worse is yet to come in other encouragements of public activity. Women are encouraged to spend their time in public places, such as at the performances of lewd plays—a source of further moral instruction—and tavern entertainment where, the speaker emphasizes, they should never be seen blushing:

Turpia sive vides sive percipis aure, putato
    Tingere virgineas turpe rubore genas:
Conscia commissi tibi criminis esse fereris,
    Purpura si malas pinxerit illa tuas.
Sin color in vultu semper tibi manserit idem,
    Illa via ad laudem pronior esse potest:
Non res te credent intellexisse profanas,
    Quod fugiant annos turpia dicta tuos.

(3.8.1409–16)

Whether you naughty words do heare, or beastly sights do see,
To blush at either of them both is not beseeming thee.
For one which for some great offence hath suffred some disgrace,
You will be thought, if blushing colours are within your face.
Let nothing in your cheekes a red unseemely colour raise,
Keepe still this rule, there can be found no neerer way to praise.
All men will thinke that you the way to vice did never know,
If in your gestures you no signe of blushing use to show.

(3.8.4266–73)

On the streets, female grobians are instructed to be seen eating as they walk about; unblushingly brazen, they gratify their appetites in public.

In this attempt to assimilate the female to an ironic didactic order, the parallels with male subjects cannot be sustained. Simply in deline-ating the space of social life "Grobiana" depends on important structural differences. In a moral environment that offers women the chief pre-cepts to be chaste, silent, obedient, indecency is produced the moment a woman appears in public or speaks. Thus, addressing Vives's concern in *De institutione foeminae Christianae*, the female grobian is encour-aged to appear in public, though public appearance is obviously not a topic of concern in the sections addressed to men, where it is not (as for women) proscribed but assumed. For men, only proper or improper public deportment is at issue; for women, no public deportment is proper.[21] In addition, much of the advice to women concerning behavior toward the opposite sex ironically alludes to the conventional pedagog-ical-maternal role of women in civil society and thus emphasizes setting an example—a very bad one, of course—for men. In frequenting tav-erns, for example, the grobian woman is advised to seduce men with intoxicants and her sexual powers:

Quis scit an obtineas animos faciente Lyaeo,
    Ut tibi promittat foedera sancta tori?
Quoque magis laetum videas et amore calentem,
    Non nimium tuus est dissimulandus amor.
Ingentem cyathum iuveni tu laeta propines,
    Sic erit exemplo laetior ille tuo.

. . . . . . . . . . . . . . . .

Indubiisque suum signis iam prodet amorem,
Tempore qui longo dissimulatus erat.
Iam teretes manibus volet attrectare papillas,
Ceteraque, in toto quae latuere sinu.
(3.8.1439–44, 1455–58)

Perchance the wine and you may urge him promise for to make
That very shortly for his loving wife he will you take.
If he consent, love domineering o'er the captive boy,
You must not hide your love too long, nor must you be too coy.
Beginne to drinke a cup of wine unto him for his sake.
Thy good example will enforce the youth more wine to take.
. . . . . . . . . . . . . . . . . . . . . . . .
And then by many publike signes his love he will betray,
Which from you he so long before in jeast had kept away.
Then heele beginne to holde your tender dugs within his hand,
And range in all those snowie vales which round about them stand.
(3.8.4294–99; 4310–13)

But Grobiana differs from Grobianus in other important ways as well. Although many of her coarse actions are similar to those described for the male grobian—that is, she will belch and fart with the "best" of the men—aggression and assault, so prominent in the male grobian, are unsustained. Though the female grobian confronts men with bold looks and complains that men mistreat women, the instructions proceed with ever more drastic advice to a scene of seduction and fondling of the woman. Just as calculating as a grobian—a quality that well befits her role as seducer and corrupter of men—she does not treat men in the way that Grobianus abuses women but rather conspires against her own sex in encouraging abuse from men. Thus when the speaker offers precepts with the encouragement of declaring that *he would be happy to see* the reader put them into action, this shaming device from the advice to men takes on an additional charge when he advises women to expose their breasts:

Non ego tam stupidus nec ero tam barbarus unquam,
Quin mihi te talem saepe venire velim.

Quae bona sunt oculis manifesta, merentur amari,
Quaeque latent nulli cognita, nullus amat.

(3.8.1351–54)

I neither will so sencelesse nor so bashfull ever bee,
But that I will desire a maid in such a case to see.
Those lovely partes which may be seene of all men, all will love,
But no man chooseth hidden things, before he do them prove.

(3.8.4208–11)

In the special case of Grobiana, her immodest exposure makes her the
object of a predatory and evaluating male gaze that transforms her indecency into his scopophilic opportunity.

There are limits to disruption in "Grobiana," and even in exagger-
atedly bad female behavior the author contains the potential for disruption. There is no scene in which a female grobian produces the kind
of social chaos offered in chapter 9 of book 1, where the speaker presents Xantippe as ironic exemplar to the youth serving at table, advising
him to emulate her techniques for making hospitality so unpleasant as
to drive away the guests.[22] Slipping from the ironic posture, the speaker
takes care to warn his female audience that, despite the considerable
liberties they should encourage men to take with them, they should
preserve their reputations (that is, their virginity):

Non mea res agitur, tua saltem fama laborat,
Fama nequit multos integra ferre iocos.
Heu mihi quam facile est amittere nomen honestum,
Quod periit ingens est reparare labor.

(3.8.1461–64)

and yet thus much you ought to know,
If this you suffer, you your credites cracke must undergoe.
Your credite and your honest name may quickely both be lost,
But to repaire them both againe, a greater price twill cost.

(3.8.4316–19)

Thus, like every "straight" manner book for women of the period, the
text holds up chastity as the chief precept for female behavior, indicat-

ing that it has the status of absolute taboo, staunchly resistant to humor and ironic reversal.

As in the rest of the work, textual irony works off the humorous gap between narcissistic delusion and civilly constructed social perception: in the instructions to perform boorish actions because they will provoke admiration, both grobian and grobiana, inflated by the speaker's claims of triumph, stand blinded to the humiliation and defeat the reader knows their actions are guaranteed to earn them:

> Commodius tamen et civilius esse putarem,
>   Vicino ambesam proposuisse dapem.
> Accipiet laetus, gratesque tibi in super addet,
>   Te quod adhuc memorem sentiat esse sui.
> Argumentum ingens non ficti erit illud amoris,
>   (Secula quem raro nostra videra solent)
> (1.5.699–704)

But yet I thinke it is a tricke more civill, and more fine,
To loade thy neighbours trencher with those scraps that lie on
  thine.
Hee'le thanke you with a ioyfull heart for that so royall fare,
And saie he sees (he thankes you) that you mindefull of him are.
T'will moove you for to be his friend most faithfull and most kinde,
And yet a faithfull friend in these bad dayes is hard to finde.
(1.5.586–591)

Yet the projected didactic reversal of such precepts becomes complicated for women. Everything women are told to do by the speaker reproduces the social passivity expected of them in conventional society. What Grobianus forcefully takes, Grobiana aggressively offers in the form of sexual favors that work to diminish her sexuality and her person, as well as the reputation that convention demands she preserve as the ambivalent signifier of feminine legitimacy. Cultivating this kind of passivity—allowing herself to be fondled and molested—hardly constitutes an automatic reversal of the decent behavior of women whose passivity differs in degree of refinement only, not in kind.

Finally, not wishing to burden his readers with excessive length (a great irony indeed!), the speaker tells his female audience they may

simply transport the precepts from the earlier parts of the book and
apply them to women's behavior; that is, *almost* all of them:

> Omnia quae generi iam sunt praecepta virili
> Tradita, tu vitae transfer ad acta tuae.
> Nec tamen esse putem tibi congrua cuncta, sed ipsae
> Cernere quid deceat dedeceatque potes.
> (3.8.1553–56)

> Those wholesome precepts which I lately unto yongmen gave,
> To serve your turne, whenas you lacke you may them also have:
> But yet I dare not say that all their precepts will be fit,
> But take the best; as for the worst, to others them commit.
> (3.8.4408–11)

The ironic-didactic method, by which the author seeks to internalize
civil discipline and produce a self-governing civil subject with an anxiety
level high enough to control his potentially boorish actions before they
take place does not work for the female audience (at least to the extent
that there is one). In the author's treatment, the female civil subject
has an identity that is "by nature" problematic:[23]

> Pauca loquar saltem mores formantia vestros,
> Pauca sed illa tamen commoda multa dabunt.
> Nil opus est longo vos carmine multa doceri
> Vincitis en ipsos rusticitate viros.
> Ad mala vos ultro facilis natura, vel omnes
> Instruit, officio nil eget illa meo.
> (3.8.1317–22)

> Some precepts I will give whereby your manner for to frame,
> They shall be few, but you shall reape great profite by the same.
> It is not nede for your instruction many trickes to tell,
> You are so prone, that all men you in clownish trickes excell.
> Nature her selfe, which scornes the helpe of any others trade,
> Unto all kindes of vice your sect most tractable hath made.
> (3.8.4174–79)

Women might provide the author with ironic examples, might furnish vital material from which to formulate reverse precepts for male subjects; but woman herself lies outside the zone of the ironizable.

By the internal logic of her female nature, Grobiana is destined to behave coarsely. This propensity separates her from Grobianus, who, when so tutored, acts like a peasant without actually being one, who is "effeminate" without being female.

> Simplicitas antiqua virum laeta arva colentum,
> Rusticitasque rudis sit preciosa tibi.
> Sed quaecunque solent homines laudare severi,
> Neglige, quid rigida cum gravitate tibi?
> (3.8.1301–4)

The simple life of country farmers which the field doe plow,
And all their rusticke trickes must be esteemed deere of you.
Those things which other curious Crittickes doe exhort thee too,
Neglect them all, with gravities you nothing have to doe.
(3.8.4158–61)

Grobianus is not by nature a boor and a lout; he chooses to become one by willfully resisting the right (civil) path and placing himself in bondage to female influence, to the goddess Rusticity, invoked as the speaker's muse in the preface. The utterly essentialized Grobiana, by contrast, has her particular vices—and really all vice—linked directly to her sex. She acts as she does because she is a woman.

> Hinc igitur semper quae multa queraris habebis,
> Utere naturae dote puella tuae.
> Foemineum omne genus fecit natura disertum,
> Id mulier donum coelitus omnis habet.
> Ergo diu nihili de rebus multa loqueris,
> De nihili rebus discere multa voles:
> Illa decem durat tibi fabula coepta per horas,
> Ante tibi turpe est velle redire domum.
> (3.8.1367–74)

That use of tongue which Nature gave thee, freely thou maist take.
Your sect hath store of eloquence its weakenes to defend,

That gift to woman-kinde, I thinke, great Jove himselfe did send.
Then since it is yorr gift to talke, have something still to say,
With trifling matters it is good to drive the time away.
For ten houres space at least your talke begun had neede to last,
By no meanes you must cease till then, although you have great haste.
                                                    (3.8.4225–31)


Presumably you can take the Grobiana out of Grobianus and produce
the civil subject. That is, in fact, the project of the civilizing process,
which views coarse behavior as a lack of manliness, as evidence of effeminacy. We have by now seen sufficient evidence of the futility of
this claim, but even if it were possible to excise every imaginable "feminine" trace from the male subject, you cannot take the Grobiana out
of Grobiana.

Instead, therefore, of pursuing internalization of shame and inculca-
tion of self-discipline through ironic reversal, Dedekind constructs a
paradox in which he is caught trying to cure women of vices endemic
to their sex. Likewise, his moral satire of the harassment of women only
leads, in its didactic trajectory, to the sequestering and public exclusion
of women. And similarly, as the very foundation of the civil society
whose manners he seeks to reform and refine, misogyny can be nuanced, perhaps endlessly, but not eliminated.

Our awareness of such contradictions is so strong for several reasons.
First, women have already been introduced in the earlier parts of the
text. Rusticitas, the author's ironic muse (as opposed to Apollo, the
nonironic muse of civil virtues), inspires (by negative association)
the speaker to write the text. In her relationship to Nature—also a
female, maternal figure—and to the goddess Rusticitas (identified in
the preface as "nostro dea maxima saeclo"), the female grobian is easily
identified as the agent of Simplicity, which civility appropriates in its
scheme of second nature. Second, one of the problems of a grobian is
a tendency to reproduce the behavioral characteristics traditionally associated with women: vanity, a desire for ornamentation, garrulousness,
being "materialistic" or bogged down in the physical and sensual realm.
The speaker often justifies a coarse action (wearing long hair and not
brushing the teeth, wiping the nose, or otherwise following the socially

required hygienic procedures) by claiming that it is "manly," meaning, by ironic reversal, that it is anything but.

> Cuncti homines quondam longos habuere capillos,
> Quos modo virgineus curat habere chorus.
> Regna pater quando Saturnus prisca tenebat,
> Tunc fuit in longis gloria magna comis.
> (1.1.105–8)

When father "Saturne" rulde the world, all men did use long haire,
And gloried in it, though now wenches use it most to weare.
(1.1.91–92)

> Qui nimios ambit, muliebria munera, cultus,
> Ridendus merito cui libet ille venit.
> (1.2.297–98)

He that regardeth cleaneliness, which onely women use,
At him let all men mocke and scoffe, let all men him abuse.
(1.2.248–49)

As student and initiate to a reverse civil standard, the grobian reader is addressed as male. Yet in offending against the standard, the grobian claims to be—and is everything but—manly. Using grobianly reasoned arguments about the threat that conventional grooming poses to his health and allusions to a fictitious past golden age and misplaced past values in the age of Saturn, *Grobianus* justifies the wearing of un-combed, uncut, unclean hair by claiming that it is not only manly but that grooming the hair, like many other equally perilous hygienic mea-sures, is a sign of effeminacy. Yet with his unlimited vanity, his garru-lousness, his curiosity that causes him to eavesdrop on conversations or to read everyone's letters over their shoulders, his Xantippe-like acts that drive out his master's guests, he embraces nearly all the vices pop-ularly associated with women in his time. It goes without saying that his notion of ornamenting his body with excreta and filth from the street is somewhat at odds with hygienic guidelines, but the grobian idea of what constitutes fashion combines both the vanity that women are taken to task for in civil society and his slovenly habits under justification of "natural" authority; it links his boorishness to the sphere of peasants and animals as well as to the purported excesses of women. The more he claims masculinity for himself, the more "grobian" his actions, the farther he departs from the code of civil behavior and cultural manhood and approaches animal, peasant, or female status. Then, like unreflecting animals, like his model of the natural world and his muses, the goddess Ceres and god Bacchus invoked in his preface, he stands in the enemy camp, the hostile Otherland, which civility must conquer and control. Yet because femaleness is not really part of the civil (second) nature, he (unlike women or the Others) can be cured by excising those proclivities.

Being the slave of simplicity, serving Rusticitas, means giving way to one's female proclivities, and is the consequence of lacking civil self-control—by definition an exclusively male provenance. Thus whereas the male grobian revolts against the (civil) nature appropriate to men—denatured and perverting nature—a grobiana acts out her officially constructed female nature. Finally, though, having encountered the overcoming of the female in Erasmus's model of civil behavior and its injunction against effeminacy enables us to see the logical conclusion of Erasmian moderation as the realization that the extreme of effeminacy is not merely out there to be avoided but rather, like lurking instinctual life, an enemy within.

But here is where an overarching irony disrupts a homogeneous, simple-ironic reading. Nature projected from the code of civility must retain and preserve the threat of the unruly and (unmediated by civil regulation) "natural." Civility needs and creates indispensable enemies, needs an alien nature. The civil subject who must obey the code can do so only by preserving the threat or repressed power of nature as instinctual gratification; and what that means is clear: Grobiana is part and parcel of Grobiana, but Grobiana is in Grobianus as well.

To create an internalization in women equivalent to that in the greater part of the text, addressed to males, is to socialize passivity and decorous seduction practices. In the civilizing process, through limited and controlled sexual enticement, women serve the institution of marriage as indeed they serve the institution of civility itself. Their "rule" stems from and reinforces their subordination to patriarchal order. In the ritualized practice of civility and etiquette, women would become,

as for Rousseau, the representatives and the police of civilization's col-
onized desires, both nature and nurture. Manners entrusted to women's
guardianship would follow the narrative of disappearance and forgetting, become part of the "conductorless orchestration" that Bourdieu
describes. Yet just as manners, as a modern discourse on the body,
preserve the power of instincts as opposition, so marginalization, or even
demonization, preserves the resistance potential of woman as Other,
inimical to the civilizing process.

# 5 / Scheidt's *Grobianus*: Revolting Bodies, Vernacular Discipline, National Character

> Damit das sewisch volck bey sich ain spiegel het, darin es sich besehen möcht.
>
> So that the swinish people have a mirror in which they may view themselves.
>
> —Kaspar Scheidt, Preface to *Grobianus, von groben sitten und unhöflichen geberden*)

Kaspar Scheidt enthusiastically tasked himself with vernacularizing and adapting Dedekind's 1549 *Grobianus* and published *Grobianus, von groben sitten und unhöflichen geberden* (Grobianus, on rude manners and impolite gestures) in 1551. Scheidt's adaptation extends the civilizing regimes of humanism to national and vernacular spheres and aims to take the revolting bodies of an untutored nation, stamp them with the indelible marks of humanist civility, and develop from them a reformed German national character. What emerges from his efforts, however, is a character named Grobianus. Pressed into the service of civility, he and his unholy household transform Dedekind's text and take conduct into a popular, material, early modern milieu.

Scheidt is joined in this labor of national reform by Hans Sachs, whose *Tischzucht* poems—five poems of the six thousand in his oeuvre—make a minor contribution to the genre but one that shares Scheidt's preoccupation with transforming revolting bodies to produce docile bodies and vernacular discipline for the masculine subject of a protonational Germany.[1] Sachs was a shoemaker and meistersinger;

Scheidt, in comparison, was a schoolmaster and academic whose use of
the popular forms and modes would bring Dedekind's humanist text to
a wider audience. Comparing their respective contributions to conduct
literature and protonationalist ideology tells us much about the concerns
of those who sought reform of and through the vernacular in the sixteenth century, a way of ideologically knitting together a nation centuries before it achieved the political status of nationhood.[2]

Reading Scheidt's *Grobianus* and taking the discussion to a brief
comparison with Hans Sachs, I will suggest links in discourses of conduct and bourgeois discipline from humanist texts to their vernacularization and self-conscious bourgeoisification. By the time we get to
Sachs's poem, "Die verkert dischzuecht Grobianj" (Grobianus's inverted
etiquette) of 1563, the pedagogical procedures for teaching good behavior seem thoroughly mechanized and exhausted, the lessons sufficiently internalized, perhaps even enough to please the Kaspar Scheidt
of my epigraph. Added to their conduct pedagogy, however, is a concern
not only with the material body but with the economic-material world.[3]
While the two authors share awareness of the intrusions of material life,
their attitudes toward it diverge significantly.

When we bring Hans Sachs and Kaspar Scheidt into a discussion of
conduct, we travel from the courtly setting of Castiglione, the humanist
pedagogy of Erasmus, and the humanist text of Dedekind to a self-
consciously bourgeois literature. Yet Scheidt and Sachs mark no significant break from their finer, more influential predecessors; indeed,
Scheidt's *Grobianus* and Sachs's five modest *Tischzuchten* precipitate
from what came before, are the very realization of it and, at least in a
textual sense, fully in collusion with it. They follow the historical logic
of bourgeoisified and bourgeoisifying regimes of conduct, regimes that
are composed of specular regimes occupied by the rulers and delinquents of civility.

Scheidt never met or corresponded with Dedekind before he published his *Grobianus* adaptation and acknowledged, in his prefatory letter, that he did so without Dedekind's prior knowledge.[4] He may not
have known Hans Sachs or visited the city of Nürnberg, but he was
well acquainted with popular verse forms such as those practiced and
polished by the Meistersinger and would likely have admired Sachs's
partisan and Protestant spirit in such poems as the encomiastic and

proselytizing "Wittembergisch Nachtigall" (The Wittenberg nightingale) dedicated to Luther and his cause.[5] An active Protestant moral reformer himself, Scheidt addressed a popular audience and sought to shape popular taste even as he appealed to it.

As Scheidt was aware, the international reputation of Germans was not the best in the sixteenth century. Philip Stubbes's encyclopedic *Anatomie of Abuses* (1584) offers English readers "a terrible example of Swabian drunkards," a story of eight German men carried off by the devil for drinking and carousing on Sunday; and another story of drunks from Neckershof and Strassburg.[6] Shakespeare has Portia comment about her German suitor that she likes him "very vilely in the morning, when he is sober; and most vilely in the afternoon, when he is drunk."[7] Thomas Nashe locates the birthplace of drunkenness in Germany in *Summers Last Will and Testament* (1592):

> Drunkennesse of his god behaviour
> Hath testimoniall from where he was borne:
> That pleasant worke "De arte bibendi",
> A drunken Dutchman spued out few yeares since.[8]

When Thomas Dekker takes up Dedekind's *Grobianus* for *The Guls Horne-booke* he carefully puts distance between the gull and the "Dutchman" (i.e., German) and alters the work to get "an Englishman" out of it. Scheidt's preface shows that he knows what he sarcastically calls the "gar adeliche subtile und höfliche namen" (absolutlely noble, subtle, and polite names) bestowed by other nations on the Germans: "Porco tedesco, inebriaco, Aleman yurogne, . . . Comedones und Bibones" (4).

Seeing the Germany shamefully compared to other European nations, Scheidt focuses on a German audience. Like the neo-Latin original, Scheidt's vernacular *Grobianus* uses reversals to teach and reform. It, too, responds to the historical crises of authority experienced in the rising urban middle classes of the transitional sixteenth century, but Scheidt's *Grobianus* tells us much about his views on the place of vernacular literature in the development of this kind of didactic satire and its contribution to a popular fashioning phenomenon of the period.

His attraction to the project of translating *Grobianus* is understandable; he himself had published pamphlets on the subject of bad behavior and specifically on drunkenness. One of these, titled *Die volle Bruoderschafft* (The fraternity of drunks and gluttons), pursues the theme of the degenerative and bestial metamorphoses of human beings through their excessive drinking, and it is further exploited in Scheidt's adaptation of *Grobianus* as an important addition to Dedekind. Alcoholic metamorphosis is emblematized in the pamphlet's woodcut illustration, a scene of animals drinking and carousing in human clothing and postures, which also becomes the title page of *Grobianus* (see figure 1).

Scheidt seemed to approach German culture and literature as a reforming humanist activitist. We know, for example, that his student Fischart's versification of *Tyl Ulenspiegel, Eulenspiegel Reimensweiss* (Eulenspiegel in rhyme, 1569), realized Scheidt's intention to adapt the work himself, a plan (unfulfilled because of Scheidt's early death in 1565) that further attests to his interest in presenting the heritage of popular texts for morally improving purposes.[9] In *Die volle Bruoderschafft* and the preface to *Grobianus*, Scheidt appropriates the German folk book to save the German national reputation and seems to align himself with other German reforming writers such as the pre-Reformation Sebastian Brant and the Catholic polemicist Thomas Murner as well.[10]

Certainly Dedekind's speaker, who slyly defends crude behavior by taking classical authorities out of context and constructing opportunistic syllogisms from crude material, also suggests affinities with folk-book figures such as Markolf or Eulenspiegel, and such affinities are made more explicit in both the form and the content of Scheidt's adaptation. Much more than Dedekind, Scheidt takes pains to shine the light on Germanic early bourgeois culture, even as he holds up his own investments in classical erudition through his added marginal commentary and his peculiar adaptations.

Perhaps nothing illustrates this mixing and opportunistic adapting better than Scheidt's use of Plutarch's character Grillus of the *Moralia* dialogue "Beasts Are Rational." Plutarch makes Grillus the intriguing figure encountered by Odysseus on Circe's island who refuses Odysseus's offer to liberate him with the rest of the men, choosing instead to remain a beast (a pig, a "grunter") under Circe's enchantment.[11] Grillus holds his own in an extended debate with Odysseus which has

# Grobianus/

## Von groben sitten / vnd vnhöflichen

geberden / Erstmals in Latein beschriben/durch
den wolgelerten M. Fridericum Dedekindum/vnd
jetzund verteutschet durch Casparum
Scheidt von Wormbs.

*Hic nullus uerbis pudor, aut reuerentia mensæ,*
*Porcorum uiuit gens pecuina modo.*

Liß wol diß büchlin offt vnd vil/    Vnd thü allzeit das widerspil.

*Figure 1.* Title page of Kaspar Scheidt, *Grobianus, von groben sitten und unhöflichen geberden* (1551). Beinecke Rare Book and Manuscript Library, Yale University.

much in common with the popular Renaissance humanist exercise of the mock encomium, but Plutarch uses him as the ironizer who gets the best of Odysseus, not only arguing for the moral superiority of animals on the grounds that they at least do not exhibit the vices and treachery of men but going on the attack against the great strategist himself and suggesting Odysseus's failure of courage in refusing to explore a particular change of shape:

Evidently it was farce, that talk of your cleverness and your fame as one whose intelligence far surpassed the rest—a man who boggles at the simple matter of changing from worse to better because he hasn't considered the matter. For just as children dread the doctor's doses and run from lessons, the very things that, by changing them from invalids and fools, will make them healthier and wiser, just so you have shied away from the change from one shape to another. At this very moment you are not only living in fear and trembling as a companion of Circe, frightened that she may, before you know it, turn you into a pig or a wolf, but you are also trying to persuade us, who live in an abundance of good things, to abandon them, and . . . sail away with you, when we have again become men, the most unfortunate of all creatures! (497–99)

Perhaps Plutarch had some prescient insight into the critique of Odysseus as the self-sacrificing, instrumentalizing bourgeois hero he was to become in Horkheimer and Adorno's *Dialectic of the Enlightenment*; he thus gives Grillus lines that put Odysseus in a less than exalted position.[12] Not only does Plutarch play with the argument that change is good (or don't knock it till you've tried it) as reductio ad absurdum; in addition, he has some fun with readers whose knowledge of *The Odyssey* and its outcome—in the epic, as we know, every man "rescued" by Odysseus from Circe's enchantment will be sacrificed on the trip home; not one will return to Ithaca—sees an underlying irony with an irreverent and less than affirming view of classical authority.

Though he assigns them a prominent position in his text, however, Scheidt appreciates pigs far less than Plutarch does. The woodcut frontispiece to Scheidt's *Grobianus* shows a sixteenth-century Circean scene of riotous eating and drinking: animals (all male) in human clothing perform various indecent actions against a bacchanalian background of grapevines (figure 1). In the lower right-hand corner a boar squats and vomits. Several animals fight or make broad, hostile gestures at each other. One dog has raised a sword to threaten another while to his right another animal, seated at the table, holds a staff and bears a menacing expression on his face. The floor is littered and dirty; a large spilled mug and an axe are two prominent objects. A goat playing the bagpipes would indicate a noisy scene in itself, but the animals at the table are also talking, loudly enough, it would appear from their open mouths, to compete with the musical din. Most interesting, perhaps, are the six animals conversing in pairs at the table. Two figures seated in the upper right-hand corner of the print each wave a free hand, while the cat holds food in the other hand, and the monkey blocks the cat's face with his hat or helmet, and gazes into his reflected image. The other two pairs make physical contact: a fox, with a large, half-empty beverage mug in one hand, has the other hand on the arm of the pig next to him, as does the figure to their right. The deictic Latin motto above the woodcut begins, "Hic nullus verbis pudor, aut reverentia mensae, / Porcorum vivit gens pecuina modo" (Here there is no modest word, or respect for the table, / A beastly tribe [nation] lives like pigs). The second part appears below in vernacular advice to the reader: "Liß wol diß büchlin offt und vil / Und thuo allzeit das widerspil" (Read this little book often and well / And always do the opposite).

Though Scheidt, too, follows the mock encomium, he has far less interest in Plutarch's ironic play on the theme of mutability and seems far more anxious about human malleability and the choices that, following Pico della Mirandola's example, human beings are likely to make. (As he asks in his conclusion to *Grobianus*, should a man act like a pig?) Scheidt adapts Plutarch's Grillus to his own purposes and re-forms the Plutarchan irony of the tale, reinscribing it with civil irony; and as he freely adapts Dedekind's work, he underscores popular elements and adds items from his own moral agenda.

To Dedekind's major theme of *simplicitas* Scheidt contributes the topic of will and applies it to an appropriated Plutarch. His conclusion to *Grobianus* identifies will as what distinguishes the human being from an animal such as a pig. Whereas it is the pig's nature to roll around in filth (beasts are *not* rational), man chooses to be filthy:

Es ist nicht not daß ichs alls sag,
   Man sichts (leider) es ligt am tag,
Daß auch der mensch wirt erger schier,
   Dann ein grob unvernünfftig thier,
. . . . . . . . . . . . . . . .
Hat nicht Plutarchus das betracht,
   Und ein Dialogum gemacht,
Da er uns thuot von Grillo schreiben,
   Der lieber selbs ein saw wolt bleiben,
Dann daß er solt auff diser erden,
   Erst wider zu eim menschen werden.
            (4229–32; 4945–50)

(It's not necessary for me to say everything; unfortunately, it is quite evident: man will choose to be worse than a coarse, irrational animal. . . . Didn't Plutarch say this in the dialogue he wrote about Grillus, who would rather remain a pig than become a man again on this earth.)

Thus Scheidt domesticates Grillus's provocative choice for moral purposes and lets Odysseus off the hook.

In his prefacing letter, Scheidt amplifies Dedekind's statements on boorish perversity and willful recalcitrance as he warms to the subject of the vices he seeks to cure:

Es ist je die menschlich natur zu allem guoten, das gebotten wirt, so träg, unwillig, und widerspenstig, daß sie zu allem, das verbotten ist, ein lieb, lust, und wolgefallen hat, Und haben die ersten zwei Menschen mit der verbottenen frucht im Paradis angfangen, und ist von den nachkomenèn biß auff uns, von tag zu tag gröblich gebessert worden, daß der Poet nicht unbillich hat sagen mögen: *Nitimur in vetitum semper, cupimusque negata.* (6)

(It's just human nature to be unwilling, obstinate, and contrary toward everything's good and commended and to be inclined toward what's forbidden. The first two human beings began in paradise with the forbidden fruit, and it's come down from them to us, getting coarser every day. It's not for nothing that the Poet [Ovid] could say: *We strive ever for the forbidden and desire what is denied.*)[13]

I have already mentioned the importance for humanist education of initiation into official language and an elite, extrafamilial culture, the shedding of immature and unrefined habits and the mother tongue and *mundus mulieris*, the home and the mother herself. Separation and rejection are taken one important step farther in Scheidt's *Grobianus*. In vernacularizing and characterizing, Scheidt transports the text back to a household setting. Civility's values return to occupy the once-rejected domestic space.

First, Scheidt takes to the labor of translation and adaptation of the work for the "mother tongue" with apparent relish. As he explains in his prefacing letter to Dedekind, he has "mit mancherley Scholien gespickt und gesaltzen" (spiced up [the text] and salted it with various comments) and improvised a little, "wie die Musici offtermals under die fürgeschribne notten jre läufflin machen und das gesang colerieren doch alweg wider in schlag Kommen" (7) (as musicians often improvise on the written notes and embellish the song, yet always return again to the beat). He nearly doubles the length of the original text because, as he explains, Dedekind's examples need to be embellished: the work is "nit grob genuog" (not coarse enough), and the Latin elegiacs are simply too elegant to bear the burden of depicting such repulsive vices. Furthermore, the work needs to reach a popular audience; whereas Dedekind writes for a universal academic or learned audience, Scheidt's folk book makes specific references to German customs, characters, locations, and to German national notoriety.

In his desire to aim the satire and humor at a specifically German audience, Scheidt expands the text and increases its appeal not only by adding many colloquial expressions and proverbs or by transforming the rather elegant and pedigreed Latin distichs of the original into the rough and ready *Knittelvers* of the *Fastnachtspiele* but by greatly amplifying the popular traces in Dedekind's text and making specific references to German places and national vices.[14] Among other things, this Germanization and popularization means developing the character of Grobianus in order to rival other folk-book figures such as Eulenspiegel or Marcolf (both of whom are included in Scheidt's work in a pantheon of grobian saints). The word *Grobian* had entered the German vocabulary at least three-quarters of a century before and Sankt Grobian had already appeared in Brant's *Narrenschiff*, but in Scheidt's hands the character is a self-identified teacher, artisan, householder, and grobian, and he is German.

Walter Ong notes the relationship in pedagogical writings between learning Latin as the official language of male authority and maturing as a man in the sixteenth century. Scheidt, however, claims in his introduction that his version will bring Dedekind's text to more readers and make its purpose more intimately accessible. His vernacularization will intensify the lessons and make Scheidt's text a new way to learn even the native tongue. He emphasizes the significance of this idea, explaining that the text

> werde diß Teutsch bey dem groben gesind, welchs das Latein gar nit oder wenig versteht, etwan auß innerliche einsprechung, biß weilen schand, spottens, und vexierens halb, der andern so darauff mercken, noch mehr nutz und frucht bringen. (p. 6)

> (this German [translation of the text] will better benefit the coarse populace who understand little or no Latin at all by offering them an inner voice, that is, shame, mockery, and anger that others may remark upon it.)

The ancient Spartans are said to have paraded drunken slaves before their children in order to impress upon them the repulsive effects of overindulgence, but Scheidt intends that his readers observe themselves as the distasteful spectacle; he uses the German language, "damit das sewisch volck bey zeiten ain spiegel het, darin es sich besehen möcht" (so that the swinish people betimes have a mirror in which they may see themselves). In Scheidt's treatment the mirror reflects a repulsive image of the national-masculine subject as he might be and offers introverted projections of individual anxieties, the anxieties of the virtual identity of the bourgeoisie. In his vernacular translation, therefore, Scheidt brings the puberty rite of physical discipline from the academic setting to the native realm, where the male initiates learn their bodily rhetoric in a more personal way. Scheidt's version and its appeal to an "innerliche einsprechung," while not philologically bound by the Latin text, transports, translates, and disseminates the official language and cultural values into the popular realm.

The English translator of Dedekind's *Grobianus*, R.F., also had his
problems with transmitting Dedekind's elegiacs to an English audience.
In seeking "to unmaske these Roman manners, and put them on an
English face" (preface), he also thought the "scurrile harshnesse of this
subiect" demanded a more "rugged cadence," apologizing for the author and for himself: "Perhaps thei'le wonder that a man of such wise-
dome as my Author, being neyther borne a Roman, nor a 'Naso', should
with such confidence of a general applause publish so elaborate a trifle:
from which admiration of you I hope your curtesie will derive a miracle
viz. my pardon, especially considering that both 'Ovid' and 'Virgill' (both
Poets Laureat) have beene metamorphosed into as indigest and breath-
lesse a kind of verse as this" (p. 3). For R.F., however, transforming
the Ovidian elegiacs into fourteeners, or heptameter couplets, offered
him an appropriate way to represent Dedekind's elaborate trifle, bringing it down to a still more risible and indecorous plane.[15] For Scheidt,
by contrast, using the meter of the *Meistersang* meant both embodying
the lessons in a more accessible form and filling the popular form with
an appropriate moral-humanist lesson.

Hauffen summarizes Scheidt's treatment of Dedekind's text at length
and concludes that Scheidt faithfully and fully transmits the content and
structure of the 1549 *Grobianus* but adds episodes and other material
that double the length of the text.[16] Like R.F., Scheidt takes advantage
of the larger (than Latin) vernacular lexicon and apparently cannot resist
enlivening and embellishing the original, even more than R.F., "taking
pains to make the mode of expression lively, folksier and coarser to the
smallest detail." But Scheidt expands the work and adds other grobian
scenes, ironic chapter titles (which Dedekind's first edition still lacked)
and often pithy marginal commentary, a mixture of learned and popular
proverbs (58). In comments that lean heavily toward the vernacular
adaptation, Hauffen claims that Scheidt's additions and changes improve the parodic scheme and bring more focus to the work (60). Finally, Hauffer concludes, "His contribution lies in the mode of delivery.
*Grobianus had to speak German.* . . . Scheidt's adaptation not only
makes *Grobianus* interesting and popular, it remakes it into a truly
German work" (48).[17]

Scheidt's adaptation of Dedekind's poem amounts to a cultural translation. Whereas Dedekind takes some of his material from the folk-

book, takes *Grobian* from the vernacular and Latinizes it, Scheidt returns this material to the vernacular. In that sense it is interesting that Hauffen's summary comparison omits what is the most important alteration of the Latin text, namely, that in place of Dedekind's un-named speaker and the ambivalent identity of Grobianus, Scheidt gives us a speaker and character named Grobianus who is a spoon maker and master of what amounts to a paramilitary school for the ill-mannered. This Sachs-like craftsman, whose personal introduction follows on the heels of Scheidt's prefacing humanist letter, addresses his apprentices in the fictional guild of makers of eating implements and simplicity. Scheidt surrounds his character with several apprentice grobians, who are addressed as his "grobian children," beginning with his mock dedication: "Den unflätigen, groben, und unhöflichen, seinen lieben Schulern, und angenomenen Kinder, wünschet M. Grobian von Lour-demont[18] vil unförmlichen sitten, und dölpischer geberde" (p. 8) (To the indecent, coarse, and discourteous, his dear pupils and adopted children, M. Grobian from Hick City wishes many chaotic manners and stupid gestures). He is not only teacher but father and master of gro-bians, whom he addresses intimately and affectionately as members of a family. "Hör mich fein zuo mein lieber son / Was ich dich lern ist guot zu thon" (Listen closely, my dear son, what I teach you is good to do [406–407]), he tells them, offering sage paternal advice, such as,

> Also lern ich alle meine kinder
> Lang negel han, wie schelmen schinder:
> Dann unser regel kan nicht leiden,
> Schwarz wüste negel zu beschneiden.
> (625–28)

(So I teach all my children to wear long nails like slaughterers of horses [knackers], for our order cannot abide cutting long, dirty black nails.)

Thus this figure goes beyond the antisocial egomaniac projected as the result of taking Dedekind's speaker's advice. Scheidt's Grobianus is not simply antiauthoritarian but counterauthoritarian, and he bears some institutional weight. When the text introduces the domestic consort

Grobiana, it makes this *Grobianus* something of an early modern house-hold book as well.[19]

Creating a grobian protagonist is no minor alteration to Dedekind's text. Scheidt has said in his preface, after all, that he has vernacularized the work because German is a more appropriate linguistic medium; Latin is "not coarse enough" ("nicht grob genuog"). By transforming Dedekind's unidentified Grobianus into a character who speaks as Grobianus Scheidt concretizes the speaker as part of a coarsening and enlivening strategy. His prefacing remarks show him to be intent upon sharpening the didacticism of the work, but the actually identifiable character alters the response to the text, tends rather to ameliorate the painful pleasures of Dedekind's didactic effect and to make the reading more comfortable and entertaining.

It is not that Scheidt's Grobianus doesn't know his grobianism; he praises and recommends drastically bad behavior in lessons filled with the familiar repulsive images, the scenes of erupting bodies. From Dedekind's advice on postnasal ornamentation (1.2.181–90) Scheidt produces the following:

> Drumb hör was zu deinr nasen hört:
> Win wüster kengel rechter leng,
>   Auß beiden löchern auß her heng,
> Wie lang ei zapffen an dem hauß,
>   Das ziert den nasen uberauß,
> Und kansts bekomen liederlich,
>   Das also wol wirt zieren dich.
>
> (228–34)

(Now hear what you are to do with your nose: When a filthy rope of a goodly length hangs from both nostrils as long icicles hang from the house, that is really becoming to your nose; and if you can get it in a vile way, then it's becoming to you as well.)

Scheidt's *Grobianus* addresses the reader in the second person singular and takes him through the steps of being a grobian for a day; it thrusts him into imagining himself acting in the most boorish ways conceivable. He, too, rises late, parades naked before other members of the household, publically flaunts his filthy appearance and unrestrained habits, assaulting the senses of projected witnesses as well as readers of the text. But now the perpetration is shared with a character who is also the speaker dispensing advice, and the shaming effect is accordingly diluted.

In Scheidt's *Grobianus* the male readers see themselves performing the grotesque and unmannerly actions described, as in Scheidt's second chapter, "von hoeffligkeit des nasen butzens, niesens, lachens, huostens, und vil anderem wolstand der kleider" (On the niceties of blowing your nose, sneezing, laughing, coughing, and other refinements of dress), in which the reader is advised to ornament himself with "jewels" from his nose, his clothing with dirt from the street, and to make himself still more conspicuous with a widely gaping mouth, loud laughter, and coughing. It is a palpably and viscerally vivid performance, especially with its nationally specific speaker and its direct address to the reader. As in Dedekind's text, there are commensurable infractions of bodily expression: a smile, a facial expression, become the equivalent of a snotty nose or filthy clothing.

Reproducing Dedekind's homeopathy, Scheidt describes bad behavior as a disease the moralist must "cure"; like a physician, he treats a poisoned patient with an antidote. Irony, negative examples, reverse precepts will produce a shock of recognition and shame where traditional authorities (Plato, Cicero, Erasmus) have failed with a direct appeal to reason. As Scheidt explains in his prefacing letter to Dedekind with a vernacular gloss on Ovid, the world is perverted. Everyone knows what good manners are, but human nature, its faculty of reason held prisoner by the body, compels men to pervert the rules: "Es ist je die menschlich natur zu allem guoten, das gebotten wirt, so traeg, unwillig, und widerspenstig, daß sie zu allem, das verbotten ist, ein lieb, lust, und wolgefallen hat" (It's always human nature to be obstinate, contrary and averse to every good thing that's bidden; and to love, crave, and be disposed toward everything forbidden [p. 6]).

Even as a reformer, therefore, one must not try to swim against the current ("so muoß man der zeit dienen, und nach dem gemeinen lauf handlen"); why not, then, present a countermodel of behavior? When, true to their perverse natures, the readers reverse these rules, they'll act as they should, substituting sobriety for drunkenness, decency for indecency, temperance for excess, self-control for self-indulgence. Scheidt teaches decent social behavior by heartily recommending its dramatic opposite, but he portrays it so vividly and so unattractively— all the while proclaiming it the model—that the reader of the text will be anxious not to be seen doing such things, even when they involve something as minor as facial expressions:

> Du aber laß stets auff und nider
> Beide kalbs augen umbher schiessen,
>     Acht nit, wen solches möcht verdriessen.
> Verker die augen, rümpff die stirn,
>     Das zeigt in dir ein fräches hirn:
> . . . . . . . . . . . . . . .
>     Solch sitten muoß ein junger hon,
> Der lob erwerben will von leuten,
>     Daß sie auff jn mit fingern deuten,
> So jedem sein weiss wol gefelt,
>     Und jeder spricht, das wirt ein heldt.
>                     (206–10, 216–20)

(But you, let your calves' eyes shoot up and down. Pay no attention if you annoy anyone. Roll your eyes, wrinkle your forehead: it's the sign that you have a bold mind. . . . Such manners are essential for a young man who wants to earn praise from people, so that they all point to him; his wisdom will please everyone and everyone will say he'll be a hero.)

Or in what a marginal note describes as "Ein meisterstuck eines unflats" ("A masterpiece of indecency"), more serious measures are urged to ensure that you have enough to eat by spoiling everyone else's appetite, using the power of bodily effluence and the strategy of Eulenspiegel from the episode in the folk book with the self-explanatory title, "Wie Ulenspiegel ein Weissmus allein usaß, darum er ein Klumpen us der Nasen darin ließ fallen" ("How Eulenspiegel got to eat a pudding, by letting a gob from his nose fall on it"). Here Scheidt takes Dedekind's reference to the same material and develops it significantly for the vernacular audience. For Dedekind, Eulenspiegel (= owl + mirror) is used

as a word game, through which he encodes a vernacular and popular
work in his Latin text:

> Sic reliquos dapibus citus absterrebis opimis,
>   Quodque erat appositum solus habere potes.
> Fecit idem quondam vir famigeratus ubique,
>   Nomina cui speculo noctua iuncta dedit.
> Hunc homines cuncti laudant, mirantur, honorant,
>   Atque viri mores posse reserre student.
> Alius quoque tu quantum potes, indue vitam,
>   Et poteris gestis clarus abire tuis.
>
>                                        (1.5.767–74)

> And by this meanes the company will straitway loathe their meate,
> And all the delicates remaining, thou thy selfe maist eate.
> A man well knowne in everie place did often doe the same,
> Who from an Owle joynd to a Glasse did first derive his name.
> This Owle glasse all in everie place praisde, honoured, and admirde,
> And to relate his prettie pranks each merrie man desirde:
> Wherefore his life, and his behaviour doe not thou refuse,
> And then no doubt but times to come thy merrie trickes will use.
>
>                                        (1.5.650–57)

Eulenspiegel's very crude action and the admiration the character has
earned provide Dedekind with a specular example that represents as
well the return of the specter of the peasant: the peasant-agrarian past
appears in the mirror. For Scheidt, the episode can be further exploited
in vernacular publication. It retains all the repellent and specular values
that work in the shaming discipline of civil values; in addition, however,
shaming and horror are carried to a larger sphere as the example becomes a ringing indictment of popular taste:

> Also shreckstu die andern ab,
>   Daß keiner lust zu essen hab,
> So bleibt dir dann allein die tracht,
>   Da du ein grawen hast gemacht.
> Das steht vom Ulenspiegel gschriben
>   Der hat diß stücklin auch getriben

Den jederman helt hoch und werdt,
  Und man seins buochs vil mehr begert,
Dann aller Philosophen leben,
  Magst dich auch auff sein regel geben.
                                        (915–24)

(Thus you'll so disgust the others that no one will want to eat; then
the dish will be yours alone, because you've produced such revulsion.
That's written of Ulenspiegel: he did this little trick, too; everyone
holds him high and worthy and they follow his book much more than
all the lives of the philosophers. You too should follow his rule.)

In the corresponding episode in *Ulenspiegel* a hungry Eulenspiegel enters the house of a peasant woman sitting by the fire, cooking a pudding.
When he asks for food she replies, "Ja, mein lieber Ulenspiegel gern,
und sollt ich das selber enbehren, so wollte ich Euch das geben, dass
Ihr das allein essen" (Yes, my dear Eulenspiegel, and if I myself dis-
pense with it, I'll give you what you can eat alone), he tricks her out of
the dish by taking her *at her word*, taking her answer literally.[20] Ulenspiegel's pranks confront language and culture with a triumphant material body. In *Grobianus*, however, the advice lacks the context of this
conflict and reduces the incident to one repulsive image of a boor in-
flicting himself on a silent and victimized society.

Grobianus's advice to act like Eulenspiegel because people approve
not just of the behavior but of the book, value it above philosophical
works, becomes a profound reproach to popular taste, linked to an action repulsive enough to spoil appetites. Even worse is that popular
taste makes *Ulenspiegel* a "best seller" and starves serious and learned
authors. Just as in his preface Scheidt rages like Diogenes against the
neglect of the learned, who receive fewer rewards for their accomplishments than cripples get charity for their handicaps, so he treats bad
manners and the folk book on the level of a venal and materialist simplicity:

Diß sage ich nur, daß so bald der Mammon die groben steinechten
hertzen eingenomen, und für ein Gott gehalten wirt, treibt und ver-
jagt er alle tugent hinwegk, und besetzt die statt mit lastern und

unbilligkeit. Darumb Diogenes nicht unbillich ein Question bewegt, Warumb wir ehe den krüpplen und aussetzigen unser almuosen geben, dann den gelerten und weisen, so die selbigen arm und dürfftig uns fürkomen, Und solviert sie also, Daß wir nemlich (unsers groben unordenlichen lebens halben) ehe besorgen wir werden krumm, lahm, und außsetzig, dann gelehrt, weiß oder geschickt. Aber solt Diogenes widerkommen, er würde bald sagen, man ließ beide die gelerten und andere armen not und mangel haben. (4–5)

(I'm only saying that as soon as Mammon enters the coarse, stony hearts and becomes a god, he confronts and hunts down all virtue and replaces it with vices and false ideas. About which Diogenes not mistakenly posed a question: Why do we give alms to cripples and the homeless before the learned and wise who also come to us poor and needy. His answer was that namely it is on account of our coarse, disorderly lives that we care for the crippled, lame, and homeless rather than the learned, wise, and skilled. But if Diogenes were to return he would soon say that [these days] one leaves both the learned and the other poor in want and need.)

Base taste, bad manners, and vice endanger philosophy and true learning, pervert the values that would exalt them.

To cure the perverse will, Scheidt means to substitute for the traditional, external authority of ancient authors an internal authority, and to do so through the autoproduction of shock and shame. Scheidt's preface repeats Dedekind's disease-physician metaphor, adding that once the antidote has taken effect, the cure will continue; "sie möchten sich vor solcher unform entsetzen, und sich darfür hüten, und als vor einem schedlichen gifft ein grawen haben." (5–6) (they'll be repulsed by such disorder and take precautions against it, regarding it with horror, like a dangerous poison). In the case of effeminate behavior, then, the internal mirror that shows the male reader an image of an "effeminate" self produces an example shocking enough (as shocking as nose picking or public incontinence) to correct his faults. In this way, self-repression and self-control can become a second nature of civility, successfully supplanting "perverse" nature.

In the vernacular *Grobianus* peasants and peasant customs are paraded before the reader not as the object of edifying mockery and laughter but as inwardly borne remnants of a class caught between its origins and its aspirations. In the aristocratic literature of the late Middle Ages, too, the peasant was the countermodel, the negative example for a noble paradigm; at the same time the peasant was the outsider. Now, in *Grobianus*, it is the peasant within who threatens to expose the ill-mannered subject and earn him exclusion from the realm of urban society. Scheidt uses Dedekind's allusion to comment on the tradition because he sees continuity from the popular works of the past to the deplorable state of present culture. In this, he reflects the need of his class to separate itself from its origins in a distinct way, and then to sit in stern judgment on those very origins. Although the text was undoubtedly written in an atmosphere of the increasing hostility toward the peasantry and toward the threat of the "common man," when the speaker proudly declares, "Nun will ich euch beschreiben geschwind, / Was beurisch grobe sitten sind" (Now I will craftily describe for you what rustic, coarse manners are [29–30]), the satiric attack is not meant to follow the tradition of the medieval satire of the estates, in which all strata were held up for general ridicule. It is not Scheidt's purpose, either, to mock the manners of real peasants, surely a pointless task; rather, his targets are the recalcitrant *Stadtbürger* who exhibit what the author deems rustic behavior and who needs to refashion his manners and attitudes to conform to a newer urban standard.[21] The growing cultural voice is self-focused and harshly self-scrutinizing. Laughing at yourself is not the goal, although laughter may sweeten an otherwise bitter dose of medicine, as Scheidt's speaker takes pains to point out ("und under dem schein eines suessen puelverlins, auch das bitter zu jrem nutz und gesundtheit einbringen" [and with the appearance of a sweet little pill deliver the bitter pill for their use and good health [p. 5]). The goal is to link laughter to shame.

Yet to claim that Scheidt's *Grobianus* has nothing to say about peasants or that peasants function only marginally in the satire would be a serious error. Civility organizes an image of dominated nature as nature itself, that is, a second nature of the civilized world in which it is "natural" to behave according to codified rules. As for Dedekind, for Scheidt primary simplicity (*natura naturans*) gives way to second-nature simplicity (*natura naturata*). But this form of self-control and self-repression has its other side as well. It marginalizes those groups that are positioned outside the value sphere of civility. Thus, it brings with it a particular attitude toward nature, peasant, and woman. After all, for the adolescent boy to whom so many of these lessons in manners are addressed, masculine identity does not come "naturally," any more than mastery of Latin grammar does. Renouncing the authority of his instincts and controlling his bodily self in order to become civilized and manly also means renouncing what has been negatively projected as the maternal and female realm, both threatening manhood both from outside and, as the "other" part of himself, from within.

Unlike Dedekind, who presents the conventional apologia and disclaimer of moral satire, Scheidt also relishes the task of presenting the work to a German audience. He remains unapologetic about the possibility of offending sensitive readers with indecent language and anecdotes, unconcerned that they might confuse what is presented with his better intentions. At the end of the work he states that only those guilty of the offenses depicted could be offended by them:

> Ein troffner hundt nur schreyen will
>   Ob schon die andern schweigen still.
> Und kratzen allweg jren grind,
>   Die reudig oder krätzig sind.
>
>   (4917–20)

(A kicked dog will only bark if the others are quiet, and those who scratch are those who itch.)

Scheidt concludes by joining his editorial voice to that of the speaker Grobianus as one and the same person, in whom the battle between instinctual and physical demands and decent self-restraint is never ending:

> Meins theils steck ich so tieff darinnen,
>   Daß ich mich nit kan rauß gewinnen.
>   . . . . . . . . . . . . .
> Weil ich dann je der letst bin worden,
>   In disem Grobianer orden,

Bitt ich mein guote gsellen all
　　Zum bschluß, daß jn doch wol gefall,
Mich in die groß Gsellschafft zu nemen,
　　Und sich meins namens [Kaspar Scheidt]
　　nicht beschemen.
                            (4883–84, 4889–94)

(For my part, I'm stuck so deep in the battle that I can't get myself
out.... Since I'm the last of this order of grobians, in closing I ask
my good apprentices that they be so good as to accept me into their
society and not besmirch my name [Kaspar Scheidt].)

This identificatory embrace with his literary persona works ironically at
the same time that it collapses the ironic divisions, Scheidt reveals still
another ironic touch but also a powerful dialectical tension within which
the civilized male self of the sixteenth century is continuously fashioned.
At least for *Grobianus*, although the satire attacks an old version of the
self and simultaneously works toward constructing another version, for
the lesson of the text to be truly effective it is necessary that the old
version be perpetually canceled and preserved. In order not to be a
grobian, you must see yourself as a grobian, must retain the images of
the worst possible behavior imaginable. Really good behavior, according
to the now revised standard of the urban bourgeois milieu, requires that
one retain the internal negative image. For the naturalized civil subject,
approval comes but rarely from without, and condemnation continues
to come from within.

Scheidt's specular didacticism receives iconographic support from
two emblematic illustrations. I have mentioned the bestial *speculum* of
the frontispiece, the clothed animals who, like Plutarch's Grillus, would
remain beasts instead of returning to a human state. The second illustration, placed to introduce the second part of the work, offers the
inverted ideal to the indecent extreme and specular seduction of the
frontispiece (figure 2). It shows a banquet scene in an aristocratic setting. Two richly attired couples, seated at a large, cloth-covered table
and being entertained by three musicians standing before them, are
about to be served by a young male servant seen approaching by stairs
from the left. The seated figures are shown conversing amid food and
the usual sparse eating and drinking implements of the period. A

# Das ander Büch

## Grobiani / Von groben
### vnhöflichen sitten.

Das erste Capitel vnderweiset / welcher massen
ein Grobianer / so er zu gast geladen / ein
gedenck zedel machen / den besten
sitz einnemen / vnd mit
prouiand sich ver-
sehen soll.

Ißher hab ich dich glert vil sachen /
Wie du die gest solt frölich machen /
Doch als das einem knecht gezimpt /
Der kost vnd lohn von Herren nimpt.

K ij

---

*Figure 2.* Illustration to the second book of *Grobianus, von groben sitten und unhöflichen geberden* (1551). Beinecke Rare Book and Manuscript Library, Yale University.

woman at the left end of the table gestures gracefully with her hands as a bearded man seated next to her listens, holding the only visible drinking goblet in his left hand. The other woman has her hands in her lap, and her partner rests with his chin on his hand. The figures do not touch, eat or drink. In the lower left corner a monkey on a leash crouches with table scraps. The composition is divided vertically by pillars and horizontally by lines of the table and stairs, proportioned into four unequal but decorously composed parts, dominated by the table scene. The musicians playing instruments in the lower right foreground are smaller than the figures at the table, as though perspective followed social status.

This mottoless picture of decorous sociality and juvenile initiation, which keeps animal life well leashed and segregated, negatively mirrors and reverses but also tacitly refers to the crude frontispiece. Just as the precepts of civility express the virtual identity of the bourgeoisie, so they contain anxiety about what they might do to make things go wrong. The reader is ultimately much closer to the crassly sensual, excretory life of bestial behavior illustrated by the first woodcut than to the distanced, cool, dreamlike world of the aristocratic model. We can call the second woodcut an ennobling dream image of an unreal and unreachable aristocratic ideal, so distant from the popular audience that Scheidt would reach, yet the very dream of ennoblement that informs bourgeois conduct discourse.

———————

Compared to Scheidt's lengthy work, Hans Sachs's specific contribution to conduct literature seems minor indeed, but placing his *Tischzuchten* in the setting I have just discussed suggests how psychically complex the contents of the lessons he presents are, how fully and economically they bear their civil legacy. Sachs's five rhymed *Tischzuchten*—the first three "straight" didactic, the last two ironic-didactic or grobian *Schwänke* (farcical poems)—carry the heavy freight of the specular regimes of Castiglione and Erasmus to the vernacular sphere and to other classes to promote the civic virtues of industriousness and discipline. Like Kaspar Scheidt, if not directly under his influence, Sachs promotes self-specularization to a national-masculine level.[22]

Sachs's interest in conduct developed in the sixteenth-century city of Nuremberg, a thoroughly regulated Reformation *Reichsstadt* (imperial city)—by some accounts as well regulated as the meter of Sachs's *Meistergesänge*—and thoroughly regulated for business and trade, the materialist profit that went hand in hand with the wages of civic virtue. City regulations governing the treatment of visiting craftsmen, for example, themselves serve as examples of civically authored *Tischzuchten*:

> First of all: profanity, cursing, or blaspheming are absolutely forbidden, and will be severely punished by the Council, esp. when done with intent and malice.
> When a foreign journeyman visits the city he may be entertained with drink and food, but no more than 5 Kreuzer may be spent for wine and bread.
> No more than two measures of wine shall be consumed at any one sitting.
> No journeyman shall sit armed at table.
> No foreign journeyman shall rise from table without permission.
> Those present shall elect four journeymen as heads of the banquet.
> These four shall be obeyed in all matters.
> No one may pound the table with his hand, nor call anyone present a liar.
> [There shall be] . . . no toasts, no gambling. . . .
> Apprentices shall have nothing to drink.[23]

Like the *Tischzucht*, such regulations tend to micromanage the urban bourgeois subject. Yet like the *Tischzucht*, such legislation, in containing bad behavior, also records transgression; one does not codify or regulate what is not always already taking place. Thus sumptuary legislation is the attempt to arrest the unarrestable, the crossing of class and income levels creating situations in which lower classes could afford to consume above, dress above their status, the mobility that destabilizes the sense of the body.

In his autobiographical "Summa all meiner gedicht vom MDXIII jar an biss ins 1567 jar," Sachs encapsulates his lifelong literary handwork:

> Und im Teutschland an allen orten
> Bey alter und auch bey der jugend
> Das lob aller sitten und tugend

> Werd hoch gepreiset und perhümt,
> Dargegen veracht und verdümt
> Die schendlichen und groben laster,
> Die alls übels sind ein ziehpflaster,
> Wie mir das auch nach meinem leben
> Mein gedicht werden zeugnuss geben.
>                                              (227–35)

(Everywhere in Germany, for young and old alike, praise of decency and virtue is prized and renowned; in contrast, the shameful and coarse vices, are despised and condemned. They act as a plaster that draws out the evil. As my poetry bears witness to what my life has also been.)

That cheerfully rhymed binarism, "sitten und tugend . . . perhümt [ver-rühmt]" / "groben laster . . . verdümt" (the rhymed witticism is lost in translation: morals and virtue famed / coarse faults blamed), well describes his *Tischzuchten*. In the 1534 "Tischzucht," Sachs presents his disciplinary catalog of mainly proscribed behavior:

> Nit schnaude oder sewisch schmatz.
> Nit ungestümb nach dem brot platz,
> Das du kein gschirr umbstossen thust.
> Das brot schneid nit an deiner prust;
> Red nicht mit vollem mund. sey messig.
> Sey in der schüssel nit gefressig,
> Der aller-letst drinn ob dem tisch.
> Zerschneid das flaisch und brich die fisch
> Und kew mit verschlossem mund.
> Schlach nit die zung auss gleich eim hund,
> Zu eckeln.

(Don't snore or smack piggishly. Don't grab wildly for the bread, so that you don't upset the table wares. Don't cut bread against your chest; don't talk with your mouth full. Be moderate. Don't be glut-tonous about what's in the platter, leave the last portion on the table. Cut meat and break fish. Chew with a closed mouth. Don't let your tongue hang out like a dog; it disgusts people.)

In his last treatment, the 1563 "Verkert dischzuecht Grobianj" the just-
say-no strategy becomes an ironic and lengthier just-do-it; the proscrip-
tions are readily recycled as encouragements; both call up the familiar
visceral, self-shaming response.

Sachs's grobian reversal is framed as Saint Grobianus addressing the
brothers of his order. The poem concludes by cloistering the addressee
in the monastery, exiled from any other, properly Protestant society:

> Den spricht iderman wol dein wiczen
> Vnd helt dich fuer ain ordensman
> In dem kloster Sant Grobian,
> Drin man lert weder scham noch zuecht,
> Der auch kein mensch mehr bey dir suecht.

(Everyone will recommend your wittiness and regard you as a member of the monastery of Saint Grobian. In it one learns neither shame
nor discipline, and you'll be without company.)

In addition, unlike Scheidt's, Sachs's conventional signature, which usually concludes his poems as a mark of work and ownership, stands outside the frame of the text. If we can regard the *Meistersang* as literary
craft (*Handwerk*) with uniform rules, measures, and themes, practiced
by middle-class craftsmen and tradesmen in tightly organized societies,
then we can speak of Sachs's contributions to the *Tischzucht* as especially serviceable poems, a utilitarian literature in support of practical
values of self-control, industriousness, a socially perceptive sense that
could knit together the urban dwellers in a harmonious, self-censoring
unity.

Sachs, however, sees material rewards for control of the material ody
which do not exist for Scheidt. In a poetic dialogue praising his city,
"Ein Lobspruch der Stadt Nürnberg," Sachs underlines the connections
between bourgeois virtues and the rewards of prosperity:

> Ich sprach: "Wer wohnt in dieser Stadt,
> Die so unzahlbar Häuser hat?"
> Er sprach: "In der Stadt um und um
> Des Volkes ist ohn Zahl und Summ,

> Ein emsig Volk, reich und sehr mächtig,
> Gescheit, geschicket und fürträchtig.
> Ein grosser Teil treibt Kaufmannshandel;
> In alle Land hat es sein Wandel
> Mit Spezerei und aller War.
> Allda ist Jahrmarkt über Jahr
> Von aller War, die man begehrt.
> Die meist Teil sich mit Handwerk nährt,
> Allerlei Handwerk ungenannt,
> Was je erfunden Menschenhand. etc."

(I said: "Who lives in this city of so many houses?" He said: "In this city of countless people there live industrious people, rich and very powerful, modest, skilled and prudent. Some of them are merchants; they trade in all lands with spices and all kinds of goods. All year long there is a fair with every sort of ware that one could want. Most of them are craftsmen who make their living with every sort of craft known to man. etc.")

Sachs's urban morality of industriousness rewarded by well-earned prosperity, then, eventually diverges from the humanist morality of Scheidt. Scheidt's *Grobianus* figure is a simulated craftsman, constructed through the ironic-didactic strategy of the the text to instruct readers in a morality that links the vital and aggressive material body to corrupting materialist values.

Both Dedekind and Scheidt show that grobians can interrupt and subvert polite table conversation, changing worthy subjects into trivia and ignorant chatter and even in some cases destroying the conversation altogether when inebriated talk degenerates and grobian gestures produce a drunken slugfest. Like the excremental functions and gluttony they bring to the table to repel other guests, bad conversation interrupts and drives out good. But Scheidt takes particular pains to link grobian boorishness with more serious and ominous social and moral consequences. In Scheidt's preface, Grobianus combines his intimate direct appeal with an aggressive threat to virtuous society, as he explains that he has vernacularized the work in order to increase the family ranks and wipe out social decency altogether, "damit dise unsere löbliche

gesellschafft gemehret, darneben alle tugent, zucht, scham, und mes-
sigkeit, wie schon (lob sey Baccho) zum theil geschehen, ganz auss-
gerottet und vertilgt werde" (p. 10) (so that our praiseworthy society
increases, and that therefore all virtue, discipline, shame, and moderation, as has already happened in part [praised be Bacchus], be entirely
done away with and exterminated). In the context of a standard of civil
decency, a category that covers everything from restraining belches and
farts, to greetings on the street, to table manners and repect for women,
dignified conversation and reverence for learning, grobian reversal is
not just inverting precepts but reversing the response to humorous situations from amusement to a sense of danger and anxiety. Not just
personal embarrassment is elicited but, linked to it, the feeling that such
actions—from drunkenness and gluttony to a decline of morality—can
subvert the entire social order.

The numbers of grobians swell to correspond to a growing perception
of "civil decency," a reflection on what one is surrounded by in limited,
urban, social space. The consciousnesss of vulnerability and the power
of an undefined, un-unified middle class, in the throes of formulating
and articulating its cultural identity, make all these actions not just disgusting but perilous.

With Scheidt's mirror of negativity and the calling up of an inner
voice—Scheidt's "innerliche Einsprechung"—of internalized, autocon-
trol, there is no covering up: any physical urge that body communicates
to mind becomes suspect. His *Grobianus* attempts to fashion a kind of
collective and national identity for a class on the foundation of the
painful pleasures of indecency and cultivated shame. For him the one
recognizable restraint, that which makes and keeps men grobian, comes
under the rubric of materialism.

In an extended attack on materialism in his preface, Scheidt presents
and links two versions of the golden-age *topos*. One is the age of Saturn
when precivilized men wore their hair long and kept the "simple" and
coarse habits that Grobianus holds so dear. The other is the man-made
"golden" age of the money economy, a kind of Renaissance earthly and
material paradise. As Scheidt complains in his prefacing letter, "Es wolt
dann jemand sprechen, es er die recht Guldin zeit eben jetzund, . . .
das gold nie so lieb und werdt gehalten, und begert worden, Das nicht
unbillich die Medici gesagt, das golt sterck und erfrewe das herz"

(Someone could say that we really live in the Golden [and guldin = currency] Age now, . . . for never has gold been so prized and sought after. It's not for nothing that the Medici have said that gold strengthens and gladdens the heart [p. 4]). Linking the traditionally edenic and utopian age of the past with the present age of commerce and economic activity, Scheidt identifies both as impediments to decency. These are the constituent parts of the materialism—instinctual and economic— that enslaves the populace to vice and condemns true learning to obscurity and poverty. "Gold" as the sign of the money economy is what shapes men from without, as their vices work from within to prevent them from properly fashioning themselves.

By attacking the precivilized rural past of the natural (that which contains the female realm as well) and casting a negative eye on the only too present conditions of the money materialism that underpins the urban bourgeois world, Scheidt serves a bourgeois ideology of freedom, envisions—outside the specular horror—a place unrestricted by tyranny of the instincts, on the one hand, or by the subtle and inscrutable powers of the money economy, on the other. For Sachs, then, the body is at odds with values of material productivity; for Scheidt it is, really, in cahoots with corrupting materialism. For both, the body, whether undisciplined or disciplined, remains the problem.

It is possible to understand the importance of the grobian literature, and the body of literature on manners as well, not as merely anthropological documents or historical curiosities of subliterary value but as literature that can tell us something about the social function of irony in a critical historical moment. The issue is certainly not whether, by some universal or objective standard, an accurate evaluation of etiquette standards could ever be possible or whether manners in the later fifteenth and early sixteenth centuries were in need of reform. Rather than dismiss this work as the product of a historian's mythical "grobian age," we might far more appropriately see it as another manifestation of the conscious shaping of behavior, specifically, masculine behavior, in the period of self-fashioning. For Scheidt, the appeal to fashion a civil self is generated from the text's ironic-satirical method, and the purpose is not just to create an identity and not only to "naturalize" it but to nationalize the masculine subject of civility.

Scheidt's *Grobianus* reveals the efforts made by the male members of the emerging middle class to create an identity of both class and gender for themselves. The model of nobility and courtly behavior was visible in tradition but remained outside. It offered traditional authority's codified precepts but not the identity needed to reestablish authority in a time of its crisis. These rules stood as empty forms awaiting appropriation and a content that could speak, intimately and awesomely, to their successors. Self-made men, or self-fashioned *Bürger*, had to deal with the enemies within: the tyranny of instinctual life, which perpetually threatened to run out of control, exposing one's anxiously imagined inadequacy to compete for a place in an alien society or destroying the carefully constructed patriarchal world of social artifice.

The body is not always grateful for the efforts made to render it decent and docile. Even when it is successfully contained, when it is docile, national or protonational, classed and gendered, the body remains the archive (memory container) of what the subject of civility, on the ideological level, so happily sacrifices. When, in Plutarch's text, Grillus and Odysseus face each other in their specular relationship, we could now imagine, from reading that great work of German exile, *The Dialectic of Enlightenment*, that Grillus knew a few things about cultural masculine identity and that he wasn't all that wrong to turn down an opportunity to sail with the great and savvy instrumentalizer.

# 6 / Gulls from Grobians: Dekker's *Guls Horne-booke* and the Circulation of the Body in Renaissance England

Men that would have all in their owne handes. Cormourantes, gredye gulles; yea, men that would eate vp menne, women, and chyldren, are the causes of Sedition!

—Robert Crowley, *The Way to Wealth*

*The Guls Horne-booke* (1609) begins as a prose translation of Friedrich Dedekind's *Grobianus*; but as Thomas Dekker frankly remarks in his foreword, "Not greatly liking the subject, I altered the shape and of a Dutchman [i.e., a German] fashioned a mere Englishman." Presenting himself as the queasy English reader of the German author's Latin text, Dekker makes an uneasy exchange and fashions in translation English gulls from German grobians. In writing *The Guls Horne-Booke* in the setting of Jacobean England, some sixty years after Dedekind's *Grobianus*, Dekker takes up the figure of the gull and reconfigures the conduct book to make it an entertaining mock guide to social mobility.

Dekker's declared distaste may have been for the ironic-didactic style as much as the extraordinary coarseness of *Grobianus*, but although we could say that both the didactic and the indecent—at least as treated by Dedekind—were apparently untranslatable to early seventeenth-century English conditions and tastes, that would not be enough to address the real work of translation going on in Dekker's pamphlet adaptation and the context in which the translation is produced. This is the task of this concluding chapter, the last stop of a historical, literary, and conceptual itinerary that has attempted to locate the end of conduct.

R.F.'s earlier, more faithful English translation of *Grobianus* (unknown to Dekker), whose heptameters and embellishments exploited Dedekind's crude material, was no popular success; the equally obscure later translation of 1739, by the pseudonymous Roger Bull, freely adapted the work for an audience with Swiftian expectations.[1] The first three chapters of Dekker's eight-chapter prose work are recognizable, if cosmeticized, adaptations of *Grobianus*; they follow the attention to traditional precepts on rising in the morning (very late), on grooming (long hair is praised, as is nakedness exposed to household members), and on setting out for the day. The remaining five break from the source text and place the gull in specifically English conditions and social sites: St. Paul's Walks, restaurants ("ordinaries"), the theater, city streets, and the tavern. In the transition to local themes and topics, Dekker trades in Dedekind's navigation trope for tropes of fashion and dress and begins with a brisk and comprehensive, fashion-conscious tour of Paul's Walks: "Being weary with sailing up and down alongst these shores of Barbaria, here let us cast our anchor and nimbly leap to land in our coasts" (88). Taking an Anglocentric turn, he dedicates his efforts to the gull, "that true humorous gallant that desires to pour himself into all fashions" (88) and whose social-climbing goal, tropically laid out and exploited by Dekker, is to *publish his suit*.

Those who have compared the two works have routinely stressed their clear differences, emphasizing contrasting contents and characters—gull versus grobian—as much as the change of genre from poetry to prose. Douglas Bush, for example, states that Dekker's text "owes little to the crude Latin poem. Dekker's gull is not a mere nasty boor but an ignorantly pretentious young man from the country who wants to cut a dash as a sophisticated man about town, and whose behaviour is inspired by the one motive of attracting attention to himself."[2] Rühl sees the work unsuccessfully divided into two unrelated parts: the first part translating *Grobianus*; the second developing the figure of the gull alone. Rühl sees Dekker's gull as more broadly comical than the grobian and only weakly satirical, and he sees "fundamental differences at all points of contact" between the two figures (xxxvii, xlviii). C. H. Herford also sees a jarring thematic discontinuity in the change of the figure:

"The portrait begins decisively to change character, and a new subject emerges, of totally unlike habits and ideas, no regretter of the primitive age 'when all men were "Grobians",' but the most fanatical devotee of the latest fashion."[3]

While it is true that Dekker himself remarks on the deliberate and abjecting discontinuity in his text and seems eager to put distance between his pamphlet and its source, it might be more productive to investigate continuities between the seventeenth-century English work and its sixteenth-century German text than to stop with the indisputable differences. Considered in this way, Dekker's work continues and transports grobianism, writes and "translates" grobian literature. While Dekker shows his aversion to taking on the indecent and makes every effort to clean up Dedekind's act, he retains the grobian materiality of the body and a famiiar autoscopic body-consciousness as a cultural-thematic precipitate. The gull, whose single-minded pursuit of attention is less than boorish, is nonetheless a kindred derivitive of the civilizing and self-fashioning process in which the grobian is found, a process in which the defecating, farting, and belching body and the self-promoting, fashionably attired body share a central space. Even more than the work of Dedekind or Scheidt, for whom the gross materiality of the body is central, Dekker's work concerns itself with links between the bodily material and the commodifying materialism of urban life. Dekker's gull is both fashion conscious and body conscious; the text enforces no real distinction. The ironies exploited in Dekker's structuring trope of "publishing your suit," skillfully pursued and developed in his satirical portrait of the gull, begin with an Adamic suit that soon receives a social-economic wardrobe. But Dekker's ironies are also the indecent ironies of the *Grobianus* texts. Dekker takes the unlocalized and quotidian events of *Grobianus* and turns them into a travelogue on life in London, a life of trade, consumption, display, and performance: in short the early modern material world of exchange. In cleansing his adaptation of the sensational crudeness, the effluent and excremental coarseness of *Grobianus*, Dekker reveals more about that material world as well as about the central connection of both gull and grobian to it. Not unlike Dedekind's reworking of the conduct book, Dekker's treatment is a repudiation of its source which repeats it with a difference and even, perhaps, with a vengeance.

*The Guls Horne-booke's* satirical critique of the materialism of its contemporary setting embeds more than just a commentary on the tradition of conduct literature; it reflects as well on the fashioning of the early modern subject and the social order in which that subject circulates, publishing his suit in pursuits of exchange and the profits or fruits of exchange. One of those strange fruits will turn out to be the conduct book itself, yet another circulating commodity and ticket to exchange in early modern life.[4] In that sense, then, Dekker's work contributes yet another reading of *Grobianus* and the tradition of conduct literature.

As we have seen, *Grobianus* presents us with a disordering of signifying practices, a semiotic economy that skips the middleman and constructs a scheme in which bodily production or bodily excess—forms of effluence and excretion—constitutes the sign of material wealth. As commodities, such signs can be exchanged for recognition and prestige, themselves exchange-sign values.[5] Effluence as affluence: the praise of yellow (gold) teeth offers one comparatively bland example, but there are really graphic ones, such as praise for the aesthetic value of nose "jewelry," the excremental "accessorizing" of apparel, or the radical *enrichez-vous* advice of mining body scabs. It is when the grobian speaker claims that rude behavior gains the profit of approval by witnesses, that all this can be cashed in for cultural capital, that the reversal in the text becomes coercive. Do this, he urges through the intimate and imperative vehicle of second-person address; no man (appealing to the reader's socialized sense of an observing and evaluating audience) will be more praised for his civility.

At the center of the contradictions of the text stand twin horrors: a horror of the body whose eruptions and drives write a catastrophic script that civil discipline would suppress, and a horror of the inscrutable forces of the modern economy. The horror of body, controlled by keeping the image of horror ever present, creates and maintains a repressive self-consciousness that renders one marketable or, as Dekker expresses it so well, allows one to publish one's suit; it is that investment in horror which is the necessary precondition in the urban world for the professional exchange relations that mark the mobile, negotiable, fluid economic urban environment. In the politics of the self-regarding, self-repressing gaze, however, body horror is more the consequence of than the conspirator with new socioeconomic relations.

That Dekker expresses a certain distaste for the subject of *Grobianus*, comes as no surprise to those now thoroughly initiated into the ironic *rites de passage* of this literature of indecency. Yet Dekker's distaste for grobianism shows only too well that *Grobianus*'s "failure" already marks its success. The grotesque bodily spectacle of conduct and courtesy books has done its internalizing work; what Norbert Elias calls the "shame threshold" of civilization is demonstrably lowered in Dekker's revisionist labors. At the same time, in adapting the work to suit altered conditions and goals, Dekker also capitalizes on the specular apparatus of the civilizing process and retains interest in the micropolitics and psychic economy of the self-promoting spectacle of the civil subject. It is in stating his distaste, however, that Dekker suggests the continuous legacy of *Grobianus*: readers like Dekker, increasingly civilized and sensitized in the intervening sixty years, find the work indecent; even as it marks an end of sorts to the genre of conduct literature, Dekker's translation continues to negotiate with indecency.

========

Dekker is not the first English author to make use of the nationally unique and fashionable figure of the English gull. Popularized by the minor Elizabethan poet Sir John Davies in his "Epigrammes" and "The Gullinge Sonnets," this late sixteenth-century "would-be" or "wannabe" became, in the Jacobean period, a highly exploitable stock literary figure for authors such as Thomas Dekker and Ben Jonson.[6] References to the gull, generically defined as "credulous fool" or "dupe," appear throughout Elizabethan and Jacobean drama.[7] In the *Oxford English Dictionary*, the verb "to gull" means "to make a gull of," and "to swallow, guzzle, devour voraciously" (from the French, "je engoule"). The sea gull is a raucous, greedy, scavenging bird that feeds ravenously and indiscriminately. In the early modern sociocultural lexicon, the gull becomes the signifier of the vulgar materialist par excellence, a creature who asserts the absolute primacy of *gula* (throat or gullet) over considerations of order, decency and in particular, hereditary duty and financial obligation.[8] He—for there are no female gulls—also possesses an impressive, if necessarily reprehensible, elasticity and versatility. "I name a gull," one of Davies' epigrams begins. "But this new terme will many questions breede."

Seventeenth-century gulls, such as Jonson's Master Stephen, the "country gull" in *Every Man to His Humour*, are most commonly young country upstarts who come to the city to squander the family fortune (by being gulled or conned) or to live as though they had a fortune to squander, gulling their creditors, as does Jonson's Master Matthew in the same work. They could also, according to the multiple portraits of them in *The Guls Horne-booke*, be found among pretenders to many ways of life. Yet in the mobile social milieu of the early seventeenth century, with James I's "inflation of honors," the dependency of the absolute monarchy on instruments of financial credit and the frequent impoverishment of the hereditary nobility, the distinction between social-climbing pretense and fixed class authenticity was more seriously compromised than ever.[9]

Thus Douglas Bush's ham-handed compliment, that in Dekker's text "even the gull has social significance," is surely disingenuous.[10] The gull could be considered the signifier of social relations in the early seventeenth century and also an object of disdain, a satirized scapegoat, the product of a process of projection and displacement. Dekker's attention to the elasticity of the figure of the gull corresponds to his observations on increased social mobility and on the invasive and disruptive role of money and exchange in a social and political structure still officially dominated by feudal and monarchical forms.[11] But the gull, in turn, further imprints the culture that produces him.

In his *English Epigrammes* (1594), Davies identifies himself as the one who writes about "this new terme" and proposes to "expresse at full, / Who is a true and perfect gull indeede."[12] He represents the gull as a pretentious and ignoble fop who cannot come up with the goods that his attire and outward gestures promise:

> A gull is he, which while he prowdlie weares
> A silver hilted rapier by his side:
> Indures the lyes, and Knockes about the eares,
> Whilst in his sheath, his sleepinge sword doth bide.
> A gull is he which weares good hansome cloathes,
> And standes in presence stroaking up his hayre,
> And filles up his unperfecte speech with othes,

> But speakes not one wise word throughout the yeere:
> But to define a gull in termes precise,
> A gull is he which seemes, and is not wise.
>
> (5–14)

Davies' concluding epigrammatic couplet sums up the gull's qualities as the generic fool or dupe, but the poem makes clearer (if not in "in termes precise") that the name takes in more.

Edward Guilpin's *Skialetheia; or, A Shadow of Truth* (1598) portrays the gull as the man of fashion and an in-your-face resister of Protestant values of thrift and financial restraint.[13] Disregarding filial decency and obligations to patrimony, he spends beyond his means and dissipates the family fortune with a lack of fiscal restraint that recalls the lack of physical restraint in *Grobianus*:

> He is a gull, whose indiscretion
> Cracks his purse strings to be in fashion;
> . . . . . . . . . . . . . .
> He is a gull who runnes himselfe in debt.
> For twelve dayes wonder, hoping so to get;
> He is a gull, whose conscience is a block,
> Not to take interest, but wastes his stock:
> . . . . . . . . . . . . . .
> He is a gull, that for commoditie
> Payes tenne times ten, and sells the same for three:
> . . . . . . . . . . . . . . .
> And to conclude, tho selfe conceitedly,
> Thinks al men gulls, ther's non more gull then he.
>
> (7–8, 11–14, 17–18, 21–22)

As Guilpin's concluding epigram suggests, the gull was a useful and timely figure of ridicule, but the new fashion of mocking the upstart gull included a certain uncomfortable aspect of self-criticism as well, and one that could backfire. As the clumsy figure of worldly ambition, material greed, and social pretense, the inept and self-deluded socially mobile male stood in the midst of the self-interested, ever more intrusive money economy of the early modern world and mingled with those who managed their ambitions with greater discretion and success. Like others who deal with the gull figure, Davies participates in this unwitting cultural critique, composed of divers parts of self-privileging and self-confessional mockery.

Davies's gull functions to comment on early modern subject and sonnet construction. His *Gullinge Sonnets* (c. 1594) exploit and immortalize the gull and offer a metapoetic reflection on the Elizabethan-Renaissance sonnet as an all too easily appropriated vehicle for the socially mobile and the culturally and financially pretentious.[14] Davies begins the dedication to his friend Sir Anthony Cooke, probably on the occasion of Cooke's knighting in 1596, by invoking a muse of mutability to take on the ambitious and pretentious figures who, either as poetasters or as credulous and undiscerning readers, also deal in the currency of sonnets:

> Here my Camelion Muse her selfe doth chaunge
> To divers shapes of gross absurdities,
> And like an Antick mocks with fashion straunge
> The fond admirers of lewde gulleries.
> Your judgement sees with pitty and with scorne
> The bastard Sonnetts of these Rymers bace,
> Which in this whiskinge age are daily borne
> To theire owne shames, and Poetries disgrace.
> Yet some praise those, and some perhappes will praise
> Even these of myne: and therefore thes I send
> To you that pass in Courte your glorious dayes,
> That if some rich, rash gull these Rimes commend,
> Thus you may sett his formall witt to schoole,
> Use your owne grace, and begg him for a foole.

Davies offers Cooke nine of these "gross absurdities" as a pedagogical tool that is also a tool of power. Sonnets circulate at court and at the Inns of Court; these sonnets have a policing and disciplining role: they circulate to expose and mock the "Rymers bace" who write "bastard Sonnetts." Cooke and presumably others who "pass in Courte your glorious dayes" can use them to examine the bad taste of courtiers and poseurs who can't distinguish between bad sonnets and good ones. Written in the voice of a gull, the sonnets gull the unknowing and credulous-because-pretentious reader, expose his ignorance and (dare we say anachronistically?) gullibility. Those who know good sonnets from bad, knowing as well as the purpose of these sonnets (i.e., to mock, to gull, to shame, teach, and test), gain the private pleasure of an initiated elite, silently (or otherwise) ridiculing the "fond admirers of lewde gulleries" who are no connoisseurs of sonnets or good lyric poetry. It is also quite possible that a large part of the payoff is the self-satisfaction, not unlike what the well-schooled and civilized writer and readers of *Grobianus* receive, of one's own competence, the enjoyment of the privileged observer's position as incompetent readers expose their limits.

But there is also a very personal pleasure to consider in the *Gullinge Sonnets*. How much, after all, can one enjoy writing or reading a really bad sonnet? Perhaps sonnet 6 can serve to illustrate how exuberantly bad things can get:

> The sacred Muse that firste made love devine
> Hath made him naked and without attyre;
> But I will cloth him with this penn of myne
> That all the world his fashion shall admyre:
> His hatt of hope, his bande of beautye fine,
> His cloake of crafte, his doblett of desyre;
> Greife for a girdell shall aboute him twyne;
> His pointes of Pride, his Iletholes of yre,
> His hose of hate, his Codpeece of conceite
> His stockings of sterne strife, his shirte of shame;
> His garters of vaine glorie, gaye and slyte,
> His pantofels of passions I will frame;
> Pumpes of presumption shall adorne his feete,
> And Socks of sullennes excedinge sweete.

Typical of the nine sonnets, number 6 belabors the Renaissance poetic convention of the blazon of love (392), copiously inflating and trivializing allegorical personification with inappropriate tropes of amorous and exaggerated affect, and juxtaposing alliteration and incongruity. *Amplificatio ad absurdum*, copious dilation, meets with the humorously deflationary effect of the closing couplet, where the Codpeece of conceite is taken down to the Socks of sullennes.

Others in the sequence play with sonnet conventions in other ways. Number 3 ("What Eagle can behould her sunbrighte eye") overuses *gradatio*, the technique of beginning a line by repeating the last words of the previous line, working to death Petrarchan tropes on Cupid's wounding darts; number 4 ("The hardnes of her harte and truth of myne") produces Petrarchan fire from the lovers' friction, only to have it ludicrously extinguished by the "snuffers of her pride" (13); and number 5 ("Mine Eye, myne eare, my will, my witt, my harte") is composed entirely of correlative verse and can be read both horizontally and vertically.

In its parody of Petrarchan conventions of love and poetic composition, at times tied to a legal lexicon and references to the courtly milieu in which love sonnets, like the subject status of poets, circulate, Davies' sonnet sequence mocks those constituents even as it dissects and recomposes the conditions of subject construction.[15] Thus Davies' project in popularizing and exploiting the name "gull" constitutes an important reflection on the sonnet, the early modern subject, and the social order in which both subjects and sonnets circulate.

Arthur Marotti mentions Davies' sonnets as one of the many responses to the Elizabethan fashion of writing sonnet sequences.[16] Davies' editor comments that his *Gullinge Sonnets* progress to meaninglessness and "succeed brilliantly in saying nothing" (392). I might suggest another, more significant role for them. Although the thought of such connection would undoubtedly surprise Davies, the *Gullinge Sonnets* have a certain unwitting, intertextual debt to *Grobianus* and to conduct literature. Enjoying the work of exposing gullers and the gulled entails occupying and straddling the positions of the knower and the offender. Yet, like *Grobianus* in relation to the conduct-book tradition, the *Gullinge Sonnets* are not simply a reaction to the fashion of Renaissance sonnet sequences in which parody then marks the exhaustion of the form. Rather, they play out of the constitutive elements of the sonnet sequence. If there is one example that can illustrate this aspect it would be sonnet 7, which begins with the speaker mapping out the terrain of the heart as one of the Inns of Court and playing host to a personified Cupid who pledges the lover's wit in a promise of good behavior:

> Into the Midle Temple of my harte
> The wanton Cupid did himselfe admitt,
> And gave for pledge your Eagle-sighted witt
> That he would play noe rude uncivill parte.
>
> (1–4)

In the tediously elaborated conceit, Cupid soon misbehaves—"But at the last he gan to revell it / To break good rules, and orders to perverte" (7–8)—and an aged judge, Reason, passes a sentence—"That love and wit for ever shold departe / Out of the Middle Temple of my harte" (13–14)—which circles back to the first lines of the poem while it both comically takes the sonnet to the point of the speaker's unwitting self-ridicule and takes the ludicrously elaborate image to the point where sense itself is evacuated from the poem. The eviction of love and wit from this sonnet, however, makes it perhaps the quintessential antisonnet or (like R.F.'s subtitle to *The Schoole of Slovenrie*) the Renaissance sonnet, characteristically composed of the love *topos* and techniques of wit, turned inside out through the gull.

In Davies' courtly pedagogy, the sonnet is part of a regime of conduct, even an exercise in grobianism.[17] The mechanism recalls strongly and uncannily the ironic-didactic techniques of *Grobianus*, which, in the the courtly setting of sonnet circulation, resonate with the experience of humanist Latin schools: to appreciate the sonnets, the reader must know the difference between pretense and putatively authentic experience. He also needs to know that there are those "fond admirers of lewde gulleries" who don't know what he knows.[18] Gulled by bad sonnets, the nouveau riche pretender is entrapped by the suave courtier-sonneteer in a scam.

Joel Fineman, in *Shakespeare's Perjured Eye*, argues powerfully for the connection between the sonnet sequence and subject construction. Fineman's thesis is that Shakespeare's metapoetic sense of Renaissance sonnet conventions marks an acutely self-conscious moment in subject construction, resulting in the innovative development of a protopostmodern speaker, quite removed from traditional notions of a sovereign subject: the production, in other words, of "the literary effect of a subject."[19] Fineman sees Shakespeare and Oscar Wilde as "bracketing the epoch of subjectivity" (47). Davies, however, brings another kind of reflection, albeit one that in no way approaches the self-consciousness of Shakespeare, into a historically pointed existence. His is a reflection on the sonnet as a regime of conduct and consumption for poet and reader alike, on the breaking of conventions, in horrifically bad sonnets dedicated to horrifically bad readers, as a way of adding to their authority and legibility while putting that authority and legibililty of sonnet and subject in question. Without finding an equivalent position or an identically sustained literary self-conscious for Davies, Dedekind, or Dekker, it nonetheless seems possible to suggest an important conribution. The gull, like the grobian, is the figure of reversal and inversion, a subject inside out, and the reflections in their grossly absurd works on conduct books, sonnet construction, and reader construction participate in the work of early modern subjectivity effects.

=======

When, in treating Dedekind's *Grobianus*, Dekker takes up Davies' project of popularizing the English gull, he apparently senses that the neo-Latin work has no "currency" for an English audience. In Dekker's hands, a gull emerges, but essential parts of the grobian remain. The first three chapters of the eight-chapter prose work follow Dedekind's poem closely in structure or at least in spirit; then the work departs abruptly from its model and sets out for the London scene to address the topic of what are, clearly, not the most winning, though not viscerally repulsive, of modern English manners and the sociocultural context that nurtures them. Whereas Dedekind's work focuses on the body and sets out to create a self-conscious, self-controlled, and civilly marked male subject in grobianism's project of cultural embodiment, Dekker's treatment of the body as a suit to be published amplifies and expands on the theme of materialism in *Grobianus*.

If Dedekind's speaker recommends, ironically, going naked before the household and assaulting the gaze and modest sensibilities of its female members, and Dekker's speaker in chapter 1 reproduces the advice, he also contrasts a "suit" of naked and Adamic honor to present-day fashions in way that satirizes contemporary values and points toward the exchange mechanism that produces the contrast:

No, no! the first suit of apparel that ever mortal man put on came neither from the mercer's shop nor the merchant's warehouse. Adam's bill would have been taken then sooner than a knight's bond now; yet was he great in nobody's books [i.e., recorded in debt] for satin and velvets. . . . For Adam's holiday hose and doublet were of no better stuff than plain fig-leaves, and Eve's best gown of the same piece; there went but a pair of shears between them. . . . "Fashions" then was counted a disease, and horses died of it. (77–78)

The text presents a view of the economic refashioning of the body—and a rereading of body semiotics—under English conditions in which Adamic "honor" stands above the indebted aristocracy, juxtaposed to the convoluted condition in which being "great" bears the double meaning of being in debt and being in aristocratic dress. These are conditions that also require Dekker to take "fashion" and the body that occupies a place in fashion seriously, inasmuch as it is the body that moves the clothing, makes the turns, exhibits through gestures. Although Dekker repudiates the "Dutch" model and declares his departure from Dedekind after three chapters, in chapter 4, "How a gallant should behave himself in Paul's Walks," the suit goes with him:

Where in view of all you may publish your suit in what manner you affect most, either with the slide of your cloak from the one shoulder (and then you must, as 'twere in anger, suddenly snatch at the middle of the inside if it be taffeta at the least, and so by that means your costly lining is betrayed) or else by the pretty advantage of compliment. But one note by the way do I especially woo you to, the neglect of which makes many of our gallants cheap and ordinary: that by no means you be seen above four turns, but in the fifth make yourself away either in some of the sempsters' shops, the new tobacco office or amongst the booksellers where, if you cannot read, exercise your smoke and enquire who has writ against "this divine weed", etc. For this withdrawing yourself a little will much benefit your suit, which else by too long walking would be stale to the whole spectators. (89)

Unclothed, the Adamic "suit" spites fashion and the mechanisms of extravagant consumption which clothe the urban subject with bills and debts.[20] Once fashionably attired, the body circulates in published and extravagant form as a commodity on parade. Exposure is the goal of the publishing subject, but it must be preserved and sheltered. Withheld, withdrawn, it should perform for select, but not all, spectators; it must not be cheapened by the wrong kind of exposure. In a restaurant, this calculated publishing is taken farther, as the gull is advised to enter the ordinary "scornfully and carelessly" and to "select some friend, having first thrown off your cloak, to walk up and down the room with you. Let him be suited if you can worse by far than yourself: he will be a foil to you, and this will be a means to publish your clothes better than Paul's, a tennis-court or a playhouse" (93). The repertoire of socially signifying trappings and gestures grows to include facial expressions ("laugh in fashion, and have a good sour face to promise quarrelling, you shall be much observed"), boasts of adventures and highly placed acquaintances, foreign languages ("fragments of French or small parcels of Italian to fling about the table" [95]), amorous and courtly suits, epigrams and sonnets, and finally, in an inclusion that comes as close as Dekker can to the explicitly scatological indecency of Dedekind, privy conversations. The gull who holds court in this closet loudly publishes his "natural" suit, boasts of lavish purgative expenditures, and combines that broadcasting with crude insinuations on the current state of circulating print publications:

> You may rise in dinner-time to ask for a close-stool, protesting to all the gentlemen that it costs you a hundred pound a year in physic besides the annual pension which your wife allows her doctor. And if you please you may, as your great French lord doth, invite some special friend of yours from the table to hold discourse with you as you sit in that withdrawing-chamber; from whence being returned again to the bord, you shall sharpen the wits of all the eating gallants about you, and do them great pleasure, to ask what pamphlets or poems a man might think fittest to wipe his tail with. (95–96)

By focusing on display, observation, and calculated effects, Dekker continues the autoscopic concerns of Castiglione, Erasmus, and the authors of the *Grobianus* texts, adding to them a foregrounded economic interest. In treating the clothed and circulating body, Dekker certainly has a "corpus of strategic gestures" in mind, but this repertoire of publishing gestures and fashions belongs to the marketplace and places conduct in that locus of exchange.

For Dedekind and Scheidt, it is the link between the material body and worldly materialism that underpins bad behavior; the aversive conditioning that the text promotes works to cultivate aversion to both kinds. Taking his cue from Dedekind's condemnation of the effects of materialism in the early modern world, the world that accelerates the civilizing process and "discovers" the grobians in its midst, Dekker pays little attention to the bodily reform plank of grobianism's platform but preserves and expands its associated concern with materialism. In satirizing the special "threepence" ordinary, "to which your London usurer, your stale bachelor and your thrifty attorney do resort" (96), he echoes Scheidt's tone of outraged innocence at the intrusion of exchange and opportunistic mobility into social life, of besmirched traditional values at the hands of these peculiarly appetitive social types for whom "every man's eye . . . is upon the other man's trencher to note whether his fellow lurch him or no" (96), and "if they chance to discourse it is of nothing but of statutes, bonds, recognizances, fines, recoveries, audits, rents, subsidies, sureties, enclosures, liveries, indictments, outlawries, feoffments, judgments, commissions, bankrupts, amercements, and of such horrible matter than when a lieutentant dines with his punk in the next room he thinks verily the men are conjuring" (96–97). But despite the speaker's special disdain for this arrangement of commensurable discourse—"I can find nothing at this ordinary worthy the sitting down for"—it has a certain material affinity with "your grand ordinary," where a gallant "shall fare well, enjoy good company, . . . proclaim his good clothes, . . . and, no question, if he be poor he shall now and then light upon some full or other whom he may skelder, after the genteel fashion, of money" (97). Usurers and attorneys may eye each other's trenchers, but "the genteel fashion" is equivalently appetitive and predatory. In the world of gulls distinctions matter less than common denominators.

If the uncontrolled outflow of the grobian body and the orifices-as-exits dominate in the *Grobianus* texts, for Dekker excessive intake and consumption are the controlling figures. Tropes of food and eating abound in the work, as the narrator urges his readers to "con my lessons, and therefore be sure to have most devouring stomachs." He assures them that the rules are not "indigestible" and presents them with an array of scenarios and characters, a veritable "Feast of Fools," a cup that "is full, and so large that I boldly drink a health unto all comers." To Dedekind's grobian pantheon—Silvanus, Bacchus, Rusticity (Ceres)—Dekker adds two more modern deities: Comus, the "clerk of Gluttony's kitchen," of whom the speaker begs, "Let me not rise from table till I am perfect in all the general rules of epicures and cormorants" (75); and the veritable icon of seventeenth-century material and imperialist life, Tobacco, the addictive luxury from overseas exploration and exploitation, which contributes stinking breath to the social arena.[21]

In the neo-Latin *Grobianus* "simple" manners corrupt the "true" noble simplicity of an orderly, civilized world and twist virtue's straight path. Straightening the twisted path is the task that the first English translator of *Grobianus* happily calls negotiating the "tedious laborinth of simplicity." By the time Dekker was writing, however, the comparatively clear, though falsely premised and symptomatically projected, opposition between an uncivil, rustic world and a simple, civil one had disappeared. Dekker's is a place of urban satire, its representation more entertaining and less didactically pointed. The relativism, humorous resignation, and superficial cheeriness often noted as characteristic of Dekker's work are marked here, though the light satirical tone does not prevent him from producing a social representation with serious undertones. Even when Dekker follows his source text and praises the pastoral-rustic simplicity of a lost golden age in chapter 1 ("The old world and the new weighed together: the tailors of those times and these compared; the apparel and diet of our first fathers" [77]; and chapter 3, with its encomium on long hair [86–87]), an almost utopian nostalgia for a space and time before the intrusion of exchange littered the streets and theaters with promenading, self-promoting gulls colors the satire: "Certain I am that when none but the Golden Age went current upon earth it was higher treason to clip hair than to clip money" (87).

Some reasons for Dekker's changes are suggested when we consider briefly the different historical settings and the relationships of the two authors to political and economic power in their time. Dedekind, a third-generation humanist, wrote as a member of the rising German middle class, as a regionally prominent Protestant clergyman engaged, with official approval, in anti-Catholic polemics. Dekker, by contrast, wrote from the social margins; he was a struggling professional writer, with middle-class sympathies perhaps, but negotiating a precarious, usually unpatronized existence under difficult and often hostile conditions. His sojourns in debtors' prison from which his publisher, Philip Henslowe, frequently rescued him and his eventual seven-year stretch there (1612–1619) certainly offered him an education in the school of hard economic lessons.[22]

Denied the enjoyment of the progressively successful life, not a self-identified gull and eager to distance himself from gullishness, Dekker lived at the mercy of publishers and fickle patrons. Such adverse conditions may in part account for the differences in the presentation of his "buffet" of English manners and customs in *The Guls Horne-booke*, which are in distinct contrast to Dedekind's repetitive, circular, often lengthy, and tedious wit. But Dekker also seems to be aware that he deals in words and fashions as commodities, that he is both accessory to and victim of exchange values, that he publishes his own suit for the sake of his very livelihood, his own bodily sustenance. In the often quoted chapter 6, "How a gallant should behave himself in a playhouse," for example, Dekker represents the much mediated conditions of the writer who also publishes his suit:

> The theatre is your poets' Royal Exchange upon which their Muses— that are now turned to merchants—meeting, barter away that light commodity of words for a lighter ware than words—plaudits and the breath of the great beast which, like the threatenings of two cowards, vanish all into air. Players are their factors who put away the stuff and make the best of it they possibly can, as indeed 'tis their part so to do. Your gallant, your courtier and your captain had wont to be the soundest paymasters and I think are still the surest chapmen. And these by means that their heads are well stocked deal upon this comical freight by the gross when your groundling and gallery commoner buys his sport by the penny and like a haggler is glad to utter it again by retailing. (98)

In Dekker's chain of publishing and performing, muses become merchants, players become agents, gallants function as paymasters and accountants, and all produce and circulate "comical freight" for popular applause and consumption or even the opportunity to recycle and retail the play production in taverns. But the mediated life of the playwright is underscored when it comes into competition with gullish behavior as the speaker lengthily advises the pretentious ticket buyer to share the stage with the performance. "Sitting on the stage," "spreading your body on the stage," "being a Justice in examining of plays," the gull who publishes his suit in the theater is in his own social-theatrical element:

> Present not yourself on the stage . . . until the quaking Prologue . . . is ready to give the trumpets their cue that he's upon point to enter. For then it is time, as though you were one of the properties or that you dropped out of the hangings, to creep from behind the arras. . . . For if you should bestow your person upon the vulgar when the belly of the house is but half full, your apparel is quite eaten up, the fashion lost, and the proportion of your body in more danger to be devoured than if it were served up in the Counter amongst the Poultry. (100)

Further advice follows the pattern of *Grobianus*'s specious reasoning and the comically ironic anticipation of observers' approving reactions:

> It shall crown you with rich commendation to laugh aloud in the middest of the most serious and saddest scene of the terriblest tragedy and to let that clapper, your tongue, be tossed so high that all the house may ring of it. . . . all the eyes in the galleries will leave walking after the players and only follow you; the simplest dolt in the house snatches up your name and, when he meets you in the streets or that you fall into his hands in the middle of a watch, . . . he'll cry "He's such a gallant!" . . . you publish your temperance to the world, in that you seem not to resort thither to taste vain pleasures with a hungry appetite but only as a gentleman to spend a foolish hour or two because you can do nothing else. (100)

This ironic advice on the gullish man of fashion's distracting counterperformance lets readers easily imagine the disapproval that will ensue, but it also gives us the nightmare projection of the publishing playwright:

Now, sir, if the writer be a fellow that hath either epigrammed you
or hath had a flirt at your mistress, or hath brought either your feather
or your red beard or your little legs, etc., on the stage you shall
disgrace him worse . . . if in the middle of his play, be it pastoral or
comedy, moral or tragedy, you rise with a screwed and discontented
face from your stool to be gone. No matter whether the scenes be
good or no: the better they are, the worse do you distaste them. And,
being on your feet, sneak not away like a coward but salute all your
gentle acquaintance that are spread either on the rushes or on stools
about you, and draw what troop you can from the stage after. (101)

What may be most nightmarish about Dekker's imaginary scenarios,
however, is the tacit recognition that the man of fashion and the man
of theater are interchangeable in a world in which both publish their
suits and both spread their bodies on an economic stage.

The Guls Horne-booke follows through on the internal logic of Grobianus as metacommentary on conduct literature. In Grobianus the
structuring irony builds in reflexivity. But The Guls Horne-booke takes
this further: it self-reflexively mocks conduct literature as instrument of
commodification and as commodity itself, and links it as well to Dekker's own theatrical practice. In doing so, however, it gestures toward
the context in which it is written and to which it responds. The gull is
the shifting signifier of social difference, the cipher of new economic
conditions (for new awareness of those conditions as well) and the "personification" of the mobile subject in the civilizing process. Dekker
"capitalizes" in locating with the gull a central characteristic of English
society: the crisis of mobility, especially in the Jacobean era, when the
monarch James I actively pandered, marketed nobility, conspired in the
creation of his own gulls and sycophants. Nor would those members of
the traditional hereditary nobility, seeking to exploit commercial possibilities through the practices of regional enclosure, merit exemption
from the title. As the epigraph to this concluding chapter suggests,
"gredye gulles" could be found wherever and whenever wealth was
sought in sixteenth- and seventeenth-century England.

Although Dekker's text and its source are written with amusement
and entertainment in mind, both gulls and grobians have their more
sinister sides as well. When Herford compares Grobianus to Faust as

the divine and demonic, elevated and debased, fine-minded and mean-spirited binary pair, his description reads like an allegory of abjecting civilization and canonization; it resonates as well with the conventional depiction of a "street-wise" Dekker whose literary accomplishments are eclipsed by the brilliance of Shakespearean creation.[23] Yet as we know, Grobianus is not a mere boor, nor is the gull the mere fool or dandy to which many a glossary reduces it. Both *The Guls Horne-booke* and *Grobianus* make pacts with demoniacal magic, fraternize with impossibilities, the metamorphoses of life through forces of money materialism and social mobility of which Marx speaks in *The Economic-Philosophical Manuscripts of 1844*.[24] Dedekind sees in Grobianus's bodily material excess a mortal danger against which civility must maintain its defenses. As for the gull, we might place it with its more prestigious contemporaries, Jonson's *Volpone*, Shakespeare's *Timon of Athens* and even *Coriolanus*, or with Shakespeare's *Henriad*, where in *1 Henry IV* Worcester's rebuff to Henry IV depicts the king as an "ungentle gull" who, devouring and duping, usurps a position in a nest and murderously disposes of (deposes) the legitimate nester (Richard II) rightfully residing there:

> And, being fed by us, you used us so
> As that ungentle gull, the cuckoo's bird,
> Useth the sparrow—did oppress our nest,
> Grew by our feeding to so great a bulk
> That even our love durst not come near your sight
> For fear of swallowing; but with nimble wing
> We were enforced for safety sake to fly
> Out of your sight and raise this present head;
> Whereby we stand opposed by such means
> As you yourself have forged against yourself
> By unkind usage, dangerous countenance,
> And violation of all faith and troth
> Sworn to us in your younger enterprise.
>
> (5.1.59–71)

What Phyllis Rackin has called a clash of the modes of power in the play also testifies to the intrusion of the economic world of mutability and *negotio*, and the early modern author's awareness of it.[25]

Dedekind concludes the neo-Latin *Grobianus* with the excuse that he could continue at infinite length and never exhaust the possibilities of his subject. Having set the psychic mechanisms of bodily self-consciousness and shame in motion, having made his contribution to civilization's regulatory regime—the last chance to instill traditional precepts in what is to him an untraditional manner—he leaves the continuation of his ironic-didactic lessons to his readers. In *The Guls Horne-booke*, on the other hand, Dekker again distances his work from its model and demonstrates a more refined (and thus grobianized) sensibility. He declares his intent "to close up the stomach of this feast . . . lest too many dishes should cast you into a surfeit," and he holds out the promise of more at some future time. Although today it is considered among Dekker's best prose works, *The Guls Horne-booke* was not a popular success in its time. But concluding in this way only points up Dekker's significant distance from the more moralistic stance of his German humanist predecessor. It emphasizes his awareness that, at least under English conditions in the early modern period, with the growing power of money in bourgeois society, in which pretense goes hand in hand with the kind of fraternizing with impossibilities that Marx addressed in his remarks on money, gulls and gulling will continue to increase in form and frequency and, like the grobian, will remain the dirty little secret of conduct and courtesy literature, as well as masculine subject formation.

# Notes

## Author's Note

1. Interested readers should note that Aloys Bömer's edition of the 1549 *Grobianus*, with the chapter "Grobiana" added from the 1554 edition (*Lateinische Litteraturdenkmäler des XV. und XVI. Jahrhunderts* 16 [Berlin: Weidmann, 1903]), and Milchsack's edition of Scheidt are combined and reprinted in Friedrich Dedekind, *Grobianus, de morum simplicitate; Grobianus, von groben sitten und unhöflichen geberden, Deutsche Fassung von Caspar Scheidt*, ed. Barbara Könneker (Darmstadt: Wissenschaftliche Buchgesellschaft, 1979).

2. R.F.'s preface informs readers that "though in the minority of my grammarschollership, I was induced by those whom dutie might not withstand, to unmaske these Roman manners, and put them on an English face." Some part of the work, he adds, was published without his permission or knowledge. As for the accuracy of the translation, let R.F. speak: "Those which mislike the verse in English, let them reade it in Latine" (pp. 2–3).

3. Ernst Rühl sums up R.F.'s reception and influence: "In spite of his success in recreating Dedekind's work in a livelier, more vivid and folksier, certainly often coarser and dumber manner, through his minor changes, additions and editing, the translator got little from the effort. Nothing is known of a later edition. There is no evidence of the translation's influence nor any mention of it." Rühl, *Grobianus in England: Nebst Neudruck der ersten Übersetzung "The Schoole of Slovenrie" (1605) und erster Herausgabe des Schwankes "Grobiana's Nuptials" (c. 1640) aus Ms. 30 Bodl. Oxf. Palaestra* 38 (Berlin: Mayer und Müller, 1904), p. xxv.

4. Like many other students of early modern cultural and textual studies, I have found my thoughts on translation in *Grobianus* much marked by the work of Margaret Ferguson and Thomas Greene on the role of *translatio* for Renaissance treatments of classical texts and models in an age when reception and refunctioning of a past and a cultural heritage so preoccupied humanist writers. See Margaret Ferguson, "The Exile's Defense: Du Bellay's

*La Defence et Illustration de la Langue Françoyse,*" *PMLA* 93 (1978): 279–94; and Thomas M. Greene, *The Light in Troy: Imitation and Discovery in Renaissance Poetry* (New Haven: Yale University Press, 1982). To their work I would add Stephanie Jed's remarkable feminist philology on the "chaste thinking" evidenced in humanist transmissions of the civic myth of Lucretia; her comments on chaste-making, contaminating, and castigating practices of textual transmission are suggestive (and "translatable") for this discussion of grobian texts and grobian thinking. Stephanie Jed, *Chaste Thinking: The Rape of Lucretia and the Birth of Humanism* (Bloomington: Indiana University Press, 1989).

5. Thanks to Jonathan Crewe and e-mail for this typically incisive and succinct definition.

6. Adolf Hauffen, *Caspar Scheidt, Der Lehrer Fischarts: Studien zur Geschichte der grobianischen Litteratur in Deutschland,* Quellen und Forschungen, 66 (Strassburg: Trübner, 1889), 66–77, summarizes the revisions to the 1549 text: "Dedekind takes almost every grobian stroke of his first edition further. Most of these additions, however, no longer constitute satire, for they teach impossibilities, relate examples that are neither plausible nor, in their compulsive inventiveness, comical" (p. 68).

7. While he does not concur with Hauffen's claim that Dedekind changes every part of his text (or with Hauffen's negative evaluation of the changes), Bömer does note that Dedekind finds revision irresistible. See Bömer, Introduction, pp. xxxvi–lxvi.

## Introduction

1. Cf. Ovid, *The Art of Love and Other Poems,* trans. J. H. Mozley, Loeb Classical Library (Cambridge: Harvard University Press, 1962), pp. 46–48:

> Sed tibi nec ferro placeat torquere capillos,
> Nec tua mordaci pumice crura teras.
> Ista iube faciant, quorum Cybeleïa mater
> Concinitur Phrygiis exululata modis.
> Forma viros neglecta decet; Minoida Theseus
> Abstulit, a nulla tempora comptus acu.
> Hippolytum Phaedra, nec erat bene cultus, amavit;
> Cura deae silvis aptus Adonis erat.
> Munditie placeant, fuscentur corpora Campo:
> Sit bene conveniens et sine labe toga:
> Lingula ne ruget, careant rubigine dentes,
> Nec vagus in laxa pes tibi pelle natet:
> Nec male deformet rigidos tonsura capillos:
> Sit coma, sit docta barba resecta manu.
> Et nihil emineant, et sint sine sordibus ungues:
> Inque cava nullus stet tibi nare pilus.
> Nec male odorati sit tristis anhelitus oris:
> Nec laedat naris virque paterque gregis.
> Cetera lascivae faciant, concede, puellae,
> Et siquis male vir quaerit haber virum.
>
> (505–24)

But take no pleasure in curling your hair with the iron, or in scraping your legs with biting pumicestone. Bid them do that by whom mother Cybele is sung in howling chorus of Phrygian measures. An uncared-for beauty is becoming to men; Theseus carried off Minos' daughter, though no clasp decked his temples. Phaedra loved Hippolytus, nor yet was he a dandy; Adonis born to the woodland, was a goddess' care. Let your person please by cleanliness, and be made swarthy by the Campus; let your toga fit, and be spotless; do not let your shoe-strap be wrinkled; let your teeth be clear of rust, and your foot not float about, lost in too large a shoe; nor let your stubborn locks be spoilt by bad cutting; let hair and beard be dressed by a skilled hand. Do not let your nails project, and let them be free of dirt; nor let any hair be in the hollow of your nostrils. Let not the breath of your mouth be sour and unpleasing, nor let the lord and master of the herd offend the nose. All else let wanton women practise, and such men as basely seek to please a man.

2. Jakob Burckhardt, *The Civilization of the Renaissance in Italy*, 2 vols., trans. S. G. C. Middlemore (New York: Harper and Row, 1958). See part 2, "The Development of the Individual," especially comments in chap. 2 on "the increase in the number of complete men during the fifteenth century" (p.147). Ernst Cassirer, Introduction to *The Renaissance Philosophy of Man*, ed. Ernst Cassirer, Paul Oskar Kristeller, and John Herman Randall Jr. (Chicago: University of Chicago Press, 1948), pp. 16–20.
3. Pico della Mirandola, *Oration on the Dignity of Man*, trans. Elizabeth Livermore Forbes, in the *The Renaissance Philosophy of Man*, p. 225.
4. Cf. also Juan Vives, "A Fable about Man" (1518), ibid., pp. 387–93. In Vives's fable, it is the protean and theatrical character of "man" that earns him divine admiration and makes him suitable to socialize with the gods, for whom, like a courtier or a resident humanist at a royal court, he gives a command performance.
5. The most notable and extended critique of "essentialist humanism" is offered in Jonathan Dollimore, *Radical Tragedy: Religion, Ideology, and Power in the Drama of Shakespeare and His Contemporaries* (Chicago: University of Chicago Press, 1984). Jonathan Goldberg, "The Politics of Renaissance Literature: A Review Essay," *ELH* 49 (1982): 514–42, remains a useful map of scholarly positions that challenge traditional approaches; to it should be added important feminist work such as Carol Thomas Neely, "Constructing the Subject: Feminist Practice and the New Renaissance Discourses," *English Literary Renaissance* 18 (1988): 5–18; and Lynda E. Boose, "The Family in Shakespearean Studies; or, Studies in the Family of Shakespeareans; or, The Politics of Politics," *Renaissance Quarterly* 40 (1987): 707–42.
6. Stephen Greenblatt, *Renaissance Self-Fashioning: From More to Shakespeare* (Chicago: University of Chicago Press, 1981). Cf. also Thomas Greene, "The Flexibility of the Self in Renaissance Literature," in *The Disciplines of Criticism: Essays in Literary Theory, Interpretation, and History*, ed. Peter Demetz, Thomas Greene, and Lowry Nelson Jr. (New Haven: Yale University Press, 1968), pp. 241–64. Finally, cf. Gramsci's interesting and historicizing reflection on fashioning:

What does it mean that the Renaissance discovered "man," that it made him the centre of the universe, etc.? Does it mean that before the Renaissance "man" was not the centre of the universe? One could say that the Renaissance created a new culture of civilization, in opposition to the preceding ones or as a development of them, but one must "limit" or "specify" the nature of this culture. Is it really true that before the Renaissance "man" was nothing and then became everything or is it that a process of cultural formation was developed in which man tended to become everything? ... It is because this way of thinking became widespread, became universal leaven. Man was not "discovered," rather a new form of culture was initiated, a new effort to create a new type of man in the dominant classes.

Antonio Gramsci, Q17, para. 1, in *Selections from Cultural Writings*, ed. David Forgacs and Geoffrey Nowell-Smith. (Cambridge: Harvard University Press, 1985), p. 217.

7. The published record of debate is voluminous, and usually revolves around "major figures": Greenblatt and Shakespeare. Representative positions can be seen in Ivo Kamps, ed., *Shakespeare Left and Right* (New York: Routledge, 1991); the special issue on new historicism in *New Literary History* 21 (1991); and Brian Vickers, *Appropriating Shakespeare: Contemporary Critical Quarrels* (New Haven: Yale University Press, 1993). At least two other works should be included with Greenblatt's among the trailblazers: Stephen Orgel, *The Illusion of Power* (Berkeley: University of California Press, 1975), on cultural artifacts, power, and theatrical performance; and Coppélia Kahn, *Man's Estate: Masculine Identity in Shakespeare* (Berkeley: University of California Press, 1981). I mention these not only because both achievements tend to remain in the shadow of Greenblatt's greater visibility but because Kahn's study of constructions of masculinity addresses gender in newly productive ways.

8. The Thomas Hoby translation of Castiglione was first published in England in 1561.

9. Juan Vives, *Ad sapientiam, De tradendis disciplinis* (1531); Sir Thomas Elyot, *The Book Named the Governor* (1531); Roger Ascham, *The Scholemaster* (1570). Vives also wrote dialogues (or colloquies) for pedagogical purposes. Erasmus's pedagogical writings are discussed in Chapter 2.

10. I am aware, of course, of the potential links between this project on indecency and the recent important work in Renaissance queer studies. The clearly more stigmatizing discourse on conduct and the indecent tends to set it apart from more local and also less determinate concerns with same-sex relationships and questions of normative sexual behavior. I will refer to this work and suggest potential comparisons where relevant, but see Jonathan Goldberg, *Sodometries: Renaissance Texts, Modern Sexualities* (Stanford: Stanford University Press, 1992); Goldberg, ed., *Queering the Renaissance* (Durham, N.C.: Duke University Press, 1994); Gregory Bredbeck, *Sodomy and Interpretation* (Ithaca: Cornell University Press, 1991); and Valerie Traub, "Desire and the Difference It Makes," in *The Matter of Difference: Feminist Materialist Criticism of Shakespeare*, ed. Valerie Wayne (Ithaca: Cornell University Press, 1991), pp. 204–27.

11. Among the major contributions of Renaissance scholarship on conduct, many of which I shall have occasion to address, I include Nancy Armstrong and Leonard Tennenhouse, eds., *The Ideology of Conduct: Essays in Literature and the History of Sexuality* (New York: Methuen, 1987); Jonathan Goldberg, *Writing Matter: From the Hands of the English Renaissance* (Stanford: Stanford University Press, 1990); Francis Barker, *The Tremulous Private Body* (New York: Methuen, 1987); Peter Stallybrass and Allon White, *The Politics and Poetics of Transgression* (Ithaca: Cornell University Press, 1986); Frank Whigham, *Ambition and Privilege: The Social Tropes of Elizabethan Courtesy Literature* (Berkeley: University of California Press, 1984); Gail Kern Paster, *The Body Embarrassed: Drama and the Disciplines of Shame in Early Modern England* (Ithaca: Cornell University Press, 1993).

12. Gustav Milchsack gives a list of editions and translations up to his own edition, *Friedrich Dedekinds "Grobianus" verdeutscht von Kaspar Scheidt*, Neudrücke der deutschen Litteraturwerke des XVI. und XVII. Jahrhunderts (Halle: M. Niemeyer, 1882), pp. xxiv–xxviii. Among them is a dauntingly lengthy German version of 1567 (over 6,000 lines) by Wendelin Hellbach which combines the additions of Dedekind's third edition with Scheidt's adapta-

tion. The last translation into English, by the pseudonymous Roger Bull, appeared in 1739 and was dedicated to Swift. There is no record of Swift's acknowledgment.

13. On the context of the German Reformation, standard texts include G. R. Elton, *Reformation Europe, 1517–1559* (New York: Harper Torchbooks, 1966); H. J. Hillerbrand, *The Protestant Reformation* (New York: Harper and Row, 1965); A. G. Dickens, *Reformation and Society in Sixteenth-Century Europe* (London: Thames and Hudson, 1966); Dickens, *Martin Luther and the Reformation* (London: English Universities Press, 1967); Dickens, *The English Reformation* (New York: Schocken, 1964); Steven Ozment, *The Reformation in the Cities: The Appeal of Protestantism to Sixteenth-Century Germany and Switzerland* (New Haven: Yale University Press, 1975); R. Po-Chia Hsia, ed., *The German People and the Reformation* (Ithaca: Cornell University Press, 1988). On the importance of pedagogy for Protestantism, see Gerald Strauss, *Luther's House of Learning: Indoctrination of the Young in the German Reformation* (Baltimore: Johns Hopkins University Press, 1978); Strauss, "The State of Pedagogical Theory c. 1530: What Protestant Reformers Knew about Education," in *Schooling and Society: Studies in the History of Education*, ed. Lawrence Stone (Baltimore: Johns Hopkins University Press, 1976), pp. 69–94; Carmen Luke, *Pedagogy, Printing, and Protestantism: The Discourse on Childhood* (Albany: SUNY Press, 1989); John Morgan, *Godly Learning: Puritan Attitudes towards Reason, Learning, and Education, 1560–1640* (Cambridge: Cambridge University Press, 1986).

14. Details on the life of Dedekind are from *Allgemeine Deutsche Biographie*, (Berlin: Duncker und Humblot, 1877), 5:14. Aloys Börner, Einleitung to *Fridericus Dedekindus, Grobianus*, Lateinische Litteraturdenkmäler des XV. und XVI. Jahrhunderts, 16 (Berlin: Weidmann, 1903), pp. iv–ix, cites letters of introduction to potential noble patrons written in Dedekind's behalf. The two pro-Protestant plays were *Der christliche Ritter* (The Christian knight) and *Bekehrte Papisten* (Converted papists). Dedekind also translated Luther's catechism into Latin.

15. Ernst Rühl, *Grobianus in England: Nebst neudruck der ersten Übersetzung "The School of Slovenrie" (1605) und erster Herausgabe des Schwankes "Grobiana's Nuptials" (c. 1640) aus Ms. 30. Bodl. Oxf. Palaestra XXXVIII* (Berlin: Mayer und Müller, 1904), p. 9. R.F., the English translator, thought that readers should "wonder that a man of such wisdome as my Author, being neyther borne a Roman, nor a 'Naso', should with such confidence of a generall applause publish so elaborate a trifle" (p. 3).

16. On Johann Fischart and his relationship to Scheidt, see Adolf Hauffen, *Caspar Scheidt, der Lehrer Fischarts: Studien zur Geschichte der grobianischen Litteratur in Deutschland*, Quellen und Forschungen, 66 (Strassburg: Trübner, 1889); and Hauffen, *Johann Fischart: Ein Literaturbild aus der Zeit der Gegenreformation*, 2 vols. (Berlin: Walter de Gruyter, 1921).

17. Milchsack, *Friedrich Dedekinds "Grobianus,"* p. vi. Bakhtin links Fischart to the "grobianists": "At its sources German grobianism was related to Rabelais. . . . But the moral and political ideas of the grobianists (Dedekind, Scheidt, Fischart) lent these images [from grotesque realism and folk festival forms] a negative connotation of indecency. . . . Precisely this grobianist point of view (influenced by Scheidt) formed in part the basis of Fischart's free translation of Rabelais," though "Fischart was not a strict grobianist" (pp. 63–64). The issue of Fischart's putative grobianism is further taken up in Dieter Seitz, *Johann Fischarts "Geschichtklitterung": Untersuchungen zur Prosastruktur und zum grobianischen Motivkomplex* (Frankfurt am Main: Athenäum, 1974). Bakhtin's inability to secure a clear distinction between an affirmative Rabelaisian carnivalesque celebration of the grotesque bodily material, on the one hand, and grobianist disciplinary repression of body and the carnivalesque, on the other, is symptomatic of what continues to haunt the reception of his text. In 1981,

for example, Wayne Booth pointed out the aggression toward women in "Rabelais and Feminist Criticism," *Critical Inquiry*, reprinted in *The Company We Keep: An Ethics of Fiction* (Berkeley: University of California Press, 1988). More recently, Thomas Laqueur, *Making Sex: Body and Gender from the Greeks to Freud* (Cambridge: Harvard University Press, 1990), p. 121, discusses Bakhtin's "cheerful acceptance of corporeal openness, dismemberment, and mutilation; his blindness to the brutality of the language directed against women."

18. Karl Goedeke, *Grundrisz zur Geschichte der deutschen Dichtung aus den Quellen*, 2d ed., vol. 2: *Das Reformationszeitalter* (Dresden: L. S. Ehlermann, 1886), para. 158, "Grobianus," pp. 455–57. Goedeke describes Scheidt's work as a reformer, his interest in the *Meistergesang* in Worms, his pamphleteering on moral topics, and the rhymed biblical stories. Hauffen, *Caspar Scheidt*, pp. 42–43, describes Scheidt's importance: "With these writings he tied together the most diverse and more important literary strands of the century; he incorporated the humanist cultural development of his age. . . . Living in the midst of a literarily active area, he could easily be considered the mediator between French literature and the culture of the court of Heidelberg. He quoted and translated French and Italian poetry and, by his own account, spent some time in France."

19. Such qualities caused some problems for early modern scholars of the former German Democratic Republic who relied on a notion of a positive national bourgeois cultural heritage that saw its fulfillment in prose narrative. See, for example, Ingeborg Spriewald, *Grundpositionen der deutschen Literatur im 16. Jahrhundert* (Berlin: Aufbau, 1972); Spriewald, *Vom "Eulenspiegel" zum "Simplicissimus": Zur Genesis des Realismus in den Anfängen der deutschen Prosaerzählung* (Berlin: Akademie, 1974); Robert Weimann, Werner Lenk, Joachim-Jürgen Slomka, eds., *Renaissanceliteratur und frühbürgerliche Revolution: Studien zu den sozial- und ideologiegeschichtlichen Grundlagen europäischer Nationalliteraturen* (Berlin: Aufbau, 1976). Weimann suggests reasons for excluding *Grobianus* from these official cultural historical accounts in *Realismus in der Renaissance* (Berlin: Aufbau, 1977), when he uses a teleological argument in speaking of the "historical transformations of the relationship between literature and society bound up in the Renaissance," claiming that the bourgeois revolution attains a predetermined literary value in realistic prose fiction (p. 5). In this scheme, realism itself is subject to standards of decency and propriety.

20. Christoph Mühlemann remarks: "Grobian sexuality, if we can speak of it, is not directed erotically at an other; rather, it is essentially phallic or anal. Of the greatest priority is the excremental." *Fischarts "Geschichtklitterung" als manieristisches Kunstwerk: Verwirrtes Muster einer verwirrten Welt* (Frankfurt am Main: Peter Lang, 1972), p. 44. Barbara Könneker also notes that the text "holds back in the area of sexuality despite the clear lack of inhibition in corporeality. . . . This restraint is shared not only with *Eulenspiegel* . . . but with all grobian literature of the sixteenth century: it is dirty, unappetizing, fecal/scatological, but only seldom obscene in any specific sense. That is all the more remarkable since obscenity played a increasing role in German literature of the fifteenth century, almost dominating the *Schwank* and in the *Fastnachtspiel*. Dedekind had a rich body of material available." Könneker, Introduction to Friedrich Dedekind, *Grobianus, de morum simplicitate; Grobianus, von groben sitten und unhöflichen Gebärden, deutsche Fassung von Caspar Scheidt*, ed. Könneker (Darmstadt: Wissenschaftliche Buchgesellschaft, 1979), p. xv.

21. Fritz Bergmeier, *Dedekinds Grobianus in England* (Greifswald: Julius Abel, 1903), p. 3.

22. Rühl, *Grobianus in England*, p.14.

23. C. H. Herford, *Studies in the Literary Relations of England and Germany in the Sixteenth Century* (London: Frank Cass, 1886), p. 379: "As a pregnant type of sixteenth-

century Germany its hero stands beside Faustus. What Faustus is to its intellect, Grobianus is to its manners. As Faustus stands for the Titanic aspiration of Humanism which repudiates divine law for the sake of infinite power, so Grobianus represents the meaner presumption which defies every precept of civil decorum and suave usage in the name of appetite and indolence."

24. In addition to Bergmeier, *Dedekinds Grobianus in England*, a published dissertation, Rühl reprints the R.F. translation of the three-book *Grobianus*. See also Hauffen, *Caspar Scheidt*. Cf. also his entry with Carl Diesch, "Grobianische Dichtung," in *Reallexikon der deutschen Literaturgeschichte*, 2d ed., revised, ed. Paul Merker und Wolfgang Stammler (Berlin: De Gruyter, 1958), vol. 4; Herford, *Literary Relations*, pp. 379–80.

25. Cf. John Guillory, "Canon," in *Critical Terms for Literary Study*, ed. Frank Lentricchia and Thomas McLaughlin (Chicago: University of Chicago Press, 1990), pp. 233–49; and Guillory, "Canonical and Non-Canonical: A Critique of the Current Debate," *ELH* 54 (1987): 483–527. In overall agreement with Guillory's position, I have no desire to contribute to the "structural fatigue" of that institution. Cf. Michael Müller, "Künstlerische und materielle Produktion: Zur Autonomie der Kunst in der italienischen Renaissance," in M. Müller, Horst Bredekamp, et al., *Autonomie der Kunst: Zur Genese und Kritik einer bürgerlichen Kategorie* (Frankfurt am Main: Suhrkamp, 1972), pp. 9–87.

26. Rosemary Kegl sees those dynamics at work in George Puttenham's *Arte of English Poesie* (1589), a work that attempts to delineate and adjudicate realms for courtier poets in the midst of conditions of increased mobility and weakened social distinctions both at the court and in the understanding of poetic production. See Kegl, " 'Those Terrible Aproches': Sexuality, Social Mobility, and Resisting the Courtliness of Puttenham's *The Arte of English Poesie*," *English Literary Renaissance* 20 (Spring 1990): 179–208.

27. The relationship between the fate of the body in civility's *régimes du savoir-faire* and the translation of civilizing technologies to the realm of "discovery" is one in which *Grobianus* was already contemporary with the historical events of overseas exploration. The texts of discovery and conduct proliferated in the early modern period. Self-domination and the self-constituting procedures of othering were part and parcel of the prerequisites of discovery and conquest mentality. The bibliography on the literature of discovery is growing vast. A sustained and rigorously examined connection between the literature of conduct and civility and the literature of discovery remains to be made, but it would begin from the crossing point of hegemonizing projection and civil othering, and it would also recognize the inability to enforce or sustain projected oppositions. In this sense, a conceptual work such as Homi K. Bhabha, "The Other Question: Difference, Discrimination, and the Discourse of Colonialism," in Francis Barker et al., eds., *Literature, Politics, and Theory* (London: Methuen, 1989), 148–72, would be essential reading. Cf. also the special issue of *Representations* 33 (Fall 1991); Peter Hulme, *Colonial Encounters: Europe and the Native Caribbean, 1492–1797* (New York: Methuen, 1986); Francesco Guerra, *The Pre-Columbian Mind* (London: Seminar Press, 1971); and Bernadette Bucher, *Icon and Conquest: A Structural Analysis of the Illustrations of De Bry's Great Voyages*, trans. Basia Miller Gulati (Chicago: University of Chicago Press, 1981). Goldberg's remarks on sodomitic discourses in discovery literature also offers insights; see " 'They Are All Sodomites': The New World," in *Sodometries*, pp. 179–249.

28. Elias, *Civilizing Process*, vol 1, *The History of Manners* (New York: Urizen, 1978), pp. 83–84: "If the written heritage of the past is examined primarily from the point of view of what we are accustomed to call 'literary significance,' then most of them have no great value. But if we examine the modes of behavior which in every age a particular society has expected of its members, attempting to condition individuals to them; if we wish to observe

changes in habits, social rules and taboos; then these instructions on correct behavior, though perhaps worthless as literature, take on a special [extraliterary?] significance."

29. After Elias endured exile and politically motivated loss of his intended German-speaking audience, *The Civilizing Process* was republished in two volumes in German in 1968, then translated for U.S. publication in 1978.

30. Daniel Javitch, *Poetry and Courtliness in Renaissance England* (Princeton: Princeton University Press, 1978), hereafter cited parenthetically in the text.

31. Javitch builds on the earlier work of G. K. Hunter, *John Lyly: The Humanist as Courtier* (Cambridge: Harvard University Press, 1962). Hunter finds the political conditions of the Elizabethan court restrictive and sees literary expression as compensatory. Javitch takes issue with that negative view and sees a "marriage" rather than an oppressive relationship between courtly politics and literary production.

32. The quotation from Foucault reads: "Subjugated knowledges are . . . those blocs of historical knowledge which were present but disguised within the body of functionalist and systematising theory and which criticism . . . has been able to reveal. . . . By subjugated knowledges one should understand . . . a whole set of knowledges that have been disqualified as inadequate to their task or insufficiently elaborated: naive knowledges, located low down on the hierarchy, beneath the required level of cognition or scientificity. . . . With what in fact were these buried, subjugated knowledges really concerned? They were concerned with a historical knowledge of struggles. In the specialised areas of erudition as in the disqualified, popular knowledge there lay the memory of hostile encounters which even up to this day have been confined to the margins of knowledge." "Two Lectures," in *Power/Knowledge: Selected Interviews and Other Writings, 1972–1977*, ed. and trans. Colin Gordon (New York: Pantheon, 1980), pp. 82–83.

33. Whigham's *Ambition and Privilege* continues to be frequently cited in Renaissance scholarship. Despite my criticisms of what I read as its schematic limits, it has given me much to think about.

34. Cf. Michael Schoenfelt's interesting application of Whigham's approach to the poetry of George Herbert in *Prayer and Power: George Herbert and Renaissance Courtship* (Chicago: University of Chicago Press, 1991). Schoenfelt reads "Love (III)," for example, as a "comedy of manners" or a conduct text (pp. 199–229).

35. An interesting if unsustained point is made when Whigham deals with the political stakes of courtier specularization: "The typical courtier's dominant Other will be the embodiment of non-existent 'public opinion' readable in the mirroring responses of witnesses but dangerously evanescent. In fact, no one is in charge here" (p. 39).

36. This exclusion remains a problem in other new historicist studies, as feminist and queer scholarship has pointed out. Of the many critiques of Greenblatt's *Self-Fashioning*, see Marguerite Waller, "Academic Tootsie: The Denial of Difference and the Difference It Makes," *Diacritics* (Spring 1987): 2–20; Waller, "The Empire's New Clothes: Refashioning the Renaissance," in *Seeking the Woman in Medieval and Renaissance Literature*, ed. Jane E. Halley et al. (Knoxville: University of Tennessee Press, 1989), pp. 160–83. But even more recent studies seem willing to repeat Whigham's neglect of gender specificity; e.g., Richard Halpern, *The Poetics of Primitive Accumulation: English Renaissance Culture and the Genealogy of Capital* (Ithaca: Cornell University Press, 1991), includes a fine discussion of the political economy of schooling and social mobility which never identifies the masculinizing processes of the Renaissance education practices it so nicely analyzes. See "Breeding Capital: Political Economy and the Renaissance," pp. 61–100. Like Whigham, moreover, Halpern signals his awareness of the blindness in the last pages of his book, when he characterizes his reading of *King Lear* as "a strongly masculinizing one" (pp. 247–48) be-

cause it focuses on male characters and masculine values. Surely, however, reflexively identified analyses of masculinity and attention to male characters are not automatically or necessarily "masculinizing."

37. Michel Foucault, "The Subject and Power," in Hubert L. Dreyfus and Paul Rabinow, *Michel Foucault: Beyond Structuralism and Hermeneutics*, 2d ed. (Chicago: University of Chicago Press, 1983), pp. 208–26, p. 208; hereafter cited parenthetically in the text.

38. The by now familiar debate on subversion and containment in English Renaissance drama or between structuralist-functionalist tendencies of the new historicism, on the one hand, and poststructuralist indeterminacy, on the other, has much to do with readings of Foucault and critiques of power. Cf. Stephen Greenblatt, "Invisible Bullets," in *Shakespearean Negotiations: The Circulation of Social Energy in the Renaissance* (Berkeley: University of California Press, 1988), pp. 21–65; Carolyn Porter, "History and Literature: 'After the New Historicism,' " *New Literary History* 21 (Winter 1990): 253–72; Jonathan Goldberg, "Speculations: *Macbeth* and Source," in *Post-Structuralist Readings of English Poetry*, ed. Richard Machin and Christopher Norris (Cambridge: Cambridge University Press, 1987), pp. 38–58.

39. We can then understand Louis A. Montrose's admirable treatment of "subjectification" as an indeterminate and ongoing perpetual negotiation in which the making of the subject means the subject of as well as the one who is subject to. Some agency is visible here, some potential for resistance and subversion are preserved. Cf. Montrose's use of Foucault in "Renaissance Literary Study and the Subject of History," *ELR* 16 (Winter 1986): 5–12.

40. Cf. Michel Foucault, *Discipline and Punish: The Birth of the Prison*, trans. Alan Sheridan (New York: Vintage, 1979). Foucault would undoubtedly have found Scheidt's sixteenth-century neologism *Zuchthaus*—which initially meant "school" but in the eighteenth century became "prison"—pleasingly anticipatory. Cf. Scheidt's pamphlet, *Das fröliche heimfart* (Worms, 1552):

> darnach in ein zuchthausz gethan,
> da sie kein stund solt müssig gan,
> da sie in zweyer jaren frist
> schreiben und lesen hatt gewist.

A rough translation would go something like this: "and afterwards into the schoolhouse they'll go, and they won't be idle for any time, so that in two years they learn writing and reading."

41. Pierre Bourdieu, "Structures and the Habitus," in *Outline of a Theory of Practice*, trans. Richard Nice (Cambridge: Cambridge University Press, 1977), pp. 72–95, p. 89; hereafter cited parenthetically in the text.

42. "Sex/gender system" is the key critical term introduced by Gayle Rubin in "The Traffic in Women: Notes on the 'Political Economy' of Sex," in *Toward an Anthropology of Women*, ed. Rayna R. Reiter (New York: Monthly Review Press, 1975), pp. 157–210.

43. Bourdieu's use of the Latin *habitus* is as old as Cicero and Aquinas but seems derived from Marcel Mauss, "Techniques of the Body," *Economy and Society* 2 (1973): 73.

44. Cf. the important critiques of Lee Patterson, "On the Margin: Postmodernism, Ironic History, and Medieval Studies," *Speculum* 65 (1990): 87–108; and David Aers, "Rewriting the Middle Ages: Some Suggestions," *Journal of Medieval and Renaissance Studies* 18 (1988): 221–40; Aers, *Community, Gender, and Individual Identity: English Writing, 1360–1430* (London: Routledge, 1988).

45. *The Body Embarrassed: Drama and the Disciplines of Shame in Early Modern England* (Ithaca: Cornell University Press, 1993). For example, Paster summarizes the development of humoral discourses: "The suppression and silencing of the body's functions—first from view, then from mention—is also a gradual suppression and silencing of the evidence of its humorality, agential interiority, and physiological porousness" (p. 16). The interesting illustration of such suppression and silencing is the material of "Leaky Vessels: The Incontinent Women of City Comedy" (pp. 23–63), which shows how early modern gynecological and urological treatises reinforce cultural constructions of gender which work to privilege men and restrain women from public roles. Again, whereas Paster remains concerned with shame and shaming disciplines, I would look to anxiety.

46. See Jacques Lacan, "The Mirror Stage," in *Ecrits: A Selection*, ed. and trans. Alan Sheridan (New York: Norton, 1977), pp. 1–7. The very well known description of the six-month-old infant is as follows: "Unable as yet to walk, or even to stand up, and held tightly as he is by some support, human or artificial (what, in France, we call a '*trotte-bébé*'), he nevertheless overcomes, in a flutter of jubilant activity, the obstructions of his support and, fixing his attitude in a slightly leaning-forward position, in order to hold it in his gaze, brings back an instantaneous aspect of the image. . . . This jubilant assumption of his specular image by the child at the *infans* stage, still sunk in his motor incapacity and nursling dependence, would seem to exhibit in an exemplary situation the symbolic matrix in which the *I* is precipitated in a primordial form, before it is objectified in the dialectic of identification with the other, and before language restores to it, in the universal, its function as subject" (pp. 1–2).

47. Ibid., p. 4.

48. Cf. Paster's note and approving reference to the psychoanalytic work of Silvan S. Tompkins, who describes "shame as one of several innate affects working to stabilize the infant's organization of and response to stimuli." That infants have shame as a hard-wired affect is the consequence of a symmetrical structure that at the very least stands in a relationship of opposition to Elias's more historicizing approach. For Tompkins, "a pluralism of desires must be matched by a pluralism of shame" (quoted by Paster, p. 18), and he locates shame in any place where desire is thwarted. The easy movement from frustration to shame seems to evidence slippage; certainly it elides a mediating and culturally specific moment of socialization.

49. Julia Kristeva, "Ellipsis on Dread and Specular Seduction," in *Narrative, Apparatus, Ideology: A Film Theory Reader*, ed. Philip Rosen (New York: Columbia University Press, 1986), p. 236, hereafter cited parenthetically in text. The translator of Kristeva's essay finds no satisfactory English equivalent for *frayage* (in Freud, *Bahnung*) and ventures "conditioning or imprinting" (p. 242).

50. In the order of specularity (the glance) the orderly (and, let us opportunistically add, highly civil) example for Kristeva is the male scientist-gynecologist who, with the (all-too-appropriately named) instrument of the speculum, examines the female patient's vagina and sees what she does not normally see of herself: "My dreamed body, sets forth to them only that which the physician's speculum reveals: a de-eroticized surface which I concede to him in the wink of an eye by which I make him believe he is not an other, but has only to look at me as I myself would do if I were he—complicity of the barrier operating on the hither side of the retina, snare which captures him rather than me." Important, too, is that unlike the Redcrosse Knight in book 1 of Spenser's *Faerie Queene*, he knows what he sees (there is no Error here); in naming it, he makes it manageable for knowledge, assimilating the woman's body to, making it subject to a *régime du savoir* that needs docile bodies, transparent, nameable, unspeaking.

51. The debt here may be as much to Georges Bataille as to Lacan. Cf. Bataille, *Literature and Evil*, trans. Alistair Hamilton (New York: Marion Boyars, 1985); and Bataille, "L'abjection et les formes misérables," in *Essais de sociologie, Oeuvres complètes* (Paris: Gallimard, 1970). See also the discussion of Bataille's influence on Kristeva in John Lechte, *Julia Kristeva* (New York: Routledge, 1990), pp. 73–75.

52. In the "discovery" sequence of James Cameron's *Aliens*, when Sigourney Weaver backs into the "incubator" chamber, she sees the monstrous eggs, about to hatch and work their parasitic, phallic, and impregnating devilry. As she turns to see what she has just entered, she sets eyes on the mother-monster and takes in the scene, bonded with the horrified cinematic audience. Both ask, in that suturing moment, What is this? and it is the space/the moment of not knowing, of not having a name (not even, "special effect") for it, of confronting something unprecedented and yet unnamed which horrifies. In the moment when What is this? has no answer, when the effort to construct boundaries fails and panic sets in, dread, in all its seductive power, arises. The viewer of the horror is pushed back, regressively, behind symbolic boundaries, which he or she then desperately works to reconstruct. "Special effect" marks the reentry of the symbolic. "Monster" would be another way to reestablish symbolic signification. "Biological motherhood as monstrosity," yet another. Even when, as in *Aliens*, "specular fascination captures terror and restores it to the symbolic order" (241), the elements of terror/horror (*frayage*, lektonic traces, dread as encounter) remain as the memory of something that was once not controllable, not containable. The symbolic may construct the socially defined mother, may delimit the maternal, the presymbolic, prelinguistic. But it doesn't touch horror, the unnameable dread, the abject.

53. It would be possible to see in this discussion important critical references to Lacan's mirror stage, here an inversion of the ideal into a counterideal. Instead of seeing the best, against which the actual body of the one gazing in the mirror cannot possibly compare, we encounter a catastrophe, the worst imaginable version, from which we turn, averting our glance.

54. See Barbara Correll, "Notes on the Primary Text: Woman's Body and Representation in *Pumping Iron II: The Women* and 'Breast Giver,'" *Genre* 23 (Fall 1989): 287–308, for a discussion of the body as primary text.

55. In saying this, despite my obvious admiration for the new historicism, I distinguish my work from many of the studies associated with it. Cf. James Holstun, "Ranting at the New Historicism," *ELR* 19 (Spring 1989): 189–225, for another criticism of the high canonical skewing at work in new historicist practices. Montrose, for example, calls for "noncanonical readings of canonical texts" in "Renaissance Literary Study," p. 8; but without disrupting the category of the canon, and in preserving it through inversion, it is hard to imagine what the critical benefits might turn out to be. It may be that by now some of the newer questions have themselves become technologies of reading, that is, in some way canonical and canonicizing practices.

## 1. Reading *Grobianus*

1. Max Horkheimer and T. W. Adorno, "The Importance of the Body," "Notes" from *Dialectic of the Enlightenment*, trans. John Cumming (New York: Herder and Herder, 1972), p. 231.

2. Sigmund Freud, *Civilization and Its Discontents*, ed. and trans. James Strachey (New York: Norton, 1961), pp. 100–101, speculates on "the analogy between the process of civilization and the path of individual development," between a "cultural superego" in an "interlocking" relationship to the superego of the individual. This analogy has also been

developed notably by Herbert Marcuse in *Eros and Civilization: A Philosophical Inquiry into Freud* (New York: Vintage, 1962), on the one hand, and by Gilles Deleuze and Félix Guattari in *Anti-Oedipus: Capitalism and Schizophrenia*, trans. Robert Hurley et al. (Minneapolis: University of Minnesota Press, 1983). But cf. also Lacan's concluding remarks in "The Mirror Stage," in *Ecrits: A Selection*, ed. and trans. Alan Sheridan (New York: Norton, 1977), p. 7: "The sufferings of neurosis and psychosis are for us a schooling in the passions of the soul, just as the beam of the psychoanalytic scales, when we calculate the tilt of its threat to entire communities, provides us with an indication of the deadening of the passions in society. At this junction of nature, so persistently examined by modern anthropology, psychoanalysis alone recognizes this knot of imaginary servitude that love must always undo again, or sever."

3. Among the works are Michel Foucault, *The History of Sexuality*, vol. 1: *An Introduction*, trans. Robert Hurley (New York: Pantheon, 1978), Foucault, *Discipline and Punish: The Birth of the Prison*, trans. Alan Sheridan (New York: Vintage, 1979); Lawrence Stone, *The Family, Sex, and Marriage in England, 1500–1800* (New York: Harper and Row, 1977); Jean Delumeau, *La peur en occident (XIVe–XVIIIe siècles): Une cité assiégée* (Paris: Fayard, 1978); R. Po-Chia Hsia, *Social Discipline in the Reformation: Central Europe, 1550–1750* (London: Routledge, 1989).

4. Cf. Barbara Könneker, Introduction to Friedrich Dedekind, *Grobianus, de morum simplicitate; Grobianus, von groben sitten und unhöflichen geberden, Deutsche Fassung von Caspar Scheidt*, ed. Könneker (Darmstadt: Wissenschaftliche Buchgesellschaft, 1979), p. xviii, where she speaks of the grobian's "egotism and self-interest."

5. Elias, *Civilizing Process*, 1: 79.

6. Foucault's term in *The History of Sexuality* for the notion that the Victorians repressed sexuality when instead there are historical signs of increased discursive activity on sexuality, the circulation of a discourse on sexuality.

7. "The whole German *grobianisch* (boorish literature) in which, spiced with mockery and scorn, a very serious need for a 'softening of manners' finds expression, shows unambiguously and more purely than any of the corresponding traditions of other nationalities the specifically middle-class character of its writers [bourgeois intellectuals] . . . a relatively constricted, regional, and penurious intellectual stratum" (Elias, *Civilizing Process* 1: 75).

8. I mean "genealogy" in its Nietzschean and Foucauldian sense, i.e., a historicizing that thwarts the myths of origins and progressive evolution and inscribes every historical account with a "countermemory" that produces multiple accounts and causes. See also Carla Freccero, *Father Figures: Genealogy and Narrative Structure in Rabelais* (Ithaca: Cornell University Press, 1991), pp. 1–2, in which she defines genealogy as the representation of "desire to locate and fix . . . one's lineage," bearing "a certain anxiety about legitimation."

9. Barbara Zaehle, *Knigges Umgang mit den Menschen und seine Vorläufer: Ein Beitrag zur Geschichte der Gesellschaftsethik*, Beiträge zur neueren Literaturgeschichte, 22 (Heidelberg: Carl Winter, 1933), is the text that establishes the phrase and the trajectory. Cf. the chapter "Das grobianische Zeitalter."

10. Adolf Hauffen, *Caspar Scheidt, der Lehrer Fischarts: Studien zur Geschichte der grobianischen Litteratur in Deutschland* (Strassburg: Trübner, 1889), pp. 65–66, 67; Gustav Milchsack, ed., *Friedrich Dedekinds Grobianus verdeutscht von Kaspar Scheidt*, Neudrücke der deutschen Litteraturwerke des XVI. und XVII. Jahrhunderts (Halle: M. Niemeyer, 1882), p. vi: "It was not until 1739, when humanity had long passed from the grobian age to a refined epoch, that it ended nearly two centuries of fame with a second English translation."

11. C. H. Lawrence, *Medieval Monasticism: Forms of Religious Life in Western Europe*

*in the Middle Ages*, 2d ed. (London: Longman, 1989), offers an excellent overview of the
history and evolving content of the Benedictine Rule. He underscores its three main elements: absolute obedience to superiors, organization of the day around prayer and worship,
and amelioration of discipline through stress on mutual love. In vol. 1 of *Five Centuries of
Religion: St. Bernard, His Predecessors and Successors, 1000–1200 A.D.* (Cambridge: Cambridge University Press, 1923), G. G. Coulton surveys the evolution of the Benedictine
Rule. Cf. also Lewis Mumford, *Technics and Civilization* (New York: Harbinger, 1963);
Jacques Le Goff, *Time, Work, and Culture in the Middle Ages* (Chicago: University of Chicago Press, 1980). Mumford sees monastic time regulation as anticipatory of industrial ef-
ficiency (pp. 12–23). Elias, *Civilizing Process* 1: 60, lists Hugh of St. Victor, *De institutione
novitiarum*, Petrus Alphonsi, *Disciplina clericalis*, and Johannes von Garland, *Morale sco-
larium*, as representative works of medieval monastic precepts.

    12. Among the many examples from medieval romances, Wolfram von Eschenbach's
*Parzival* and the *Gawain*-poet's *Sir Gawain and the Green Knight* would be examples. We
need only think of the epic, beginning with *The Odyssey*, to find examples both positive
and negative of hospitality or food preparation and consumption.

    13. Elias's model of civilization is speculative and suggestive: "A model is evolved to show
the possible connections between the long-term change in human personality structures
toward a consolidation and differentiation of affect controls, and the long-term change in
the social structure toward a higher level of differentiation and integration—for example,
toward a differentiation and prolongation of the chains of interdependence and a consolidation of 'state controls'" (*Civilizing Process* 1: 223).

    14. See Stephen Greenblatt, *Renaissance Self-Fashioning: From More to Shakespeare*
(Chicago: University of Chicago Press, 1981), pp. 4–5, where he discusses "anthropological
criticism" and "a poetics of culture" as recognizing "that the facts of life are less artless
than they look, that both particular cultures and the observers of these cultures are inevitably
drawn to a metaphorical grasp of reality.... I remain concerned, to be sure, with the implications of artistic representation as a distinct human activity ... but the way to explore
these implications lies neither in denying any relation between the play and social life nor
in affirming that the latter is the 'thing itself,' free from interpretation."

    15. On the threat of the feminine and effeminacy, he notes: "And I would like our
courtier to have the same aspect. I don't want him to appear soft and feminine as so many
try to do, when they not only curl their hair and pluck their eyebrows but also preen
themselves like the most wanton and dissolute creatures imaginable. Indeed, they appear
so effeminate and languid in the way they walk, or stand, or do anything at all, that their
limbs look as if they are about to fall apart; and they pronounce their words in such a
drawling way that it seems as if they are about to expire on the spot. And the more they
find themselves in the company of men of rank, the more they carry on like that. Since
Nature has not in fact made them the ladies they want to seem and be, they should be
treated not as honest women but as common whores and be driven out from all gentlemanly
society, let alone the Courts of great lords" (1.19.61).

    16. Cf. the overview on mercenaries in Michael Mallett, "The Condottiere," in *Renais-
sance Characters*, ed. Eugenio Garin, trans. Lydia Cochrane (Chicago: University of Chicago
Press, 1991), pp. 22–45; and the following: Piero Pieri, *Il Rinascimento e la crise militare
italiana*, 2d ed. (Turin: G. Einaudi, 1970); Michael E. Mallett, *Mercenaries and Their Masters: Warfare in Renaissance Italy* (London: Bodley Head; Totowa, N.J.: Rowan and Littlefield, 1974); Franco Cardini, *Quell'antica festa crudele: Guerra e cultura della guerra dall'età
feudale alla grande rivoluzione* (Florence: Sansoni, 1982); John R. Hale, *War and Society in*

*Renaissance Europe, 1450–1620* (London: St. Martin's, 1985); Gilbert John Millar, *Tudor Mercenaries and Auxiliaries, 1485–1547* (Totowa, N.J.: Rowan and Littlefield, 1974).

17. See "The Courtization of Warriors," in Elias, *Civilizing Process*, vol. 2: *Power and Civility* (New York: Pantheon, 1982), pp. 258–69.

18. See Jakob Burckhardt on the *condottieri* in his "War as a Work of Art" chapter, *The Civilization of the Renaissance in Italy*, 2 vols., trans. S. G. C. Middlemore (New York: Harper and Row, 1958). On the *condottieri* as members of the Italian courts, some of whom produced lyric poetry, see Mallett, *Mercenaries and Their Masters*, pp. 220–24; see also his bibliographical essay, "The Condottiere," pp. 22–45. Garrett Mattingly, *Renaissance Diplomacy* (London: Butler and Tanner, 1963), discusses the historical development of diplomatic functions.

19. The narrator relates the unfortunate biography of the duke of Urbino, "deformed and ruined while still of tender age" and thwarted in his projects: "Everything he set his hand to, whether in arms or anything else, great or small, always ended unhappily" (1.3.42–43). The duke occupies the position of observer of the company he hosts, but he "always retired to his bedroom soon after supper, because of his infirmity" (1.4.42). Thus, he leaves the evening conversation in the hands of the duchess. Her sex martyrdom is awkwardly placed on a level with the commonplace examples of virtuous women-who-die-well-and-chastely in book 3, when Cesare Gonzaga praises her as one "who has lived with her husband for fifteen years like a widow, and who has not only steadfastly refused ever to tell this to anyone in the world but, after being urged by her own people to escape from this widowhood, chose rather to suffer exile, poverty and all kinds of hardship" (3.49.253). The duchess courteously interrupts and asks Gonzaga to "speak about something else and say no more about this subject," thus adding it to the other unmentionables mentioned in the text.

20. This feminization was first suggested by Joan Kelly, "Did Women Have a Renaissance?" in *Women, History, and Theory: The Essays of Joan Kelly* (Chicago: University of Chicago Press, 1986), pp. 44–45.

21. Cf. Joan Riviere, "Womanliness as a Masquerade," in *Formations of Fantasy*, ed. Victor Burgin, James Donald, and Cora Kaplan (London: Routledge, 1988), 35–44; cf. also Stephen Heath, "Joan Riviere and the Masquerade," in *Formations of Fantasy*, pp. 45–61. Frank Whigham writes on *cosmesis* in chap. 4 of *Ambition and Privilege: The Social Tropes of Elizabethan Courtesy Literature* (Berkeley: University of California Press, 1984).

22. Cf. Phyllis Rackin's discussion of the history plays and masculinity in *Stages of History: Shakespeare's English Chronicles* (Ithaca: Cornell University Press, 1990), especially "Patriarchal History and Female Subversion," pp. 146–200.

23. "All the same, we do not wish the courtier to make a show of being so fierce that he is always blustering and bragging, declaring that he is married to his cuirass, and glowering with the haughty looks that we know only too well in Berto. To these may very fairly be said what a worthy lady once remarked . . . to a certain man . . . who . . . would not listen to music or take part in the many other entertainments offered, protesting all the while that such frivolities were not his business. And when at length the lady asked what his business was, he answered with a scowl: 'Fighting.' The lady responded, 'I should think that since you aren't at war at the moment and you are not engaged in fighting, it would be a good thing if you were to have yourself well greased and stowed away in a cupboard with all your fighting equipment, so that you avoid getting rustier than you are already' " (p. 58).

24. *The First Part of Henry the Fourth* in *The Riverside Shakespeare*, ed. G. Blakemore Evans (Boston: Houghton Mifflin, 1974), pp. 847–85. What makes the caricature so humorous is that Hal's mocking version to some extent actually paraphrases Hotspur's previous scene with the Lady Kate:

Love? I love thee not;
I care not for thee, Kate. This is no world
To play with mammets and to tilt with lips.
We must have bloody noses and cracked crowns,
And pass them current too. Gods me, my horse!
                                                        (2.3.86-90)

25. Elias, *Civilizing Process* 1, stresses the importance of the Crusades, which began in 1096 and continued into the thirteenth century. Immanuel Wallerstein calls the period of the Crusades from about 1150 to 1300 "the expansion state of feudalism" in *The Modern World System: Capitalist Agriculture and the Origins of the European World-Economy in the Sixteenth Century* (New York: Academic Press, 1974), p. 37. Both Wallerstein and Marc Bloch consider the Middle Ages an interruption (albeit quite a lengthy one) of the Roman system of state administration and money economy. They speak not of the "rise" of a money economy but of its revival. The same might be argued for Latin *civilitas*.

26. On sumptuary laws, see Kent R. Greenfield, "Sumptuary Law in Nürnberg," *Johns Hopkins University Studies in History and Political Science* 36 (1918): 102-25; Frances Elizabeth Baldwin, "Sumptuary Legislation and Personal Regulation in England," *Johns Hopkins University Studies in History and Political Science* 44 (1925): 120-91; Lisa Jardine, *Still Harping on Daughters: Women and Drama in the Age of Shakespeare*, 2d ed. (New York: Columbia University Press, 1989), esp. chap. 5, " 'Make thy doublet of changeable taffeta': Dress Codes, Sumptuary Law and 'Natural' Order," pp. 141-68. See also the many sumptuary documents in R. H. Tawney and Eileen Power, *Tudor Economic Documents: Being Select Documents Illustrating the Economic and Social History of Tudor England*, 3 vols. (London: Longman, 1924).

27. Mary Thomas Crane gives the third century as the date of composition. See *Framing Authority: Sayings, Self, and Society in Sixteenth-Century England* (Princeton: Princeton University Press, 1993), p. 232 n. 40. See also the discussion of the work and its German influence in Friedrich Zarncke, *Der deutsche Cato: Geschichte der deutschen Übersetzungen der im Mittelalter unter dem Namen Cato bekannten Distichen bis zur Verdrängung derselben durch die Übersetzung Sebastian Brants am Ende des 15. Jahrhunderts* (Leipzig: Georg Wigand, 1852), pp. 3-7. Caxton translated and published the work in 1477.

28. Elias, *Civilizing Process* 1: 61.

29. Cf. Marc Bloch on the "economic revolution of the second feudal age" (from about the end of the eleventh century), in *Feudal Society*, 2 vols., trans. L. A. Manyon (Chicago: University of Chicago Press, 1964), p. 60; also R. S. Lopez, *The Commercial Revolution of the Middle Ages* (Englewood Cliffs, N.J.: Prentice-Hall, 1971). Lester K. Little, in *Religious Poverty and the Profit Economy in Medieval Europe* (Ithaca: Cornell University Press, 1978), discusses the effects of an emerging profit economy on the clergy; see esp. part 1: "The Spiritual Crisis of Medieval Urban Culture," pp. 1-58. In earlier scholarship, G. G. Coulton documents and discusses "monastic capitalism" in *Five Centuries of Religion*, vol. 2: *The Friars and the Dead Weight of Tradition, 1200-1400 A.D.* (Cambridge: Cambridge University Press, 1927), pp. 18-33.

30. Paul Merker, "Die Tischzuchtliteratur des 12. bis 16. Jahrhunderts," *Mitteilungen der deutschen Gesellschaft zur Erforschung väterlichen Sprache und Altertümer in Leipzig* 11 (1913): 1-52. See also the two collections edited by Perry Thornton, *Höfische Tischzuchten* and *Grobianische Tischzuchten*, vols. 4 and 5 of *Texte des Späten Mittelalters* (Berlin: Erich Schmidt, 1957).

31. For Merker, at least, the *Tischzucht* is still a literary genre, albeit of negligible aes-

thetic value; for others, it is clearly subliterary. Yet it is that generic-aesthetic separation rather than decline of aesthetic value which is historically significant here: such generic distinctions would be anachronistic for the sixteenth century.

32. Elias, in *Civilizing Process*, stresses the growth of interdependence, which requires observation and foresight, as well as practices of self-restraint and a historically conditioned "psychologization" of the subject.

33. Again, Elias, *Civilizing Process* 1: 80, reads "the new power relationships" as signifying increased interdependence, rather than the competition that I see.

34. For example, the advice to wait before eating—containing the precepts to wash hands, to remember the poor in prayers, to let the food cool—distinguishes the nobility in European courtly etiquettes. In all classes, food was eaten mainly with the hands, but waiting and washing marked the difference between the hardships of the battlefield and the leisure of peacetime. One who did not wait or wash was a peasant or an animal; those who did demonstrated that they placed a ritual of status above simple physical need or that they knew the difference between themselves, as those who wash and wait to eat, and the poor, as those with far less, even nothing, to wait for. While such precepts involve emotional restraint (and contain as well the contradictions of an ideology), acted out in unison at the table they constituted a small drama of cultural hegemony. In that respect they are certainly distinct from what would later be made of them in the derivative practices of bourgeois culture.

35. "By these terms certain leading groups in the secular upper stratum, which does not mean the knightly class as a whole, but primarily the courtly circles around the great feudal lords, designated what distinguished them in their own eyes, namely the specific code of behavior that was first formed at the great feudal courts, then spread to rather broader strata" (Elias, *Civilizing Process* 1: 62–63). It should, however, be stressed that this is no trickle-down theory of etiquette; rather, the broader strata sought to appropriate the code of behavior, with the interesting results that we are following.

36. Thorstein Veblen, *The Theory of the Leisure Class* (1899; rpt. Boston: Houghton Mifflin, 1973), p. 13. Claude Lévi-Strauss, *The Origin of Table Manners*, vol. 3 of *Introduction to a Science of Mythology*, trans. John and Doreen Weightman (New York: Harper and Row, 1978), p. 505, stresses the importance of binary structures (order/disorder, regulated/unregulated, etc.) in table manners: "Betweeen the social person and his or her own body, in which nature is unleashed, between the body and the biological and physical universe, table or toilet utensils fulfill an effective function as insulators or mediators. Their intervening presence prevents the occurrence of the threatened catastrophe." The nature/culture, inside/outside distinctions are familiar to readers of Lévi-Strauss's structuralist anthropology, as well as to readers of Mary Douglas, *Purity and Danger: An Analysis of the Concepts of Pollution and Taboo* (1966; rpt. London: Ark, 1984). Cf. also Georges Vigarello, *Concepts of Cleanliness: Changing Attitudes in France since the Middle Ages* (Cambridge: Cambridge University Press, 1988). What I believe this discussion of conduct literature will show, in its focus on indecency, is that ultimately the distinctions don't work.

37. The medieval examples come from Elias, *Civilizing Process* 1: 63. As Elias has remarked, compared to the humanist and bourgeois etiquettes and from the socialized (that is, the "civilized") perspective of modern observers, the courtly precepts of the twelfth and thirteenth centuries are marked by "simplicity" and "naivete": "There are, as in all societies where the emotions are expressed more violently and directly, fewer psychological nuances and complexities in the general stock of ideas. There are friend and foe, desire and aversion, good and bad people." The less detailed, more relaxed standard makes staunch defenders of chivalric culture uncomfortable. Merker notes: "Many of these rules intended for courtly

society, which have clearly respectable aspects, still suggest that in real life the much renowned chivalric training/education often enough gave way to situations that reflected the
naive crudeness of earlier times, and that may have degenerated to the roughness of peasant
manners" ("Die Tischzuchtliteratur," p. 23).

38. Cf. Robert Weimann, "Discourse, Ideology, and the Crisis of Authority in Post-
Reformation England," *REAL: The Yearbook of Research in English and American Studies*
(1987): 109–40.

39. Jean-Christophe Agnew, *Worlds Apart: The Market and the Theater in Anglo-
American Thought, 1550–1750* (Cambridge: Cambridge University Press, 1986), p. 9, argues
that early modern Britons were "feeling their way round a problematic of exchange . . . ,
[questioning] the nature of social identity." Agnew does not consider gender identity, however, in his admirable probing of fluid and market-mediated human identity.

40. Veblen, *Theory of the Leisure Class*, p. 23.

41. *The Malleus Maleficarum of Heinrich Kramer and James Sprenger*, trans. Montague
Summers (New York: Dover, 1971). Cf. also Katherine Rogers, *The Troublesome Helpmate:
A History of Misogyny in Literature* (Seattle: Washington Paperbacks, 1966).

42. H. G. Koenigsberger and George Mosse, *Europe in the Sixteenth Century* (London:
Longmans, Green, 1968), p. 68. See also the discussion of hostility to peasants in Erhard
Jöst, *Bauernfeindlichkeit: Die Historien des Ritters Neidhart Fuchs*, Göppinger Arbeiten zur
Germanistik, 192 (Göppingen: Alfred Kümmerle, 1976), pp. 272–78.

43. Merker, "Die Tischzuchtliteratur," p. 19: "Materially blessed and ambitious, the peasantry . . . tries to match the aristocracy and, at least externally, appropriate the allure of
prominent lords."

44. Werner der Gärtner, *Meier Helmbrecht: Versnovelle aus der Zeit des niedergehenden
Rittertums* (Stuttgart: Philipp Reclam, 1971).

45. Ibid. Dieter Seitz interprets the treatment of the son as criminalizing peasants, whom
late medieval texts represent as aggressive and living without controls over their instincts.
See the discussion in Seitz, *Johann Fischarts "Geschichtklitterung": Untersuchungen zur
Prosastruktur und zum grobianischen Motivkomplex* (Frankfurt am Main: Athenäum, 1974),
pp. 201–17.

46. Cf. Merker's evaluation, however: "It was customary to look to the older aristocratic
tradition and to aspire toward courtly manners, for the representatives of the aristocracy
frequently had cordial relations with the cities, and could influence the tone of bourgeois
society and its civic festivities. But what went as a model of courtly propriety together with
the more naive manifestations of petit-bourgeois delicacy understandably formed a social
milieu that conveniently discarded the best of the older era for coarser manifestations" ("Die
Tischzuchtliteratur," p. 23).

47. Ibid., p. 16.

48. Other important examples of such manuals can be found in the work on Renaissance
paleography and handwriting pegagogy. Jonathan Goldberg's *Writing Matter: From the
Hands of the English Renaissance* (Stanford: Stanford University Press, 1990), is the model
for such study of the building of the masculine subject of humanism. Richard Halpern's
"Breeding Capital" chapter in *The Poetics of Primitive Accumulation: English Renaissance
Culture and the Genealogy of Capital* (Ithaca: Cornell University Press, 1991) also addresses
handwriting pedagogy and the connection between Tudor schooling and the growth of the
protocapitalist economy, neglecting to note, however, that the schools bred standards of
masculinity as well. Cf. also Crane, *Framing Authority*, on the role of learning *sententiae*
in the humanist schools.

49. Elias, *Civilizing Process* 1: xiii. The often-quoted passage is "Change is in the direc-

tion of a gradual 'civilization,' but only historical experience makes clearer what this word actually means. It shows, for example, the decisive role played in this civilizing process by a very specific change in the feelings of shame and delicacy. The standard of what society demands and prohibits changes; in conjunction with this, the threshold of socially instilled displeasure and fear moves; and the question of sociogenic fear thus emerges as one of the central problems of the civilizing process." What I believe is important here is that for Elias the question of fear is a greater one than any peculiar forms—such as shame and embarrassment—it may take and that, interestingly enough, his concern with less determinate structuring spheres like this places him in a relationship to Kristeva and her explorations of horror and dread.

50. Friedrich Engel-Janosi, "Soziale Probleme der Renaissance," *Beihefte zur Vierteljahrschrift für Sozial- und Wirtschaftsgeschichte* 4 (Stuttgart: W. Kohlhammer, 1924), 72.

51. Lévi-Strauss, *Origins of Table Manners*, p. 500, observes the attention given to adolescent training in most societies: "And indeed, what condition could better demonstrate that boiling up of internal forces, which was, or still is, used, even in our European societies, as a justification for the rigours of education, since these forces are thought to be uncontrollable, unless hemmed about by various rules?"

52. See p. 195 n. 2.

53. Cf. Halpern, *Poetics of Primitive Accumulation*, pp. 63–64, 72–74, on Marx's stage of "primitive accumulation" as marked by the reality of rural dislocation and displacement. Cf. also Lawrence Stone, *The Causes of the English Revolution, 1529–1642* (New York: Harper and Row, 1972).

54. This sense of limited but latent power is illustrated in a letter from Jakob Fugger to Charles V (1523), asking for the money that had financed imperial missions. The letter's mixed rhetorical posture attempts to balance formal submission with more ominous and striking undercurrents of threats and aggression:

> It is also well known and clear as day that your Imperial Majesty could not have acquired the Roman Crown without my help, as I can demonstrate by documents of all your Imperial Majesty's commissioners. Nor have I sought my own profit in this undertaking. For if I had remained aloof from the house of Austria and had served France, I would have obtained much profit and money, which was then offered to me. Your Majesty may well ponder with deep understanding the damage which would have resulted for your Imperial Majesty and the house of Austria. Considering all this I humbly petition your Imperial Majesty, graciously to consider my faithful and humble services, which have advanced your Majesty's welfare, and to decree that the sum of money due me together with the interest should be discharged and paid to me without further delay. I shall always be found ready to serve your Majesty in all humility, and I humbly remain at all times your Imperial Majesty's to command.

*The Portable Renaissance Reader*, ed. James B. Ross and Mary Martin McLaughlin (New York: Viking, 1967), pp. 180–81.

55. Cf. Werner Sombart, *Der moderne Kapitalismus: Historisch-systematische Darstellung des gesamteuropäischen Wirtschaftslebens von seinen Anfängen bis zur Gegenwart* (Munich: Duncker & Humblot, 1928), vol. 2; and Franz Borkenau, *Der Übergang vom feudalen zum bürgerlichen Weltbild: Studien zur Geschichte der Philosophie der Manufakturperiode* (Darmstadt: Wissenschaftliche Buchgesellschaft, 1971). Borkenau claims that "in the Reformation, all pleasure is sinful because it is natural" (p. 116), but this notion would not account for the peculiarly complex pleasures of grobianism.

56. See Halpern, *Poetics of Primitive Accumulation*, on the dislocations and on the category of primitive accumulation as a "pre-history of capitalism."

57. I am thinking here of the number of handbooks published in England and Germany classifying vices and virtues. Cf. *Narrenbuch*, ed. F. Bobertag (Darmstadt: Wissenschaftliche Buchgesellschaft, 1964); Barbara Könneker, *Wesen und Wandlung der Narrenidee im Zeitalter der Humanismus: Brant, Murner, Erasmus* (Wiesbaden: F. Steiner, 1966); Adolf Hauffen, "Die Trinklitteratur in Deutschland," *Vierteljahrsschrift für Literaturgeschichte* 2 (1899): 489–516; Max Osborn, *Die Teufelslitteratur des XVI. Jahrhunderts, Acta Germanica: Organ für deutsche Philologie* 3, no. 3 (Berlin: Mayer und Müller, 1893); Philip Stubbes, *The Anatomy of Abuses* (1583; rpt. New York: Garland, 1973).

58. Aloys Bömer, "Anstand und Etikette in den Theorien der Humanisten," *Neue Jahrbücher für das klassische Altertum, Geschichte und deutsche Literatur und für Pädogogik*, 14 (Leipzig, 1904), 271.

59. The most famous example of the Renaissance ironic *encomium* is, of course, Erasmus's *Praise of Folly* (1509); others would include the infamous, anticlerical *Letters of Obscure Men* (1515), the "Encomium of the Ass" at the end of Cornelius Agrippa's *Vanity of the Sciences* (1526), and Panurge's harangue in praise of debt at the beginning of the third book of Rabelais's *Gargantua and Pantagruel* (1546).

60. *Salomon et Marcolfus: Kritischer Text mit Einleitung, Anmerkungen, Übersicht*, ed. Walter Benary (Heidelberg: C. Winter, 1914); *The Dialogue between the Wise King Solomon and Marcolphus*, ed. E. Gordon Duff (London, 1892).

61. Cf. the eleventh-century *Disciplina clericalis* by Petrus Alphonsus.

62. Hauffen, *Caspar Scheidt*, p. 65.

63. Karl Marx, "Moralising Criticism and Critical Morality: A Contribution to German Cultural History contra Karl Heinzen," *Deutsche-Brüsseler-Zeitung*, October 28, 1847, in *Collected Works* (Moscow: International, 1972), 6: 313–14.

64. The reference seems to have been an important one for Marx; he continued the attack over several weeks. For a stunning contemporary example of American grobianism, one chilling example of the current uses of indecency appeared in the right-wing congressional attacks on the funding practices of the National Endowment for the Arts as supporting morally offensive and obscene art. For another, we need look no further than Senator Jesse Helms's opposition to full funding of the Ryan White Care Act for AIDS treatment because those with AIDS acquired the disease through their "deliberate, disgusting, revolting conduct." "Helms Puts the Brakes to a Bill Financing AIDS Treatment," *New York Times*, July 5, 1995.

65. Jacob und Wilhelm Grimm, *Deutsches Wörterbuch*, rev. by Arthur Hübner and Hans Neumann (Leipzig: S. Hirzel, 1935), vol. 4, sec. 1, pt. 6, item "grobian."

66. Adolf Hauffen and Carl Diesch, "Grobianische Dichtung," in *Reallexikon der deutschen Literaturgeschichte*, Paul Merker und Wolfgang Stammler, 2d ed., revised (Berlin: Walter de Gruyter, 1958), 4: 605.

67. Thomas Murner, *Schelmenzunft* (1512), ed. Ernst Matthius (Halle: M. Niemeyer, 1890). The grobian also appears in folk songs of the sixteenth century.

68. Cf. Roger Ascham, *The Schoolmaster: The Whole Works of Roger Ascham*, ed. J. A. Giles (London: John Russell Smith, 1864): "But if the child miss, either in forgetting a word, or in changing a good with a worse, or misordering the sentence, I would not have the master either frown or chide with him.... For ... a child shall take more profit of two faults gently warned of, than of four things rightly hit: for then the master shall have good occasion to say unto him, 'No, Tully would have used such a word, not this: Tully would have placed this word here, not there.'"

69. Hans Sachs, who had his early academic education at Latin school in Nuremberg before becoming a shoemaker, wrote his "Verkehrte tischzucht grobianj" at the age of sixty-nine.

70. Christoph Mühlemann, *Fischarts "Geschichtklitterung" als manieristisches Kunst-werk: Verwirrtes Muster einer verwirrten Welt* (Frankfurt am Main: Peter Lang, 1972), p. 41 n. 22; Könneker, Introduction to *Grobianus*, p. xiv. In a study of Scheidt's *Grobianus* and other ironic *Tischzuchten*, Perry Thornton sees ambiguity in the text: "We need to decide whether the grobian element is there in order to entice the reader to take the didactic message in the bargain or whether coarseness is an end in itself. Certainly both tendencies are linked" (*Grobianische Tischzuchten*, p. 9).

71. Cf. M. A. Screech and Ruth Calder, "Some Renaissance Attitudes to Laughter," in *Humanism in France at the End of the Middle Ages and in the Early Renaissance*, ed. A. H. T. Levi (New York: Manchester University Press, 1970), 216–28; Terence Cave, "Renaissance Laughter," a review of M. A. Screech, *Rabelais* (Ithaca: Cornell University Press, 1979), in *New York of Review of Books*, July 18, 1982, pp. 31–33; and Mikhail Bakhtin's clear and nostalgically tempered distinction of "grobianism" as a corruption of the allegedly pure, "carnivalesque" humor of medieval folk culture, recuperated in Rabelais's works. See *Rabelais and His World* (Cambridge: MIT, 1968), chap. 1, "Rabelais in the History of Laughter."

72. Wilhelm Scherer, article "Dedekind," in *Allgemeine Deutsche Biographie*, p. 607.

## 2. Malleable Material, Models of Power

1. Stephen Greenblatt, *Renaissance Self-Fashioning: From More to Shakespeare* (Chicago: University of Chicago Press, 1981), chap. 4, "To Fashion a Gentleman: Spenser and the Destruction of the Bower of Bliss," 157–92.

2. Louis A. Montrose, " 'Shaping Fantasies': Figurations of Gender and Power in Elizabethan Culture," *Representations* 1 (1983): 61–94, hereafter cited parenthetically in the text. Montrose notes that the cult of Elizabeth also functioned to contain masculine anxiety (p. 63).

3. J. K. Sowards, ed., *Literary and Educational Writings*, 3 and 4, vols. 25 and 26 of *Collected Works of Erasmus* (Toronto: University of Toronto Press, 1985). *De civilitate* (Sowards, ed., 3: 272) was first translated into English in 1532; *De pueris instituendis* (Sowards, ed., 4: 294) in 1551; "Coniugium," for example, was published before 1557. Cf. Henry de Vocht, *The Earliest English Translations of Erasmus's Colloquia* (Louvain: Librairie Universitaire, 1928). Cf. also T. W. Baldwin, *William Shakespeare's Small Latine and Lesse Greeke* (Urbana: University of Illinois Press, 1944); J. A. K. Thompson, *Shakespeare and the Classics* (New York: Columbia University Press, 1952).

4. On the phenomenon of self-fashioning, see esp. Greenblatt, *Renaissance Self-Fashioning*, p. 9. As others have not been reluctant to note in making use of it, Greenblatt's influential work does not really reflect on the gender specificity of self-fashioning.

5. Cf. Montrose, " 'Shaping Fantasies,' " p. 75, where he claims that *A Midsummer Night's Dream* "discloses . . . that patriarchal norms are compensatory for the [projected? representational?] vulnerability of men to the powers of women." Gynophobic fantasy is similarly exploited by Janet Adelman in *Suffocating Mothers: Fantasies of Maternal Origin in Shakespeare's Plays, "Hamlet" to "The Tempest"* (New York: Routledge, 1992). The horror of the feminine such authors want to locate in the Elizabethan setting is also seen and complicated by class issues in Erasmus's civility lessons. The question arises as to whether or not such regiocentric scholarship might be taking an effect for a cause.

6. Cf. the conclusion to book 2 of *Il Cortegiano*, where the characters Gaspare and Ottaviano serve as stalking horses for an excessive misogyny, structurally counterweighted by an idealistically chivalrous Bernardo, thus conveniently setting up the discussion of the female courtier in book 3. This is not to suggest that either the gender conflict topos or the irenic strategy is univocal or, above all, successfully and coherently constructed in the texts.

7. That the dialogues were protonovels of manners was pointed out quite early, in George Saintsbury's "Zeitgeist" account in *The Earlier Renaissance* (1901; rpt., New York: Howard Fertig, 1968), pp. 82–83: "Erasmus, though choosing to speak 'by personages,' writes what are really finished novel-scenes. . . . Colloquy after colloquy, in whole or part, gives example to the fit artist how to manage original matter in the same way. A batch of four running, the *Procus et Puella*, the *Virgo Misogamos*, the *Virgo Poenitens*, and the *Conjugium*, are simply novel-chapters; the clumsiest novelist could hardly spoil them in turning them into the narrative form, while any practitioner of spirit and gift could not but have been guided by them, if the novel-writing spirit had been at all abroad." Cf. Erasmus on the virtues of silence in women but "especially in boys," in *On Good Manners*, p. 284.

In his 1526 defense of *The Colloquies*, "On the Utility of the Colloquies," Erasmus affects a tone of righteous indignation to defend himself, claiming, "I don't think I should be reproached for attracting youth *with like zeal* to refinement of Latin speech and to godliness" (*The Colloquies*, p. 626, my emphasis). For a provocative and more general discussion of this linking of technical grammar and moral/cultural grammar in Renaissance pedagogy, see Walter Ong, "Latin Language Study as a Renaissance Puberty Rite," *Studies in Philology* 56 (April 1959): 93–110. Jonathan Goldberg meticulously links masculine subject formation to handwriting pedagogy in *Writing Matter: From the Hands of the English Renaissance* (Stanford: Stanford University Press, 1990).

8. For examples of traditional studies of images of women, see Elsbeth Schneider, *Das Bild der Frau im Werk des Erasmus von Rotterdam*, Basler Beiträge zur Geschichtswissenschaft 55 (Stuttgart, 1955); Aloys Börner, "Die deutsche Humanisten und das weibliche Geschlecht," *Zeitschrift für Kulturgeschichte* 4 (1897): 94–112, 177–97; D. Schmidt, "Die Frau in den *Gesprächen* des Erasmus," *Basler Zeitschrift für Geschichte und Altertumskunde* 44 (1945): 11–36. For examples of studies concerning notable Renaissance women, see Susan Groag Bell, "Christine de Pisan; or, The Plight of the Learned Woman," *Feminist Studies* 3 (1976): 173–86; Anthony Grafton and Lisa Jardine, *From Humanism to the Humanities: Education and the Liberal Arts in Fifteenth- and Sixteenth-Century Europe* (Cambridge: Harvard University Press, 1986), esp. chap. 2: "Women Humanists: Education for What?" 29–57, which discusses the function of the *virilis animi* idea as strategy for encouraging women's learning while, ultimately, containing the more public or active aspirations of intellectual women. For works on Renaissance pedagogy concentrating on boys, see W. H. Woodward, *Desiderius Erasmus concerning the Aim and Method of Education* (Cambridge: Cambridge University Press, 1964).

9. One study that emphasizes other important aspects of the relations between cultural representations of boys and women is Alan Bray, *Homosexuality in Renaissance England* (London: Gay Men's Press, 1982). Cf. also Stephen Orgel, "Nobody's Perfect; or, Why Did the English Stage Take Boys for Women?" and Jonathan Goldberg, "Colin to Hobbinol: Spenser's Familiar Letters," both in "Displacing Homophobia," the special issue of the *Southern Atlantic Quarterly* 88 (Winter 1989): 7–29 and 107–47. Cf. also new approaches taken in Goldberg, ed., *Queering the Renaissance* (Durham, N.C.: Duke University Press, 1994).

10. James K. McConica, "Erasmus and the Grammar of Consent," in Joseph Coppens, *Scrinum Erasmianum* (Leiden: Brill, 1969), 2: 80.

11. V. W. D. Schenk, "Erasmus's Karakter en Ziekten" (Erasmus's character and diseases), *Nederlandsch tijdschrift voor geneeskunde* 91 (1947): 702–8. Studies such as Nelson Minnich and W. W. Meissner's classical Freudian—certainly homophobic—psychobiographical essay, which painted a tragic picture of an Erasmus with homoerotic tendencies (the consequence of being abandoned by his father and searching for father substitutes), and Joseph Mangan's divided Erasmus—sickly, neuraesthenic, morbidly sensitive, unfortunate possessor of a "moral strabismus," but a genius—seek to leave us with an essential bottom line, both a sum and a guarded boundary: the judgment that Erasmus's works transcend any character flaw or psychopathological symptom. Nelson H. Minnich and W. W. Meissner, "The Character of Erasmus," *American Historical Review* 83 (1978): 598–624; Joseph Mangan, *Life, Character, and Influence of Desiderius Erasmus of Rotterdam: Derived from a Study of His Works and Correspondence*, 2 vols. (1927; rpt., New York: AMS, 1971). In another curious study, Andreas Werthemann, in *Über Schädel und Gebeine des Erasmus von Rotterdam* (Basel: Birkhäuser, 1930), reports on a team of pathologists who actually exhumed the remains of Erasmus and discovered the symptoms of syphilis.

Recent work makes progress toward fleshing out the field of Erasmus studies and shows how promising interests in this early modern figure are. While his interests are not those pursued in this chapter, Terence Cave, *The Cornucopian Text: Problems of Writing in the French Renaissance* (Oxford: Clarendon Press, 1979), relates Erasmus's *De copia* and *Ciceronianus* to tensions between Eramus's interiority ("on the plenitude of the self") and "the public, exterior nature of writing" and locates a rich rhetorical and historical constellation of problems. Lisa Jardine, *Erasmus, Man of Letters: The Construction of Charisma in Print* (Princeton: Princeton University Press, 1993), for example, examines Erasmus's self-fashioning strategies in early modern print culture. Forrest Tyler Stevens, "Erasmus's 'Tigres': The Language of Friendship, Pleasure, and the Renaissance Letter," in Goldberg, ed., *Queering the Renaissance*, 124–40, examines Erasmus's early correspondence with Servatius Rogerus and locates its significance in ideas on humanist epistolarity and emerging ideas on male friendship and homosexuality. Richard Halpern sees Erasmus's pedagogical influence on "Tudor style production" and its relationship to early modern capitalist formations; see chap. 1, "A Mint of Phrases: Ideology and Style Production in Tudor England," in *The Poetics of Primitive Accumulation: English Renaissance Culture and the Genealogy of Capital* (Ithaca: Cornell University Press, 1991), pp. 19–60. The South African novelist J. M. Coetzee examines the politics of Erasmian irenics in "Erasmus's *Praise of Folly*: Rivalry and Madness," *Neophilologus* 76 (1992): 1–18.

12. Léon-E. Halkin, *Erasme parmi nous*, translated as *Erasmus: A Critical Biography* by John Tonkin (Oxford: Blackwell, 1993), carries on this tradition.

13. J. K. Sowards, "Erasmus and the Education of Women," *Sixteenth Century Journal* 13, no. 4 (1982): 77–89, hereafter cited in the text.

14. This view is not unchallenged, of course. Constance Jordan, *Renaissance Feminism: Literary Texts and Political Models* (Ithaca: Cornell University Press, 1990), places Erasmus's views on marriage in the tradition of Aristotelian and Pauline thought. Although Erasmus argues for woman's spiritual equality in his *Institutio christiani matrimonii*, she finds, "Erasmus's wife is not only her husband's political subordinate [Paul] but also his natural inferior [Aristotle]" (61). Jordan includes brief, descriptive discussions of some of the *Colloquies* as well.

15. Teresa de Lauretis, *Technologies of Gender: Essays on Theory, Film, and Fiction* (Bloomington: Indiana University Press, 1987), hereafter cited in the text.

16. In an article in the *Sixteenth Century Journal*, the historian Merry Wiesner urges readers to think in new ways about gender questions in the Reformation as a means for

achieving new perspectives on the early modern period. Noting that Reformation studies have been marked by ignorance or neglect of gender issues, she criticizes ghettoizing studies that replicate historical marginalization in pitting "real" history (as the account of monumental political events) against marginal studies (the agenda of social history, microhistorical concerns), by circumscribing women's history in automatically equating it with—and thereby limiting it to—the history of family and sexuality. Wiesner's suggestion goes back at least to Joan Kelly's "double vision" thesis, but Wiesner takes on the issue of contemporary feminist theory in a more self-conscious way, suggesting, circumspectly, that scholars of women's history "ask the large questions, the ones that make us rethink all that has been learned until now, the ones that, perhaps, cannot be answered" (p. 321); elsewhere, more directly, she writes, "We [historians] must overcome our resistance to theory" (p. 31). Merry E. Wiesner, "Beyond Women and the Family: Toward a Gender Analysis of the Reformation," *Sixteenth Century Journal* 18, no. 3 (1987): 311–21; and Joan Kelly, "The Doubled Vision of Feminist Theory," in *Women, History, and Theory: The Essays of Joan Kelly* (Chicago: University of Chicago Press, 1986), pp. 51–64.

As an example of the kind of audience Merry Wiesner might have in mind, see Marilyn J. Boxer and Jean H. Quataert, eds. *Connecting Spheres: Women in the Western World, 1500 to the Present* (New York: Oxford University Press, 1987). This important and informative work (to which Wiesner herself contributes an essay) seeks to "integrate women's experiences into the overall pattern of historical development in the West" (p. 22)—a description composed in language of significant and unreflected conceptual density. Thus, for example, the editors speak descriptively of the "argument about women" (pp. 20–25 and 45–48) as the record of misconceptions about women (originating with Aristotle), always implying that legitimacy for women and "the feminine" might be established, equality between the sexes restored, if only one had sufficient and better information. In contrast, see two examples of feminist historical work which draw heavily from conceptual categories of continental theory: Denise Riley, *"Am I That Name?" Feminism and the Category of "Women" in History* (Minneapolis: University of Minnesota Press, 1988); and Joan Wallach Scott, *Gender and the Politics of History* (New York: Columbia University Press, 1988).

17. The "Marriage Group" is discussed in Craig Thompson, *The Colloquies*, pp. 86–88.

18. Cf. Timothy in "The Godly Feast": "Often it's our own fault that our wives are bad, either because we choose bad ones or make them such, or don't train and control them as we should" (p. 60).

19. Cf. p. 122: When men are unfaithful, instructs Eulalia, women must follow the behavior-modification model, rewarding the good and ignoring the bad; husbands, on the other hand, need no such sophisticated methods and have legitimate access to (threats of) brute force.

20. I borrow this term from Gayatri Chakravorty Spivak's discussion of another scene of domestication through language, Athena's judgment of the Erinyes in the *Oresteia* of Aeschylus, which she calls "her defeminating of the Furies, pursuing Orestes the matricide, and bidding them be 'sweet-voiced' (Eumenides) by the stroke [!] of a word." "Displacement and the Discourse of Woman," in *Displacement: Derrida and After*, ed. Mark Krupnick (Bloomington: Indiana University Press, 1983), p. 191.

21. Jacques Chomorat, *Grammaire et rhétorique chez Erasme*, 2 vols. (Paris: Société d'édition "Les Belles Lettres," 1981), hereafter cited in the text: "The result, or perhaps as well the source, of this attitude is that woman finds herself enhanced with the greatest dignity . . . , a subtle analysis which tends to place the real superiority where there is the greatest self-mastery, which is to say where it seems—deceptively—to be inferiority; this analysis is amply developed in the colloquy 'Uxor mempsigamos' ['Coniugium'] where Eu-

lalia teaches Xantippe how to dominate and educate her husband through patience and sweetness, while seeming to give in to him" (2: 896–87). Thus by a compensatory master-slave logic, woman attains the moral high ground of "une dignité plus grande," while the civic ground is cut out from under her feet. This argument, which creates a positionless position, is standard, of course, for much of modern Western political thought. Cf. Susan Moller Okin, *Woman in Western Political Thought* (Princeton: Princeton University Press, 1979). Cf. also Thompson's introductory remarks on "The Marriage Group": "When taken together, these three colloquies constitute a brilliant and entertaining addition to the vast literature of Renaissance feminism." He adds praise to the author for providing a "sufficiently light touch" (p. 87).

22. Cf. Erasmus in *Institutio Christiani matrimonii/On Christian Matrimony*: "We shall divide our functions. You will take care of the domestic, I of the professional, and we shall have nothing, save in common. . . . The authority which nature and the apostle give to the husband I hope you will not resent and mutual love will sweeten all things. You will sit on the eggs, and I shall fly around and bring in the worms. We are one and, as the Scripture says, God rejoices when we dwell together in unity." Quoted in Roland Bainton, *Erasmus of Christendom* (New York: Scribner's, 1969), 229.

23. See p. 205 n. 7.

24. For a compelling treatment of what we might well identify as the consequences of Erasmus's Western organicism in the Third World, cf. Gayatri Chakravorty Spivak's translation and discussion of Mahasveta Devi's "Breast Giver" in *In Other Worlds: Essays in Cultural Politics* (London: Methuen, 1987), pp. 241–68.

25. Erasmus, *Collected Works* 26: 296.

26. Ibid., 273.

27. Erasmus, *Collected Works* 26: 273. Cf. J. K. Sowards's "Notes" to *Good Manners in Boys*, in which he discusses the *vera nobilitas topos* and suggests that Erasmus may have been influenced by More.

28. Erasmus apologizes for his work as "crassissima philosophiae pars" and exempts the young prince of Burgundy from its lessons since, as he says, the prince's manners are inbred. Cf. also Guillaume Bude's objection to *Good Manners in Boys* as a "work devoted to that trivial task; as if so many little books do not risk tarnishing your reputation." Quoted by Franz Bierlaire, "Erasmus in School: the *De Civilitate Morum Puerilium*," in *Essays on the Works of Erasmus*, ed. Richard DeMolen (New Haven: Yale University Press, 1978), p. 239.

29. Immanuel Wallerstein, "The Bourgeois(ie) as Concept and Reality," *New Left Review* 16 (January-February 1988): 91–106.

30. *Good Manners in Boys*, 274, 275.

31. Sowards, "Notes" to Erasmus, *De pueris instituendis*, in *Collected Works* 26: 564.

32. Treatments of Juan Vives, *De institutione christianae foeminae* (1529) have become numerous in the past years; see esp. Valerie Wayne, "Some Sad Sentence: Vives' *Instruction of a Christian Woman*," in *Silent but for the Word: Tudor Women as Patrons, Translators, and Writers of Religious Works*, ed. Margaret P. Hannay (Kent, Ohio: Kent State University Press, 1985).

33. Sir Thomas Elyot, *The Book Named the Governor*, ed. and introd. S. E. Lehmberg (New York: Dutton, 1975), hereafter cited in the text.

34. To counter the projected threats of women, Elyot recommends that after age seven the boy be assigned "an ancient and worshipful" male tutor, though he "may have one year, or two at the most, an ancient and sad matron attending on him in his chamber, which shall not have any young woman in her company; for though there be no peril of offence in that tender and innocent age, yet in some children nature is more prone to vice than to virtue, and in the tender wits be sparks of voluptuosity which, nourished by any occasion or object,

increase often times into so terrible a fire that therewith all virtue and reason is consumed"
(p. 19). It is also true, however, that Elyot speaks in favor of accelerating the learning
process, "to encroach somewhat upon the years of children, and specially of noblemen, that
they may sooner attain to wisdom and gravity than private persons." To accomplish this
goal, he recommends the pupils "be sweetly allured thereto with praises and such pretty
gifts as children delight in" and that they be placed in competition with "inferior companions: they sometime purposely suffering the more noble children to vanquish and, as it
were, giving to them place and sovereignty, though indeed the inferior children have more
learning" (p. 17).

35. Natalie Zemon Davis, "City Women and Religious Change," in *Society and Culture
in Early Modern France* (Stanford: Stanford University Press, 1975), p. 77: "The Christian
humanist Erasmus was one of the few men of his time who sensed the depths of resentment
accumulating in women whose efforts to think about doctrine were not taken seriously by
the clergy."

36. Andrew Maclean, review in *Moreana* 24 (June-July 1987): 59.

## 3. Reading *Grobianus*

1. Examples of Dedekind's Ovidian borrowing include advice on personal grooming and
on winning the affections of women through ceaseless effort (book 1, chap. 6; cf. Ovid, *Ars
amatoria* 2.177–250). Dedekind, of course, takes Ovid's lover's persistence to extremes that
amount to serious street harassment. In book 2, chap. 6, the student is advised to grope his
female dinner partner:

> Illa tui magno mox coripietur amore,
>    Et tua perpetuo scilicet esse volet.
> Splendidio releves capiuntur veste puellae,
>    Virgineusque auro conciliatur amor,
> Tu quoque nonnunquam gemitu fatearis amorem,
>    Et loquitor nutu pectoris ima tui.
> Utque sui vero te norit amore teneri,
>    Virgineo duro clam pede tange pedem.
> Saepe propinabis temere non parva puellae
>    Pocula quae magni pignus amoris erunt.
>                                         (2.6.885–94)

> Of times with sighes tell her that thou till death her servant art,
> And privately before her view lay ope thy fainting heart.
> And that she may perceave that you for her do daily pine,
> As privately as may be, touch her tender foote with thine.
> What though she frowne? yet drinke unto her oft at supper tho,
> For by this meanes you shall perceave, whether shee'le yeelde or no.
>                                         (2.6.2298–2303)

2. See Lisa Jardine and Anthony Grafton, "Northern Methodical Humanism: From
Teachers to Textbooks," in Grafton and Jardine, *From Humanism to the Humanities: Education and the Liberal Arts in Fifteenth- and Sixteenth-Century Europe* (Cambridge: Harvard
University Press, 1986), pp. 122–57, for a discussion of the Erasmian system and its influence.

3. In *De civilitate* as well as in *The Colloquies*, Hauffen also sees Erasmus providing Dedekind with a wealth of ready-made phrases and other material for advice to grobians. *Caspar Scheidt, der Lehrer Fischarts, Studien zur Geschichte der grobianischen Litteratur in Deutschland* (Strassburg: Karl J. Trübner, 1899), pp. 34–35.

4. Norman Knox, *The Word "Irony" and Its Context, 1500–1755* (Durham, N.C.: Duke University Press, 1961), p. 4. See also Knox, "On the Classification of Ironies," *Modern Philology* 70 (1972): 53–62; and Knox, "Irony," in *Dictionary of the History of Ideas: Studies of Selective Pivotal Ideas*, ed. P. P. Wiener (New York: Scribner and Sons, 1973), vol. 2. In later editions of *Grobianus*, "IRON CHLEVASTES" (scoffing deceiver) became "IRON EPISCOPTES" (overseeing deceiver), an alteration that seems attuned to the scopic regime of conduct in general and to grobianism specifically.

5. J. A. K. Thomson, *Irony: An Historical Introduction* (Cambridge: Harvard University Press, 1927), pp. 10–18. Thomson also points out that the original meaning of *eiron* is "cunning, wily, sly," p. 3.

6. Knox, *The Word "Irony" and Its Context*, pp. 4–5.

7. Linda Hutcheon, *Irony's Edge: The Theory and Politics of Irony* (London: Routledge, 1994), hereafter cited parenthetically in the text.

8. Booth describes a four-part process of "reconstruction" of "stable" ironic texts, by which the reader comes to reject one statement of meaning and value and "join[s] the author in a higher position" by recognizing and thus enjoying the author's use of irony. With a foundational trust in stability of meaning and community of reception, irony for Booth represents an "astonishing communal achievement." See Wayne C. Booth, *The Rhetoric of Irony* (Chicago: University of Chicago Press, 1974), pp. 10–13. The four steps of reconstruction require the reader to "reject the literal meaning," try out "alternative interpretations," make a decision "about the author's knowledge or beliefs," and "finally choose a new meaning or a cluster of meanings with which we can rest secure."

9. In arguing that irony is not mere semantic inversion or antiphrasis, Hutcheon counters the more traditional views held by David Knox, *Ironia: Medieval and Renaissance Ideas on Irony* (Leiden: E. J. Brill, 1989), or D. C. Muecke's notion of irony as marking an "incompatibility," *The Compass of Irony* (London: Methuen, 1969); and Muecke, *Irony and the Ironic* (London: Methuen, 1982).

10. In Hutcheon's definition, offered "from the point of view of what I too (with reservations) will call the *ironist*, irony is the intentional transmission of both information and evaluative attitude other than what is explicitly presented" (*Irony's Edge*, 11). Hutcheon's remarks on subversive irony—"Even if an ironist intends an irony to be interpreted in an oppositional framework, there is no guarantee that this subversive intent will be realized" (pp. 15–16)—would also apply to the normative or moralist ironist such as Dedekind and Scheidt.

11. Cf. Booth, *Rhetoric of Irony*, pp. 28–29: "We need no very extensive survey of ironic examples to discover . . . that the building of amiable communities is often far more important than the exclusion of naive victims. Often the predominant emotion when reading stable ironies is that of joining, of finding and communing with kindred spirits. . . . Even irony that does imply victims, as in all ironic satire, is often much more clearly directed to more affirmative matters. And every irony inevitably builds a community of believers even as it excludes."

12. The distinction is used by Silvia Bovenschen in her discussion of the early modern discourses on witchcraft, "Die aktuelle Hexe, die historische Hexe, und der Hexenmythos. Die Hexe: Subjekt der Naturaneignung und Objekt der Naturbeherrschung," in Gabriele Becker, Helmut Brackert, et al., *Aus der Zeit der Verzweiflung: Zur Genese und Aktualität*

*des Hexenbildes* (Frankfurt am Main: Suhrkamp, 1977), pp. 259–312, translation in *New German Critique* no. 15 (1978): 83–119.

13. As I point out in my Author's Note, the changes to the second edition suggest that Dedekind, somewhat like Scheidt when he came to vernacularize it, wanted the text to be "coarse enough." This is evidence of a desire that was difficult to satisfy in such a project. In revising and coarsening, however, Dedekind follows the logic of the 1549 text and his changes are continuous with the project initiated in the first edition.

14. Booth, *Rhetoric of Irony*, pp. 28–29. D. C. Muecke, *Compass of Irony*, p. 25, describes "simple corrective irony" as "effective at the point at which we pass from an apprehension of the ironic incongruity to a more or less immediate recognition of the invalidity of the ironist's pretended or the victim's confidently held view. Psychic tension is generated but rapidly released." Hutcheon's position on the relational quality and edge of irony, no matter how the irony is classified, argues against the traditional position that irony is ever only semantic inversion or antiphrasis. Irony in conduct texts would take pains to generate—and preserve—psychic tension.

15. The debt here is obviously to Jacques Derrida, "Plato's Pharmacy," in *Dissemination*, trans. Barbara Johnson (Chicago: University of Chicago Press, 1981), pp. 61–171.

16. Cf. Castiglione, p. 86, where *quella sprezzata purità* (1.40.70) is (most ironically) translated as "uncontrived simplicity."

17. See Margaret Ferguson, *Trials of Desire: Renaissance Defenses of Poetry* (New Haven: Yale University Press, 1983), for a study of the poetic convention of the apologia.

18. Dedekind's uncertainty about the poetic worth of the work is expressed in an apologia that seems more than formulaic:

> Forsitan exigua est in carmine gratia nostro,
>  Et minus urbani Musa leporis habet.
> Et veniet cupido lectori parva voluptas,
>  Dulcia qui tantum scripta legenda putat.
> Heu mihi si multis etiam fastidia surgent,
>  Quod videant tenui carmina facta a stylo.
> Ergo mei studium damnabitur omne laboris?
>  Irritaque est operae cura futura mea?
> (Conclusio, 33–40)

> Some men perchance will therefore not my painefull labours love,
> Because forsooth my verses do not store of laughter move.
> What though some other thinke my verses lothsome, base, and vile?
> Because forsooth they are not written in a loftie stile,
> Will therefore every man condemne my labour and my paine?
> Is both my care, my time, and toile consumed all in vaine?
> (Conclusion, 4458–63)

> Bingius hortator veniens, audere timentem
> Iussit, et ingratum ponere corde metum:
> Emissumque domo tandem vulgare Poema,
> Quod queat a multis non sine fruge legi.
> (Conclusio, 83–86)

> He having seene the worke before, perswaded me at last
> From forth my mind such abiect thoughts and causelesse feare to cast,

> And boldly at the length to bring my poeme into light,
> That others also for their use and profite reade it might.
> (Conclusion, 4506–9)

19. Aloys Bömer, "Einleitung," to Fridericus Dedekindus, *Grobianus, Lateinische Litteraturdenkmäler des XV. und XVI. Jahrhunderts*, 16 (Berlin: Weidmann, 1903), p. vi.

20. Knox, *The Word "Irony" and Its Context*, pp. 4–5.

21. Fritz Bergmeier, *Dedekinds Grobianus in England* (Greifswald: Julius Abel, 1903), pp. 5–6.

22. Bömer also remarks on this absence in his introduction to the two-book edition of *Grobianus*: "In placing the title "Grobianus" at the top of the work, he attached to the name every vice that he attacked. In the text itself the word appears nowhere; instead we find 'simplex' and 'rusticus,' which Zeninger first germanized into 'grobian' " ("Einleitung," p. xxv).

23. Hans Rupprich, *Die deutsche Literatur von späten Mittelalter bis zum Barock*, part 2: *Das Zeitalter der Reformation, 1520–1570: Geschichte der Deutschen Literatur*, Helmut DeBoor and Richard Newald, vol. 4, part 2 (Munich: C. H. Beck, 1973), p. 218.

24.     Pinximus agrestes agresti carmine mores,
        Propositos oculis grex studiose tuis
        Vidimus a multis fieri, quae scripsimus, ipsi:
        Multa notata alio sunt referente mihi.
        Multa etiam (quid enim pudeat me vera fateri?)
        Ipse mea admisi rustica facta manu.
        Nec nisi, cuius erat nobis bene cognitus usus,
        Scripsimus hic ullum simplicitatis opus.
        (Conclusio, 49–56)

> Manners which clownish are, I have set down in clownish wise,
> Which I have set in carefull sort before the vulgars eyes.
> Most of the trickes which I have writ, my selfe before did see,
> The rest, a trustie friend of mine repeated unto mee.
> And some thereof (it is no shame to tell the naked truth)
> My selfe (as I was apt thereto) committed in my youth.
> Mongst all the precepts which my book containes, there is not one,
> Whose author (be they ne're so clownish) is to me unknowne.
> (3.4472–79)

## 4. Grobiana in *Grobianus*

1. Compare:

> Multa docendus eras, simplex ut in omnibus esses,
> Sed propero, et rebus vincor ab ipse meis.
> Ipse tuo ingenio quantum potes utere, et ista
> Dicta potes factis exuperare tuis.
> Paucula percurro saltem, ne longius ipsa
> Iliade, urgendi singula, surgat opus.
> Paucula sufficient, ipso quia doctus ab usu,
> Ipse potes monitis addere multa meis.

Singula coner enim libro comprendere in uno,
Vix istum caperet maxima terra librum.
Opprimere tanto miser ipse labore, meique
Ingenii vires exuperaret onus.
Imperium siquidem stolidorum nulla coercet
Meta, et ineptorum regia fine caret.

(1.11.1617–30)

To teach thee more, concerning this thy simple life, I meant,
But I must haste, for why mine owne affaires do me prevent.
Use thine owne wit as much as may be, for thou so maist well
By thine owne practise all my words and counsell farre excell.
I onely slightly touch those precepts which I give to thee,
Which if I should at large define, too tedious I should bee.
Few words will serve, since from thy use great learning thou hast had,
Unto my precepts by thy practise thou maist daily adde.
For me to put all thing in one booke it would be but vaine,
Because the greatest place that is, could not that booke containe.
How I (poore wretch) such labour should sustaine, I do not know,
It is a burthen, greater than my wit can undergo.
For why, no place (though ne're so wide) all fooles can comprehend,
Because their court is infinite, their number without end.

(1.11.1432–45)

2. Jean-Jacques Rousseau, *A Discourse on Inequality*, trans. Maurice Cranston (Harmondsworth, U.K.: Penguin, 1984), p. 65.

3. "The oldest of all societies, and the only natural one, is that of the family; yet children remain tied to their father by nature only so long as they need him for their preservation. . . . The family may therefore perhaps be seen as the first model of political societies: the head of the state bears the image of the father, the people the image of his children." Rousseau, *The Social Contract*, trans. Maurice Cranston (Harmondsworth, U.K.: Penguin, 1968), chap. 2, p. 50.

4. For exemplary works that address precisely this problem, see Claudia Koonz and Renate Bridenthal, eds., *Becoming Visible: Women in European History* (Boston: Houghton Mifflin, 1977); Marilyn J. Boxer and Jean H. Quataert, eds., *Connecting Spheres: Women in the Western World, 1500 to the Present* (New York: Oxford University Press, 1987); and Merry E. Wiesner, *Working Women in Renaissance Germany* (New Brunswick: Rutgers University Press, 1986).

5. See, for example, Eileen Power, "The Position of Women," in *The Legacy of the Middle Ages*, ed. C. G. Crump and E. F. Jacob (Oxford: Clarendon, 1951), p. 433, who argues that women benefited from the softening of manners in the legacy of chivalric culture passed on at the end of the Middle Ages. On revising European history to include women, see Joan Kelly, "Did Women Have a Renaissance?" in *Women, History, and Theory: The Essays of Joan Kelly* (Chicago: University of Chicago Press, 1986), pp. 19–50. For a good overview of work on women in the medieval and early modern periods, see also Mary Beth Rose, ed., *Women in the Middle Ages and the Renaissance: Literary and Historical Perspectives* (Syracuse: Syracuse University Press, 1986); and Koonz and Bridenthal, *Becoming Visible*. Since Joan Kelly posed the rhetorical question of whether women had a Renaissance, the prevailing view of feminist historians has been that the early modern period meant "a lessening of the public activity of women, a lower place in ecclesiastical opinion,

fewer roles in guild organizations, and less agricultural administration if not less agricultural labor." Susan Mosher Stuard, *Women in Medieval Society*, 2d ed. (Philadelphia: University of Pennsylvania Press, 1987), pp. 9–10.

6. Cf. Ian Maclean, *The Renaissance Notion of Woman: A Study in the Fortunes of Scholasticism and Medical Science in European Intellectual Life* (Cambridge: Cambridge University Press, 1980).

7. Cf. Joan Kelly, "Early Feminist Theory and the *Querelle des Femmes*, 1400–1789," *Signs: Journal of Women in Culture and Society* 8 (Autumn 1982): 4–28; Ann Rosalind Jones, "Counterattacks on 'the Bayter of Women': Three Pamphleteers of the Early Seventeenth Century," in *The Renaissance Englishwoman in Print: Counterbalancing the Canon*, ed. Anne M. Haselkorn and Betty S. Travitsky (Amherst: University of Massachussetts Press, 1990), 45–62; Maureen Quilligan, *The Allegory of Female Authority: Christine de Pizan's "Cité des dammes"* (Ithaca: Cornell University Press, 1991). Elaine Marks's comments on the insidious mirroring inversions in antifeminist attacks and feminist defenses alike remain incisive: "Feminist discourse has always picked up the terms of anti-feminist discourse and been determined by it. . . . Thus the feminists were always on the defensive, always pleading and, even if they affirmed the equality or superiority of women, never initiating the debate. . . . It is ironic that in the dialectic pro and con, women's reiterated affirmation contributes to the continuation of negativity." "Introduction," *New French Feminisms*, ed. Marks and Isabelle de Courtivron (New York: Schocken, 1981), pp. 6–7.

8. Joy Wiltenburg, *Disorderly Women and Female Power in the Street Literature of Early Modern England and Germany* (Charlottesville: University Press of Virginia, 1992).

9. On the literature of misogyny, see Francis L. Utley, *The Crooked Rib: An Analytical Index to the Argument about Women in English and Scots Literature to the End of the Year 1568* (Columbus: Ohio State University Press, 1944); and Katherine Rogers, *The Troublesome Helpmate: A History of Misogyny in Literature* (Seattle: Washington Paperbacks, 1966).

10. Waldemar Kawerau, *Die Reformation und die Ehe: Ein Beitrag zur Kulturgeschichte des sechszehnten Jahrhunderts*, Schriften des Vereins für Reformationsgeschichte, vol. 10, no. 39 (Halle, 1892), pp. 9–10.

11. See especially part 3, chap. 1, "Docile Bodies," in Michel Foucault, *Discipline and Punish: The Birth of the Prison*, trans. Alan Sheridan (New York: Vintage, 1977), pp. 135–69.

12. Especially important work in these areas has been done by the following: Lyndal Roper, "Luther: Sex, Marriage, and Motherhood," *History Today* 33 (December 1983): 33–38; Roper, " 'The Common Man,' 'the Common Good,' 'Common Women': Gender and Language in the German Reformation Commune," *Social History* 12, no. 1 (1987): 1–22; Roper, *The Holy Household: Women and Morals in Reformation Augsburg* (Oxford: Clarendon Press, 1989); Wiesner, *Working Women in Renaissance Germany*; Lawrence Stone, *The Family, Sex, and Marriage in England, 1500–1800* (New York: Harper and Row, 1977); David Herlihy, *Opera Muliebria: Women and Work in Medieval Europe* (New York: McGraw-Hill, 1990); Barbara Hanawalt, ed., *Women and Work in Pre-Industrial Europe* (Bloomington: Indiana University Press, 1986); Martha C. Howell, *Women, Production, and Patriarchy in Late Medieval Cities* (Chicago: University of Chicago Press, 1986).

13. Cf. Ruth Kelso, *Doctrine for the Lady of the Renaissance* (Urbana: University of Illinois Press, 1978). Having published the landmark study on courtesy for men, Kelso set out to discover in the Renaissance lady an equivalent figure, fit to complete the picture of masculine gentility, and found instead gaps and chasms, contradictions and paradoxes.

14. I say "in earnest" because the topic has already been initiated and aborted several times in the text, in the early part of book 1 and in fact every time Emilia Pia speaks

playfully and aggressively to Gaspare Palevicino. It is their misogynist-feminist *contretemps*, after all, that interrupts Bembo's neo-Platonic meditation and concludes the text.

15. Cf. Ann R. Jones's fine discussion of the woman of the court and the structural difficulties and contradictions in "Nets and Bridles: Early Modern Conduct Books and Sixteenth-Century Women's Lyrics," in *The Ideology of Conduct: Essays in Literature and the History of Sexuality*, ed. Nancy Armstrong and Leonard Tennenhouse (New York: Methuen, 1987), pp. 44–46. I admire and agree with her remarks, though here I am also interested in their consequences for the courtier.

16. The phrase comes from Luce Irigaray, *Speculum of the Other Woman*, trans. Gillian C. Gill (Ithaca: Cornell University Press, 1985), and is used to describe the desire of psychoanalysis to view women as both equivalent and at the same time inferior to men. See "The Little Girl Is (Only) a Little Boy," pp. 25–34.

17. Treatments of Juan Vives, *De institutione foeminae Christianae* (1529) have been numerous in the past years; see esp. Valerie Wayne, "Some Sad Sentence: Vives' *Instruction of a Christian Woman*," in *Silent But for the Word: Tudor Women as Patrons, Translators, and Writers of Religious Works*, ed. Margaret P. Hannay (Kent, Ohio: Kent State University Press, 1985); Gloria Kaufman, "Juan Luis Vives on the Education of Women," *Signs* 3 (1978): 891–96. A fine comparative discussion of More, Vives, and his English translator, Richard Hyde, appears in Pamela Joseph Benson, *The Invention of the Renaissance Woman: The Challenge of Female Independence in the Literature and Thought of Italy and England* (University Park, Pa.: Pennsylvania State University Press, 1993), pp. 172–81.

18. Cf. Suzanne Hull, *Chaste, Silent, and Obedient: English Books for Women, 1475–1640* (San Marino, Calif.: Huntington Library, 1982). For an important study of the philological stakes of chastity, see Stephanie Jed, *Chaste Thinking: The Rape of Lucretia and the Birth of Humanism* (Bloomington: Indiana University Press, 1989).

19. "Dann zu dem, daß mir an alter und jaren vil zuo, an sterck aber, gesicht und krefften täglich abgeht, hab ich mit rhat meiner aller liebsten zarten und tugenthafften haußfrawen GROBIANA, erwelter spinnerin der groben ungezogenen diernen und faulen mägd, ernstlich bedacht, daß wir alle ubernächtig und sterblich sind, und darzuo die Groben eben so bald, oder offtmals (wo nicht durch grosse gewonheit ein natürlicher brauch auß embsigem essen und trincken gemacht) vil ehe dann die ihenigen, so sich alle zeit subtilig und messig halten, von hinnen auß disem grobenthal scheiden, welchs nicht ein kleiner abbruch ist" (Then since my age and years increase but my strengths decrease daily, I have with the advice of my all-beloved, tender and virtuous housewife GROBIANA [experienced spinner of ill-bred wenches and lazy maids] thought seriously that we are all temporary and mortal, and especially the coarse ones who oftentimes [if not through their great habits of making a natural need of gluttonous eating and drinking] go earlier than the rest [who behave quietly and moderately] to that coarse valley, which is no minor interruption [p. 8]).

20. Cf. the discussion and survey of the flea motif in European literature in Adolf Hauffen's introduction to Fischart's misogynist (perhaps utterly untranslatable) mock epic *Flohhatz*, in *Johann Fischarts Werke: Eine Auswahl*, Deutsche National-Litteratur, 18, part 1 (Stuttgart: Union Deutsche Verlagsgesellschaft, [1895?]), pp. x–xii. L. Fränkel reviews the literature on fleas and women and claims it does not appear before the sixteenth century in "Bemerkungen zur Entwicklung des Grobianismus," *Germania: Vierteljahresschrift für deutsche Alterthumskunde*, 36 (Vienna 1891): 181–93. John Donne's poem "The Flea" is a well-known example.

21. Hull's title, *Chaste, Silent, and Obedient*, sums up the chief precepts for early modern women's behavior. "Sequestered" could be added as a fourth.

22. Compare:

Vivit adhuc fama Xantippe Socratis uxor
Quam meruit famam moribus illa suis:
Forte domum paucos convivas ille vocarat,
Artibus eximios ingenioque viros.
Colloquium gravibus doctum de rebus habebant,
Tingentes variis seria dicta iocis.
Cumque diu tererent nocturnis tempora nugis,
Res ea Xantippae non ita grata fuit.
Colloquio tandem quo finem imponeret isti,
Consilium cerebri protulit omne sui.
Iurgia convivis, convitia multa marito
Fecit, et in rixas lingua diserta fuit.
Sed sua contemni cum iurgia, seque videret,
Omnia tentandum credidit esse sibi.
Et veniens solita mensam subvertit in ira,
Convivasque suos iussit abire domum.

(1.9.1321–36)

"Xantip," wife of "Socrates," in fame shall ever live,
Who, when to certaine worthie men a banquet she did give,
They talked long and learnedly of things that lik'd them best,
Including many a weightie matter in a pleasant iest.
When halfe the night they thus had spent, "Xantip," malecontent,
Devisde some meanes whereby at length their prattling to prevent.
She being well tong'd, both her husband and her guests did chide,
But seeing that they scornde her words, this other meanes she tride.
She threw the table under feete, and forc'd them all to go
Incontinent out of her house, whether they would or no.

(1.9.1198–1207)

As though already aware of the threat such a woman could pose to the male social sphere, the narrator hastily qualifies his advice and adds his doubt that the reader would take it anyway:

Hoc ego te facinus quoque iam tentare iuberem,
Si nimis hos videas velle sedere diu.

(1.9.1337–38)

This I could wish thee eke to do, if they should sit too long,
But this I doubt thou scarce wouldst do such sober men among.

(1208–1209)

23. The issue of audience is a matter of comparison between reception of the Latin text and the English translation available in 1605. In either case, however, the question remains moot: the size of the audience of female readers of Latin texts cannot have been large; and the English translation received but a modest reception in England. Dekker's somewhat more published (for the work was no popular success in its time) *Gul's Horne-booke* (1609), though based on the early parts of *Grobianus*, makes no reference to a Grobiana character and never "feminizes" the gull.

## 5. Scheidt's *Grobianus*

1. There are more than six thousand poems in Hans Sachs, *Werke in zwei Bänden*, vol. 1: *Gedichte*, Karl Martin Schiller, ed. (Berlin: Aufbau, 1972).

2. On early modern German history, see Geoffrey Barraclough, *The Origins of Modern Germany* (New York: Norton, 1984); Michael Salewski, *Deutschland: Eine Politische Geschichte von den Anfängen bis zur Gegenwart* (Munich: Verlag C. H. Beck, 1993), vol. 1; Horst Rabe, *Neue Deutsche Geschichte*, vol. 4: *Reich und Glaubensspaltung, Deutschland 1500–1600* (Munich: C. H. Beck, 1989).

3. See Dieter Seitz, *Johann Fischarts "Geschichtklitterung": Untersuchungen zur Prosastruktur und zum grobianischen Motivkomplex* (Frankfurt am Main: Athenäum, 1974), pp. 223–33, for a discussion of "Protestant discipline" which connects Reformation restrictions on behavior with the rise of capitalism.

4. "I do not wonder, learned Frederice, that it may make you feel somewhat strange to receive a letter or greeting from one you have never met or seen, or that it may even more perplex you that I have germanized your little book Grobianus (which you wrote in Latin two years ago and which you yourself might have brought out in German verse or prose) and published it" ("und von euch selbst, so jr gewoelt, in teutsch reymen oder prosa het bracht moegen werden")(p. 1).

5. Sachs, "Wittenbergisch Nachtigall, die man jetz höret überall," in *Hans Sachs und die Reformation*, ed. Richard Zoozman (Dresden: Hugo Angermann, 1904), pp. 3–31.

6. Philip Stubbes, *The Anatomie of Abuses*, ed. Frederick J. Furnivall, New Shakspere Society (London: N. Trubner, 1877–79), pp. 111, 113.

7. William Shakespeare, *The Merchant of Venice*, 1.2.86–91, in *The Riverside Shakespeare*, ed. G. Blakemore Evans (Boston: Houghton Mifflin, 1974).

8. Thomas Nashe, *Summer's Last Will and Testament, Complete Works of Thomas Nashe*, ed. Alexander B. Grosart (London: Huth Library, 1883–1885), 6: 146–47. The author of *De arte bibendi* was German humanist Obsopoeus. In *Nashes Lenten Stuffe* (1599), Nashe also links drunkenness to a number of other nationally specific vices: "The posterior Italian and Germane chronographers, sticke not to applaude and canonize unnatural sodomitie; the strumpet errant, the goute, the ague, the droopsie, the sciatica, follie, drunckennesse and slouenry." *Complete Works* 5: 234. The effect is, of course, also to link the anal-excremental, the anal-erotic, and apparently, pleasure-seeking letting down of restraint.

9. Hauffen, *Caspar Scheidt, der Lehrer Fischarts: Studien zur Geschichte der grobianischen Litteratur in Deutschland* (Strassburg: Karl J. Trübner, 1899), p. 46.

10. Philipp Strauch published these in "Zwei Fliegenden Blätter von Kaspar Scheidt," *Vierteljahrschrift für Litteraturgeschichte* 1 (1899): 64–98.

11. "Beasts Are Rational," in *Plutarch's Moralia* 12, trans. Harold Cherniss and William C. Helmbold (Cambridge: Harvard University Press, Loeb Classical Library, 1984), 492–533, hereafter cited parenthetically in the text.

12. Cf. Max Horkheimer and T. W. Adorno, Excursus 1, "Odysseus or Myth and Enlightenment," in *Dialectic of the Enlightenment*, trans. John Cumming (New York: Herder and Herder, 1972), pp. 43–80, in which Horkheimer and Adorno discuss the insidious human domination over nature in which sacrifice of and domination over others (other human beings, natural forces) becomes, introverted, the self-sacrifice that produces the (alienated) bourgeois subject.

13. *Amores* 4, l. 17. Ovid, *Heroides and Amores*, ed. and trans. Grant Showerman (Cambridge: Harvard University Press, 1963), p. 460.

14. Stuart A. Gallacher, "The Proverbs in Scheidt's *Grobianus*," *Journal of English and Germanic Philology* 40 (1941): 489–90, argues that "a large number of the proverbs effectively counteracts the insolent coarseness of the theme" and that these proverbs "reflect conditions better than the *Grobianus*." I would emphatically counter that, used ironically as they are, these proverbs serve rather to heighten than to mitigate or diminish the coarse effects.

15. See Derek Attridge, *Well-Weighed Syllables: Elizabethan Verse in Classical Meter* (Cambridge: Cambridge University Press, 1974), p. 108, on the contemporary low regard for fourteeners, Golding's translation of Ovid's *Metamorphoses* notwithstanding.

16. "Scheidt translates Dedekind's *Grobianus* chapter for chapter, following the *content* of the original." Hauffen, *Caspar Scheidt* p. 47.

17. My emphasis.

18. "Lourdemont" was a French expression, the equivalent for which would be something like "Hick City."

19. On the German *Haushaltsbuch*, see Steven Ozment, *When Fathers Ruled: Family Life in Reformation Europe* (Cambridge: Harvard University Press, 1983); and Lyndal Roper's critique of Ozment's argument that the genre evidences a kinder, gentler early modern patriarchy in *The Holy Household: Women and Morals in Reformation Augsburg* (Oxford: Clarendon, 1989).

20. "Mein liebe Frau, das Möcht wohl kummen nach Euern Worten" (My dear woman, that may well happen according to your words). *Tyl Ulenspiegel*, in *Deutsche Volksbücher in Drei Bänden* (Berlin: Aufbau, 1979), 2:126–27.

21. Cf. Erhard Jöst, *Bauernfeindlichkeit: Die Historien des Ritters Neithart Fuchs*, Göppinger Arbeiten zur Germanistik, 192 (Göppingen: Alfred Kümmerle, 1976), pp. 272–78. Although it does not discuss in great detail the sixteenth-century violence of representation of peasants, cf. Stephen Greenblatt's reading of Albrecht Dürer's design for a monument to the defeat of the peasants in the 1525 Peasant Revolution in "Murdering Peasants: Status, Genre, and the Representation of Rebellion," *Representations* 1 (February 1983): 1–29.

22. Cf. Eugene F. Clark, "The *Grobianus* of Sachs and Its Predecessors," *JEGP* 16 (1926): 390–96, for a discussion of Sachs's sources. Clark argues persuasively that the Dedekind-Scheidt texts were not used by and perhaps were not even known to Sachs.

23. Gerald Strauss, *Nuremberg in the Sixteenth Century: City Politics and Life between the Middle Ages and Modern Times* (Bloomington: Indiana University Press, 1976), p. 103.

## 6. Gulls from Grobians

1. Roger Bull [pseud.], *Grobianus; or, The Compleat Booby: An Ironical Poem* (London, 1739). This English translation was the last edition of *Grobianus* until scholarly editions appeared in the late nineteenth and early twentieth centuries. See Ernst Rühl, *Grobianus in England: Nebst Neudruck der ersten Übersetzung "The School of Slovenrie"* (1605) *und erster Herausgabe des Schwankes "Grobiana's Nuptials"* (c. 1640) *aus Ms. 30 Bodl. Oxf. Palaestra XXXVIII* (Berlin: Mayer und Müller, 1904), pp. lxvii–lxxxii.

2. Douglas Bush, *English Literature in the Earlier Seventeenth Century, 1600–1660* (Oxford: Oxford University Press, 1945), p. 43.

3. C. H. Herford, *Studies in the Literary Relations of England and Germany in the Sixteenth Century* (London: Frank Cass, 1886), pp. 391–92, notes that "Between the two characters the whole book fluctuates, awkwardly enough," and he also sees the gull as lacking the "candour" of his predecessor; only his theatrics in chapter 6, "How a gallant should

behave himself in a playhouse," present "no doubt the best illustration of Grobianism which the society of Jacobean London afforded."

4. In that sense, cf. Whigham's "stolen honor" idea: "Elite identity was a mode of being that could be acquired, taken on in adulthood—a commodity . . . that could be bought, by means of courtesy books." Frank Whigham, *Ambition and Privilege: The Social Tropes of Elizabethan Courtesy Literature* (Berkeley: University of California Press, 1984), p. 5. Yet for Dekker, apparently, it was not so simple.

5. Cf. Jean Baudrillard, *For a Critique of the Political Economy of the Sign* (St. Louis: Telos, 1981).

6. I could also mention John Day's drama *The Isle of Guls* (1606).

7. According to the *Oxford English Dictionary*, "gullibility" first entered the English lexicon in the eighteenth century.

8. A past "Q & A" column in the *New York Times* (April 3, 1991) appropriately described gulls as "goats with wings."

9. Cf. Lawrence Stone, *The Causes of the English Revolution, 1529–1642* (New York: Harper and Row, 1972); Stone, *The Crisis of the Aristocracy, 1558–1641* (Oxford: Clarendon Press, 1965); Christopher Hill, *The Century of Revolution, 1603–1704* (Edinburgh: T. Nelson, 1961); Jonathan Goldberg, *James I and the Politics of Literature: Jonson, Shakespeare, Donne, and Their Contemporaries* (Baltimore: Johns Hopkins University Press, 1985). On the Stuart monarchy's consistent dependency on credit finance, cf. Robert Ashton, *The Crown and the Money Market, 1603–1640* (Oxford: Clarendon Press, 1960).

10. Bush, *English Literature*, p. 43.

11. Cf. Dekker's adaptation of the anonymous German monetary romance *Old Fortunatus* (1599).

12. *The Poems of Sir John Davies*, ed. Robert Krueger (Oxford: Clarendon Press, 1975), pp. 129–30, hereafter cited parenthetically in the text.

13. Edward Guilpin, *Skialetheia; or, A Shadow of Truth*, ed. D. Allen Carroll (Chapel Hill: University of North Carolina Press, 1974), p. 44.

14. John Davies, the courtier and minor Elizabethan sonneteer, was on record as a devout member of the cult of Elizabeth. Roy Strong uses his sonnets from *Celia* to introduce chapters in his *The Cult of Elizabeth: Elizabethan Portraiture and Pageantry* (Berkeley: University of California Press, 1977). In the latter part of his life, Davies became known as the man whose wife, Eleanor Davies (née Castelhaven), prophesied his demise when he burned her writings; her prophecy, the first of many, was realized three weeks later. The date of the *Gullinge Sonnets* is uncertain, but the sonnets refer to Zepheria, from an anonymous sonnet sequence (*Zepheria*), known for its mixing of legal and amorous tropes, published in 1594. Krueger dates the sonnets c. 1594 but believes the dedication to Sir Anthony Cooke, a relation of Robert Cecil and Francis Bacon who served under Essex at Cadiz and in Ireland, indicates that the dedication was added in 1596, the year that Cooke was knighted (p. 391).

15. Cf. sonnet 8 ("My case is this, I love Zepheria bright"), which pleads a legal case against an unwilling Petrarchan mistress ("I labor therefore justlie to repleave / My harte which she unjustly doth impounde" [9–10]), and sonnet 9 ("To Love my lord I doe knightes service owe"), in which the speaker figures himself as a ward complaining of a guardian's misuse of his property ("I feare he hath an other Title gott, / And holds my witt now for an Ideott" [13–14]).

16. Arthur Marotti, " 'Love is not love': Elizabethan Sonnet Sequences and the Social Order," *ELH* 49 (1982): 396–428.

17. Cf. Eve Kosofsky Sedgwick, "A Poem Is Being Written," for material that suggests

to me that if meter is spanking, the sonnet might arguably belong to the disciplinary domain of conduct. In *Tendencies* (Durham, N.C.: Duke University Press, 1993), pp. 177–214.

18. Cf. Nietzsche on that famous father of the church Tertullian, who describes the pleasures of the blessed who make it to heaven in scopophilic and sadistic terms; that is, they are privileged to witness the torments of the damned: "Beati in regno coelesti, videbunt poenas damnatorum, *ut beatitudo illis magis complaceat*" (The blessed in the kingdom of heaven will see the punishments of the damned, *in order that their bliss be more delightful for them*). On the Genealogy of Morals and Ecce Homo, trans. Walter Kaufman (New York: Vintage, 1969), p. 49.

19. Joel Fineman, *Shakespeare's Perjured Eye: The Invention of Poetic Subjectivity in the Sonnets* (Berkeley: University of California Press, 1986), p. 82.

20. On the extravagance of fashion and the costs endured by the more ambitious, see Karen Newman, "Dressing Up: Sartorial Extravagance in Early Modern London," in *Fashioning Femininity and English Renaissance Drama* (New York: Routledge, 1993), pp. 109–28.

21. Cf. Jeffrey Knapp, "Elizabethan Tobacco," *Representations* 33 (1991): 61–94.

22. This experience also bears an ironic correspondence to his earlier attraction to the German monetary romance, seen in his adaptation-dramatization of the anonymous German folk book *Fortunatus* (1509; 1550) as *The Pleasant Comedie of Old Fortunatus* (1599). See *Fortunatus-Volksbuch*, ed. Hans Gunther, *Neudrucke deutscher Litteraturwerke des XVI. und XVII. Jahrhunderts* (Halle: M. Niemayer, 1914), 140–41; Thomas Dekker, *The Pleasant Comedie of Old Fortunatus*, in *The Dramatic Works of Thomas Dekker*, ed. Fredson Bowers (Cambridge: Cambridge University Press, 1953), vol. 1; the useful introductory and comparative material in Hans Scherer, ed., *The Pleasant Comedie of Old Fortunatus: Herausgegeben nach dem Drucke von 1600* (Erlangen: A. Deichert, 1901), pp. 1–48; Herford, *Studies in the Literary Relations*, pp. 210–18. Frederick O. Waage, *Thomas Dekker's Pamphlets, 1603–1609, and Jacobean Popular Literature*, 2 vols. (Salzburg: Institut für englische Sprache und Literatur, 1977), p. 368 n. 11, suggests Dekker's connection to the Dutch-London community founded in the 1560s. Cf. esp. chapter 6.2, "*Worke for Armourers* and the Commercial Crisis," pp. 515–32.

23. Alexis F. Lange provides one example of the conventional thesis on Shakespeare as the illuminating genius and Dekker as the hack writer whose cultural insights seem simply to express an insider's experience: "Dekker owed the moulding of his genius and personality largely to the City, as distinguished from the circles of the gently born or bred. Here his robust sense for full-bodied facts learned its first lessons; here his abounding vitality and social instincts made him a part of the stirring life about him; here suffering evoked his inborn kindliness and sobered gaiety into humour; here his temperamental optimism found goodness in unpromising corners. Original in assimilating, but scantily endowed with the reactive power that converted London into an illuminating symbol for a Shakespeare, Dekker's thought glided easily into the grooves of the City mind and his ethical views and standards took shape under the influence of communal spirit and bourgeois wisdom." "On Dekker," in *Representative English Comedies, with Introductory Essays and Notes and a Comparative View of the Fellows and Followers of Shakespeare*, ed. Charles Mills Gayley, vol. 3: *The Later Contemporaries of Shakespeare: Fletcher and Others* (New York: Macmillan, 1914), p. 3; and *Dictionary of National Biography*, article "Dekker."

24. Karl Marx, "The Power of Money in Bourgeois Society," in *The Economic-Philosophical Manuscripts of 1844*, trans. Martin Milligan (New York: New World Paperbacks, 1963), pp. 165–69. Marx uses *Timon of Athens* and Goethe's *Faust I*; he might well have used Dekker, Dedekind, or Scheidt.

25. Phyllis Rackin, *Stages of History: Shakespeare's English Chronicles* (Ithaca: Cornell University Press, 1990), p. 47. In Shakespeare's *Timon of Athens*, it is the fate of Timon the protagonist to go from "flashing phoenix" to "naked gull" when he fails to realize that "the world is but a word" (2.2.150) and that the word can be mortgaged. His betrayal by the ingratitude of his parasitic acquaintances is at least in part the result of his gullish qualities, though it is his former friends who are the parasitic gullers.

# Index

# The End of Conduct

# Index